C U S T O M E R S :

ARRIVING WITH A HISTORY, LEAVING WITH AN EXPERIENCE!

How to build your sales, service or help desk call center to please customers

by Andrew J. Waite

A Flatiron Publishing, Inc. Book
Published by Flatiron Publishing, Inc.

ISBN 0-936648-84-8

Manufactured in the United States of America
First Edition, February 1996

Cover design by Mara Seinfeld
Printed at Bookcrafters, Chelsea, MI.

<u>DEDICATIONS</u>

This book is dedicated to the best of call center sellers

Brian Laske
who was prematurely promoted to a much larger territory.
Thank you Brian for the time you spent with us.

and also to

Tom Kotras
the bestof call center systems support managers.
Tom, the call center business will be a lot poorer without you.

Thank you to all those many co-workers, customers and colleagues who contributed to the knowledge collected in this book. Thanks, particularly Naomi Furukawa, Shirley Smith, Louis Suarez II, Zina Glodney, Celeste Collins, Kim Konigsberg, Kathi Shimizu, Laura Tovar, Don Owen, Joy Bagnall, Janet Barber, Carlo Brambilla, Martin Harper, Allan Petersen, Ken Ford, John Coleman, Signe Mackey, Joe Paccarotti, Cherie Torske, Kathrine Maybry, Brian Rees, Ginger Neal, Harvey Silverman, Sharon Keefer, Robert Rose and Kathy Cryer and all those customers and prospects who have allowed me to test and prove these ideas with. Without you all, my life and this book would be a lot less rich.
Now buy something!

Customers:
Arriving With A History And Leaving With An Experience!

How to build your sales, service or help desk call center to please customers

Introduction

This book began life as "The Inbound Telephone Call Center, How to buy and install an Automatic Call Distributor." Since the first edition in 1987, the business has evolved in five significant directions. Three; market driven, one technology and the final and most significant, customer call center customer frustration with the inability of "box" vendors to stay abreast of the accelerating maturity of customer call center and customer relationship management philosophy. These directions are:

1.   The realization that a customer telephone call is not simply an event but a significant milestone in a customer relationship. It is not a transaction but part of a process that may include correspondence by mail, FAX, E:mail or even the Internet.

2.   That a customer or prospect "arrives with a history and leaves with an experience." The facts and circumstances surrounding the overall relationship with a customer cannot be ignored in your customer call center. When the individual customer contact is viewed as a transaction and not a key waypoint in a business partnership, the "color" and state of the larger relationship is lost.

3.   That not all contacts with a customer are by telephone, therefore all the other "touch" events need to be woven into the contact database and process, and

4.   The wide acceptance and deployment of voice response technology and the arrival of computer telephony links.

Some businesses have benefited from the breakthrough book, "Reengineering the Corporation," authored by Dr Michael Hammer and James Champy. The whole notion of reengineering is fundamentally changing the process of business from the bottom up. Define the process in its smallest increments, use "zero based justification," analyze total cycle time by individual steps, cut unnecessary process and drive the whole customer call center. Reengineering goes way beyond throwing newer technology at a customer's call for goods or support services. Reengineering the customer call center goes to the root of the business process. Apologies are offered to Messers Hammer and Champy, as we are not going to go beyond the realm of the customer call center to reengineer your corporation, rather make note of the surrounding issues.

> **5.** By any other name computer telephony integration, is process reengineering of the customer call center. Traditional positioned customer call center vendors are not positioned to serve this market.

Consequently there are three schools of promotional thought based on vendor bias; telecentric, datacentric and workflow reengineering, consulting and systems integration. The "telecentrics;" the PBX and ACD systems vendors generally promote CTI as a tool to save money based on circuit savings and labor reduction. The "datacentrics" or computer vendors believe that the justification for CTI lies in cost savings and the efficiency driven by intermachine "plumbing." Both are right, but for very superficial reasons. The folks that grasp the vision and long term implications of CTI as workflow reengineering understand that the real success of CTI is the fact it is a platform for workflow and management changes. Reengineering of any workflow process is fundamental, disruptive and downright scary. To not grasp this and limit CTI to the realm of "plumbing" is to miss the entire point.

One of the first things we are going to do is to redefine the call center as the customer center. Because the term "call center" perpetuates the notion that customer contact is limited to calls to and from a customer or prospect. Mail, FAX, electronic mail, freight and personal contact are ignored as alternative, integrated or complementary communications with customers.

We are going to examine building, optimizing and managing a customer call center with significantly more emphasis on managing this center for the 90's and beyond.

During the intervening nine years since this book was first written, the customer call center has also gone through a significant market shift. At first the customer call center was a processor of customer transactions. With realization of the key role in the building and maintaining of a relationship with a customer. The shift has begun to full relationship documentation and management. Hence the new title: customer call center. We are beginning to move from managing transactions to managing relationships.

Successful reengineering depends on lots of information about process, understanding of the cycle time and the state of the relationship with a customer. Data and information are no longer enough; context sensitive customer knowledge is needed.

Customer call centers have grown in popularity and use as traditional methods of winning and serving a customer base have proved increasingly inadequate and expensive. In sales, a direct sales force or distribution channel are capable of significant productivity improvements when coupled with inside sales and marketing support. Philosophies such as "Sales Navigation" dramatically change the way advertising and direct response work. No longer can companies afford to squander advertising budgets nor do they have the luxuries of the 80's when any strategy seemed to work. Now every lead is vital to an immediate sale, a future sale or at minimum, a marketing intelligence in the form of a database entry.

Every year the McGraw-Hill sales cost study reports another escalation in the cost of acquiring a customer by a direct sales visit. In 1987, the average cost of acquiring a new customer rose 9.5% over the previous year to $251.63 Business to business calls average $291.10. Many sales take a minimum of five calls to close the business. In 1995 this number had risen by almost 22%.

Unsurprisingly, it costs five times as much to win a new customer than it does to keep an existing one. In the 80's Walker Research studied Citibank retail checking account sales and service in Manhattan. They found that the bank was winning 2000 new accounts a week, while the back office was losing 2500 during the same period. The key to stopping this net loss of 500 customers a week and the attendant cost of doing business badly, was linking all customer contact events into a relationship that could be managd by teleservices. Get the customers out of the branches and onto the phone. Use the telephone as a servicing channel to augment the already successful use of automatic teller machines.

Over the intevening nine years we have seen massive advances in database marketing, prospect identification and customer ranking technologies, printing, direct mail, coupled with predictive dialers and overall followup technologies. This means companies can reach prospective customers more easily and less expensively than ever before. The good news is America has 250 million plus consumer prospects. The bad news is America only has 250 million propects and with all this new marketing technology you can reach out and touch these folks as never before. Any market becomes increasingly finite.

Keeping a customer happy and maximizing the lifetime value of your relationship with that customer is more important than it has ever been. Yet often we only emphasize new customer acquisition.

The Customer Call Center is there when our customer wants to:

> **place an order**
> **check order status**
> **check delivery status**
> **answer questions on how the product works (or is meant to)**
> **troubleshoot the product over the phone (manual or remote diagnostics, and**
> **dispatch a service person (when all else fails).**

This book examines the customer call center, not only from an inbound and outbound calling perspective, but also integration with the other market contact and workflow improvement techniques a company may use to reach and serve pending and existing customers.

We'll look at basic building blocks, with particular emphasis on the switching system or automatic call distributor, the new applications made possible by client server technologies, and the strategic and tactical uses of a customer center. We will discuss the techniques, tools and technologies available to aid the customer call center owner and manager in realizing their expectations of winning and keeping customers more successfully and more profitably.

Andrew J. Waite
Phoenix ,
Spring, 1996

Table of Contents

Table of Contents

Chapter One

Why A Customer Call Center ?

Account management, customer support and service contacts have been traditionally managed through individual and personal visits by field representatives who travel to the customer. This is personnel, personality and labor intense, it has becoming so expensive and inefficient in all but major situations or courtesy visits, that alternate methods are the norm.   Enter the Customer Call Center where consistent and predictable answers are available continually, and often, around the clock. Today, the frequent   telephone conversation with a courteous, professional, and knowledgeable sales, service or support representative is more desirable, or even preferable, to the visit by the local field sales or service representative.

Today, successful pharmaceutical companies, out promoting new drugs or new uses for older products, find a distinct trend. Medical practitioners seem to prefer a telephone call from a knowledgeable telephone seller or account service person, to an office visit. The contact is faster, often more frequent, and less expensive for all parties to the contact.

A Very Brief History

The customer call center has been around for longer than officially acknowledged but really began to take definition with the introduction of the   computer controlled automatic call distributor in 1972. A functional   automatic call distributor or ACD is the core building block of any successful customer call center and computer telephone integration or CTI.

The airline and other businesses had been buying electromechanical call distribution equipment from the then Bell System for many years. These uniform call distributors were limited in their functionality and represented in microcosm the entire thinking that lead to the breakup of this monolith. They "knew what customers wanted and gave them that."

Unfortunately for them customers believed otherwise, looked elsewhere and gave birth to a healthy industry of customer call center technology specialists.

Rockwell Communications, (nee Collins Radio,) built a switching system for Continental Airlines that allowed changeable programmable inbound call routing and more extensive management reporting on service levels offered by the airline. Probably the most significant issue in the system design was philosophical. The system was built with an understanding of the mission critical nature of the airline reservation center. American Airlines recently reported that a potential outage in any critical chain component in its reservation system cost $16,000 a minute in lost revenue.

That is irrecoverable lost revenue. Today most customer center technology is built with multiple levels of "bullet proofing" and redundancy almost guaranteeing nonstop availability to customer calls.

Introduction

Over the last few years the incoming call, received by an established customer call center, has the potential to generate revenue or cost goodwill, and ultimately long term cost revenue if the call is not handled effectively. These centers therefore exist to generate or protect revenue and market position.

Outbound calling has become an increasingly important consideration in these customer call centers. First, because an inbound call or an incoming written communication may need telephone follow up. In this age of reengineering business process and assigning an agent to a "case," a complex problem may require later follow up. The second and important reasons is inbound caller demand dynamic. This combines allocation of labor, how business occurs in an inbound center and the issue of destiny.

Allocation of resources to answer callers' requests is an issue of matching supply with demand. Despite increasingly accurate forecasting systems, you cannot hire "fractions of people" or anticipate demand precisely, so assigning non-inbound call tasks to idle agents allows a desirable opportunity to justify hiring sufficient staff . These may be outbound calls or following up on correspondence or other non-telephone contacts.

To quote inbound customer call center guru, Gordon MacPherson, "calls arrive in clumps." Business occurs in predictable patterns, but typically patterns that are not ideal for rationing good service. Therefore a customer call center manager tries to modulate the whole process with an automatic call distributor, staff forecasting and attendance software and the nearest they can come to "just-in-case" staffing.

Finally most inbound customer call centers do not control their own destiny. This is because they exist to respond to prospects generated by a marketing program they not only don't control and often, are unaware of. There is the story of a bus line fare and schedule center in Los Angeles. They opened to an unprecedented volume of callers requesting information about the special fares being offered by the line. No one had notice or information about this. It was not until agents began taking their morning break and found a full page ad in the Los Angeles Times! Calls to product and customer support lines are also frequently driven by external forces such as a lapse in quality control or ambiguous documentation.

The customer call center represents the first level contact a customer or prospect has with any company. The front door to your business. With such an important mandate, it is essential that the process be thought through, well upstream and well downstream, of the actual contact. Should it occur at all? Should be strive to process the call as fast as possible? Or keep the customer on the phone for as long as possible to learn more about our products, documentation, support, etc.? How can we do this better?

At the point in the relationship a customer decides to pick up the phone and call. little things, like prompt and courteous attention, mean everything. The potential emotion bound up in this transaction, from the customer and company point of view, is tremendous. To treat the incoming caller with less than the attention they are due, (and expect,) is a reflection of the attention, concern and service they can expect from your company, should the relationship proceed. Call sometime and blind test your company. You may be in for a surprise.

The cost of acquiring a new customer, or cost of sale has increased at a steady rate and continues to do this at a rate that shows no sign of slowing. Yet ironically the average company does not know what it costs them to acquire a customer. When they do figure out the costs, the amount of money is often a stunner!" Many companies have found it is so expensive to acquire a new customer, the process is often far less profitable than retaining and servicing a new customer. It is no surprise service is has been rediscovered.

In the magazine business it costs between $15 and $25 to acquire a new paying subscriber. When you figure most consumer magazine subscriptions sell for less than $25 a year (and it costs more than that to service the subscription), you can easily see the revenue burden on the advertising side of the house. Magazines, like newspapers, commonly use the telephone as their primary sales medium. Because magazine space advertising rates are set on the basis of size and depth of the subscriber base, winning and keeping paying subscribers is a major magazine publisher's goal and industry measurement reference.

How is this $15 to $25 subscriber acquisition cost calculated? First all the marketing and sales efforts and expenses are identified and added up. Then divided by the number of new subscribers. (Think of your customers.) Lets look at some of these cost elements and what goes into pursuing a new magazine subscriber. Typically these cost include the following;

1. Creative efforts: the defining who and where the market is believed to be, obtaining the list of target prospects or selecting the media which best suits your market.

2. Acquiring these lists.

3. Creating the advertising and marketing materials necessary to pursue this campaign.

4. Purchasing the space and time necessary to reach your intended market. This may be traditional broadcast advertising, print advertising in magazines or newspapers, consumer or business vertical trade papers. This may be a direct mail/direct campaign where mail is sent to individual targets that have been identified on the lists you have acquired, via rental or purchase. Also include any list preparation necessary optimize the data to ensure you are pursuing just the prospects who represent a reasonable possibility of conversion to a subscriber.

Now the campaign is underway and the market is responding by mail or telephone and in any other manner you can accept a subscription order.

5. You must establish a processing system to actually accept this order. This may be an individual accepting a phone call or receiving a request on paper (through the mails or FAX,) or more recently, electronically (via E:Mail or the Internet. etc.)

6. Entering a subscription.

None of this process can occur in an orderly fashion unless there is a system in place, even manual. If the system is automated in any fashion, suddenly the cost and management overhead increases. With the introduction of any volume the costs and effort increase again.

The location and acquiring the staff with right skills to serve your incoming requests for subscriptions. Then there is the training and supervision for the center and staff. Otherwise known as general and administrative costs. Housing, facilities and furnishing for the subscription order processing is also a substantial cost. When all this is considered in the context of an order process that responds exclusively to subscription requests placed by telephone, the process can be illustrated as follows in Figure 1.1

FIG. 1-1

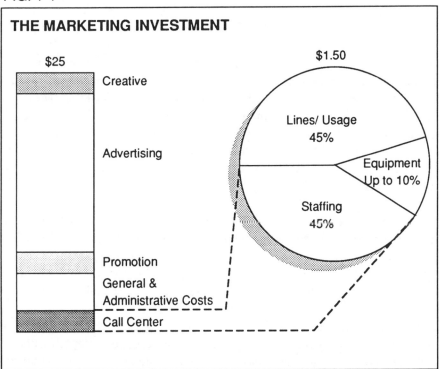

Shown here is the massive expense typically involved to induce a caller to pick up the telephone and respond to your advertisement...only to receive no or poor service because your company does not appreciate the costs and the market dynamics of acquiring a customer.

So often the cost of acquiring a new customer is given lip service by corporate management. Little is done about it before the fact, because it poses risk to equip and staff up, anticipating a busy season. Once the season has begun and callers are not being serviced, maybe this is only a temporary condition that will soon be over? Certainly it will be over when the season closes or your business is "knocked off" by smarter competition.

In this business, the "penny wise, pound foolish" rule applies with a vengeance. The illustration above shows the customer call center costs as only $ 2.30 of the entire cost of sale of $ 25.00. This amounts to less than 10% of the total marketing expense to acquire a new subscriber (customer.) Yet mismanaging the incoming customer call center by not understanding how and when your business arrives and being staffed and equipped to handle it can be disastrous. It can defeat the marketing expenditure, no matter how effectively these efforts and expenses have been applied. In fact the more effective the campaign is the greater the potential to destroy the effectiveness of the customer call center.

Good marketing and good products put heavy demand on your incoming lines, your equipment and your people. Maybe your callers get busy signals? They get put on "eternity hold." With or without announcements. They suffer through boring "music," (often on your expensive 800 WATS lines). And then they hang up. They "abandon" their calls and maybe their interest and wish to business with you. Maybe they will never call back. They become lost as prospective customers, despite your elegant, expensive marketing and you beautiful new product.

Constant inbound call volume that approaches the maximum capacity of your lines, systems and staff creates more calls. If you have a unique offer and are nearly always busy much of the call traffic is "retries." That is people who could not get through to an agent or satisfy their request the first time and are retying your number. They get through and go on eternity hold and still give up.

Much of the book will be positioned at encouraging closer communication and cooperation between your marketing and customer contact departments. The opportunities lost daily because neither group understands their respective roles, tools, techniques, technologies and challenges of their colleagues would simply amaze top management -- if they only knew.

No department in a corporation is an island, just as no process stands alone. "Upstream" and "downstream" of your particular function are others and other steps that directly influence the success or failure of your contribution. This becomes particularly critical when the workflow implications of computer telephony are considered. If this book achieves nothing else, your recognition of the crucial importance of this interaction, will be enough. Then the business of reconsidering the process of adding value to the customer experience.

Reconsider the wonderfully silly example of the bus line this lack of interaction and communication between a marketing organization and their customer call center. The case involved a bus line and the fare and schedule center. One morning the center was swamped with inbound calls. It was not until the morning break and an employee reading the daily newspaper, the customer call center discovered a huge full page advertisement pushing a new, low, fare. The center was totally unaware of the promotion and did not anticipate the increase in call volume. It was understaffed to meet the demand. It dulled a potentially good ad promotion, not to mention negating the expense.

The language of telecommunications has a wonderfully expressive term. It states in clear terms what happens to a caller who is not connected to the party they intend to reach. Brought about by inadequate or insufficient lines or equipment. That caller is "blocked" or experience "blockage." The same thing happens here...the business opportunity is blocked from almost certain success.

Good Service Assures A Future Sale

All this discussion is focused at serving the first time inbound caller, responding to an advertisement for your particular product or service. What of the existing customer calling in for service or explanation about and existing customer relationship.

The Value Of A Call

Keeping customers happy and maximizing ""the lifetime value" of that relationship is more important than it has ever been, yet the compensation plans we use to encourage our sales organizations emphasize new business. The stars of those sales teams are the people that bring in new accounts. Customer service is often seen as a backwater.

Lifetime value of the relationship is a measurement gaining in recognition. More mature companies who build ongoing account relationships with customers have worked out this effort/revenue/profitability measurement some time ago. This the exception more than the rule. Business to consumer mail order catalogers discovered their best prospect was an existing customer. Then the question became, "what was a customer "worth" over the life of the customer relationship?" Customers receive a number catalogs and promotions each year, they buy $Y, and the profit is $X. Multiply this by the expected number of years of the relationship.   There is no argument; effective customer service extends the life of a customer relationship. See Figure 1.2.

FIG. 1-2

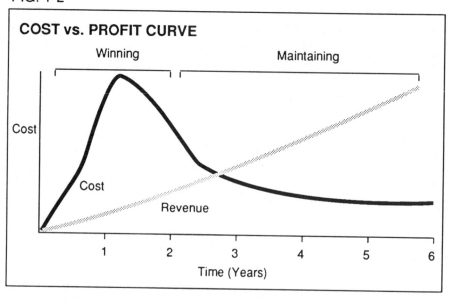

The cost/effort curve versus profitability in subsequent years. A satisfied customer is your best prospect, while a formerly unhappy customer who was promptly and effectively served is the best reference any company can have.

Making yourself available to these customers when they believe they need to speak to you is absolutely critical. Play hard to find, and when they do reach someone to talk to, the original problem is overshadowed by the perception you are difficult to find. And difficult to do business with.

Have you ever noticed that when you are put on hold, it always appears to last longer than the actual elapsed time.   Your customers have that similar perception. This compounds when there is a problem that needs resolution.

When customers have the sense that you are not particularly sensitive to their needs, there is often an increase in number of complaints. To adequately deal with these, you need to make an additional service investment so that these complaints do not escalate to accessibility then core goodwill problems.

When these complaints occur as telephone calls, placed to the same center that took he order, a displacement effect occurs that now "blocks" order calls as all your resources are now shared across two functions, sales and customer complaints.

The opportunity to take business is now displaced by the need to satisfy customers with problems. This is a perfect example of superficial treatment and partially addressing one problem creates a second and bigger problem.

There is an even more pervasive, yet less acknowledged problem and that is the effect this has on "cashflow velocity." The timeliness of invoice payment is directly proportional to the level of satisfaction a customer has about the relationship they perceive enjoy with you. Sell second grade merchandise, treat them poorly and they will find, even unconsciously, a reason not to pay you immediately. Maybe never at all. Maybe, as it turns out they really didn't need the product at all. This can be a particularly painful experience in the business consumer mail order business, where managing the rate of product returns is critical to the profitability of the business. What does it mean in your business?

The whole call contact process, when a customer or prospect initiates the call takes on a different level of importance from the customer's perception. Customer sensitivity to careless, (or callous,) treatment increases. Here is a major opportunity to fail if each aspect of your customer call center is not fully planned.

This book focuses on the strategies, techniques, and technology to ensure you get the most out of your customer call center investments.

The Cost Of A Call

Let us look at the actual cost breakdown of the call handling process. These are broadly made up of three basic elements;

☐ lines and their costs,
☐ the staff and management necessary to process the call and,

❑ the equipment necessary to answer, record and fulfill the request call represents.

FIG. 1-3

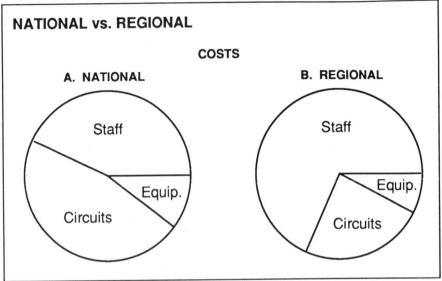

This pie chart shows the difference in operating costs in a national call center compared to a center with a regional responsibility. Because calls arrive on local and short haul lines usage costs are lower or even borne by the caller. Even so that portion of costs attributed to equipment remains a minority percentage.

The Lines

Local telephone lines, in this post divestiture age, are provided by your local serving telephone company. These people are the owners of the local telephone service franchise, and are absolutely necessary to your happy existence. We will discuss them further when we discuss lines and telephone traffic in Chapter 4.

If you are a larger phone user, there are many long distance and bulk service alternatives to the local phone company -- include stringing you own cable, hooking up with a local fiber optic company, installing your own private microwave system, anchoring a satellite antenna to your roof. Many companies have successfully installed such systems and many more are installing them.

These alternative local technologies (also called "bypass") have become more accessible, of good quality and often very cost effective.

Today the local telephone company is NOT the long distance carrier that provides long distance service, though they can provide instate long distance. The local phone company typically provides you with the connection to the long

distance carrier who in turn provides that service. They connect their local central office to a long distance carrier who provides that service. You can use the alternative of bypass as discussed in the preceding paragraph. What is important to understand at this stage, is that there are at least TWO entities involved in providing you telephone services. If your company has investigated alternate long distance carriers, your company may using one of the major carriers such as US Sprint, MCI, as well as AT&T WATS. There are sound cost reasons for using the alternatives and we will talk about this also in Chapter 4.

Now services come in a number of different flavors. Digital or analog, value added, such as ISDN (integrated services digital network) or just "plain old telephone service" (POTS.) The two pie charts in fig 3 show there are two different types of customer call centers -- those focused at serving a local population and those that receive calls from all over the country. The local electrical or municipal utility company offers service to a local customer base that does not need to call long distance to reach the center. No toll charges are incurred. Here the customer call center owner need not offer toll free long distance service. As a result customer call center costs drop substantially when compared with a national center receiving nearly all its calls from out of the local area. So the cost of making a long distance call does not become an objection to placing an order, management puts in toll free "800" service. this adds substantial operational costs. The argument for increased sales by increasing the ease and dropping the caller's cost of placing an order is said to outweigh the cost of the 800 lines in increased orders. After saying this, some very mature and successful mail order catalog houses only use 800 service for customer service. They let the customer pay the cost of long distance call to place the order. (Some do it in reverse also. They allow the customer to place the order toll-free but get assistance by dialing in on a toll-line -- one that costs the customer money.) More on this in Chapter 4.

The Staff

In a customer call center serving a local market group, people are the largest expense about 80%. In a national center, people to staff your center rank with telephone lines as the largest cost categories. Staff can equal approximately 45% each of your annual center operating expense. Staffing issues begin with selecting a location where continuity of staff availability is assured. Location is often determined by a continuing supply of adequate staff. More about this in Chapter 3.

Major direct response centers have set up shop in such unlikely places as Hobbs, New Mexico. This former oil town has an abundant supply of labor. The labor costs are low and much of the available population Spanish speaking and used in bilingual marketing campaigns. Determining the right amount of staff and balancing this to the incoming call demand is a significant management challenge. An important tool in cost effectively matching staff to call demand is a forecasting and scheduling package. We will talk about this in Chapter Five.

Once staff availability is satisfied from a planning point of view, the next issue is management structure, and staffing to the level and quality you require. There are several issues regarding labor/management relations and we will deal with these both in the context of management reporting in Chapter Twelve. Also in Chapter Fourteen where we discuss technical trends that affect customer call centers.

Training and quality control cannot be ignored. There is a finite cost to establish effective programs. Skimp on this aspect of your customer call center and you invite long term problems that return to the issue of meeting the first time caller's (prospect or customer) expectation. Training also affects the retention of a customer as a satisfied customer over the reasonable lifetime of the relationship. There have been significant developments in these areas which dramatically improve the call center manager's lot.

Go back to FIGURE 1. There's $25.00 to acquire a new subscriber, or customer. Of that $2.30 or less than 10% is the expense of the customer call center. This cost could be reduced by reverting to mail order and doing away with the customer call center all together. But the statistics are heavily favor satisfying the impulsive purchaser with a few minor questions on the phone. You could avoid providing toll free service. But there are heavy marketing arguments, reflected in sales increases that make sense to maintain toll free service.

The Equipment

Finally, and much of the reason for this book, is the equipment. This used to be simply buying a phone system and depending on your MIS department to provide you with a computer system to enter orders and track customer service inquiries. Now we have moved beyond buying telephone systems to buying a better way of doing business.

Since the original edition of this book "computer telephony" or "computer telephony integration" (CTI) has been "discovered" by mainstream vendors and customer call centers:

First this was driven by the mainframe mentality present at the large computer, PBX (private branch exchange) and ACD (automatic call distributor.) These vendors recognized the need to gather important call/caller information delivered on a call-by-call basis. This data becomes really significant when collected and used in conjunction with the customer database information stored on the company computer. The opportunity to match the caller with their account record prior to being connected to a live agent saves significant time and offers a greater potential for personalized customer focus. This linkage allowed significant gains in the speed of response, but initially remained heavily dependent on the rewriting of host code to become CTI compliant. Rewriting host code and making these links work cost significant time and money. As a result far fewer CTI links have been installed than were originally projected.

The second phase of computer telephony arrived earlier than expected by the purveyors of switch to host links. The advent of powerful personal computers and desktop operating system standards such as Windows and OS/2, has given rise to desktop call control vs. the proposed peer-to-peer call control of the first generation of CTI links. Using local area networking architectures, the desktop device has become a "client" attached to a "server" gateway that talks to the switch and possibly the host.

By moving this link into the world of Windows or OS/2 a significant breakthrough has occurred. Because Windows and OS/2 have automatic or scripted data exchange between applications programs and offer a standard for the millions of programmers striving to find "killer applications," really useful call center programs are being written daily that can take advantage of computer telephony links without the cost and expense of peer-to-peer call control as envisioned by the large computer and switch manufacturers.

When the PC arrives in a given industry, the PC and attendant culture remake the structural and economic reality of that industry in much the same way a swarm of locusts decimate a lush landscape. Many old line companies who resisted this move to PC based standards have fallen by the way side. Fortunately the aware customer call center owner can achieve dramatic productivity gains and increases in customer satisfaction. We will examine the impact of computer telephony in Chapter Fourteen.

The Customer Response Center

The inbound customer call center responds to demands that are beyond the control of the center. The destiny (i.e., success) of the customer center is satisfying caller demand when they decide to call. Caller demand may be understood to a degree, but can only be forecast within certain general parameters. And that's where a good forecasting and scheduling package can be most effective. Also there are wild card elements which exist. These can totally change call traffic demand. The example of the bus line and the sudden call volume increase turned out to be an advertising campaign rolled out by a marketing department operating in a vacuum. Marketing management "forgot" to tell customer call center management of their advertising campaign. Callers were not satisfied. Customer expectations were blunted now and maybe into the future? So much for their expensive marketing investment.

Often marketing management is unaware of the customer call center resources available to serve the expectation created by the marketing campaign. (How many catalogs do you still see without the 800 number on every page? How many print advertisements do you see with the telephone number buried or missing completely?) When they do, they compound the problem by not communicating to the people charged with serving inbound calls what is about to happen.

There are many other wild card elements that can affect a customer call center's ability to serve callers. Beyond inadequate facilities, lines, building space, equipment and people, wild card issues that affect your customer call center

include things like adverse weather (this may create increased call volume and make it difficult to get your staff to and from work,) service outages with telephone lines, telephone systems, computer equipment and electricity. We will discuss these in Chapter Ten, when we discuss "bullet proofing" your customer call center.

A Little History

Using the telephone for business was the very first application. "Watson, Come here" was the first business person-to-business-person communication using the telephone. Telephones were originally seen as a tool exclusive to the business world. Because of their intrinsic social value it is no surprise the telephone is vital to modern society and business development. Today they are a ubiquitous device and their presence considered a measure of a society's development.

Business telecommunications developed slowly from invention till the early sixties. However this is not the place to plot the development of telecommunications, other than to say high volume customer call centers were a well established fact with the development of telephone exchanges, information lines and manual central offices.

The image of the legions of operators manually connecting callers and answering their requests, are frequent images in contemporary literature. All the early work standards developed for customer call centers began in telephone company local and toll offices. Business systems were large electromechanical devices that offered little in the way of flexibility and totally without any real data about the performance of the switching system, the lines attached to the system or the personnel staffing it.

The telephone companies, particularly those of the Bell System began providing call distribution capabilities on Private Branch Exchange (PBX) systems to the heavy inbound customer call centers. The obvious users were the airline companies who accepted the technology and like Oliver Twist, wanted more, now. As is typical of a market where the demand drives development, the incumbent vendors (the telephone companies) were slow to respond and this opened up an opportunity for the electronics industry.

By the early 1970s, it was clear the Bell System was not going to respond to airline demand for sophisticated call distribution systems. Enterprising airline communications managers, like Mike Huntley, then at Continental Airlines, had established relationships with a vendor of high technology radio equipment,

Collins Radio. Together they explored the idea of building a high traffic, non blocking, software controlled, user programmable call distribution system that would provide management reports. The result was the birth of the computer controlled automatic call distributor in 1974. The Galaxy (now part of Rockwell International) system remains a standard in many large customer call centers today.

A new era began that has given birth to no fewer than twenty vendors and twice as many systems to choose from. However making the wrong choice can increase your staff requirement by up 30% over ACD systems designed to do just that.

Chapter Two

The Customer Call Center: The Implications And Applications

To succeed in the customer call center business there is one absolute! You must establish a clear role the center. The success of your customer call center is primarily a marketing issue. Both to an externally to customers and internally departments with who the call center interacts. You must set achievable goals that can measure the success of the center against these goals. As a customer call center manager making your management and client departments set reasonable expectations is key to your sanity and personal success.

You establish a customer call center to satisfy of a volume of particular requests that can be made to your company by telephone, by your customers and prospects. There are several key issues in this above statement which need explanation:

First; the volume of CALLS really represents PEOPLE calling with a request that can be satisfied by any one of a group of people.

Second; a successful customer call center can no longer look at each call as a standalone event but rather a waypoint or milestone in a customer relationship.

Third; the particular request is relatively predictable and homogeneous. It also can be served by any one of several your employees on the telephone, hence the need and logic for establishing a customer call center in the first place.

Fourth; that this service function has become a defined function in your enterprise, and your callers and other employees are made aware that the group to call for a particular service is group defined as the customer call center.

Fifth; that this group recognizes they are the focal point for customer and prospect service requests, and are prepared to effectively service the call.

Sixth; that the center is adequately equipped to process the a particular caller's and requests to the point of expectation and high satisfaction.

This list has undergone expansion and iteration since the first volume for two reasons; the arrival of computer telephony and the ability to enrich the caller's experience. "A customer arrives with a history and leaves with an experience" is a very compelling argument for placing all the tools before the customer service representative so they may respond appropriately to that one customer's particular problem, and in the context of the relationship state! . Today this is less a dream and fast becoming a market reality.

1. Call Volume?

First, how many calls should a customer center receive to justify formally establishing a customer call center? What is considered volume enough to qualify as a customer call center and therefore warrant the attention of management?

There is no simple answer to this question, though the obvious measurement is that of the importance of the caller and the business that is represented by the incoming call. What is the value of the call? How much has been invested to generate it and what is the desired call result or conclusion? A sale or a satisfied customer who will buy later on?

If it is a few important calls a day, interspersed with other non-telephone functions, then maybe it is not a customer call center per se, yet add a little more call volume, revenue and/or goodwill into the formula, and suddenly all the issues and potential to succeed or fail are present. Take another look, this department or application may be a candidate more sophisticated telephone tools. Two key properties to the call volume are the homogeneity of the caller's request and the ability for the call to be served by anyone on the staff of the customer call center.

Also, the moment such a group is identified as operating in the company, as a focus for customer or prospect call requests, new functions that can be satisfied by telephone are found and added to the responsibilities of the center. This is a factor (and there are many) that accounts for unanticipated customer call center growth.

There is no such entity as a "small" customer call center because at any size they represent a substantial cost to set up and maintain. Further, their business mission alone may be significant enough to warrant establishing the customer call center. In smaller businesses this is compounded further by the fact the business conducted by the customer call center is disproportionately large when compared to the number of people as a percentage of the total company headcount to revenue ratio.

2.   The Call is not a Standalone event but part of a larger customer relationship

With the widespread use of customer call centers and acceptance of the response center as a vital customer channel, there is growing recognition that a the customer relationship can be better managed.   With the advent of computer telephony there are many things that can be done to equip the agent to handle the customer in the context of the larger relationship.   This is beginning to show up in case and inquiry management systems.   We will talk more about this in Chapter Fourteen.

3. The Request For Service

This is a service request in technical sense, not literally "come and fix my broken dishwasher," but a service demand or opportunity that is created by the marketing of this center. The call could be to buy a plane ticket, a request for help with a complex piece of software leading to a purchase of the latest release, an emergency call for help, or an inquiry about an invoice discrepancy. It can be any one of an infinite number of requests. It is typically the first step in a sequence of events of a larger business transaction.

Many technical managers fail to look at the "big picture" in the analysis, specification and implementation of these customer call centers. Many opportunities for management convenience and insight and the resultant sales leverage, are lost at this stage by not treating the call as part of the larger business transaction.

A fact that has become increasingly important in the culture of customer call centers, and is still not recognized with the degree of importance that it deserves. This s the integration of the customer call center systems with the ultimate fulfillment and satisfaction that this call requires. Seldom is the request satisfied completely with the one telephone call. More calls may follow, inbound and outbound, and the dispatch of information, personnel or goods to the caller, to complete the transaction. There are substantial opportunities for integration of these systems and services that will result in even greater economies and efficiencies. More on this in Chapter Fourteen.

4. A Defined Service Function

It is absolutely necessary that this center has a defined function and responsibility.

Often a customer call center will be established or begun timidly -- so as not to upset an existing sales or service process or entity. The best and most amusing examples of this are typically inside sales departments that are set up to support (not compete with) a field sales organization. Field sales has managed these accounts for years and has done so quiet well. "Thank you kindly, why should we now refer our customers to some home office type, who has never visited the account, is insensitive to the needs and the politics of the account and will be taking orders and answering inquiries that should be handled by the field organization?"

A turf battle ensues and the company loses all this productivity, energy, time and money. And all for lack of a clear definition, and the tools and controls to make it work. The customer call center fails and the cost of doing business increases.

Corporate reengineering as espoused by Dr. Michael Hammer and James Champy in "Reengineering the Corporation," challenges the types of structure organizations and processes that would object to an inside sales support group where one may not have existed. Despite the logic of such a process, turf battles can kill a start up customer call center without a clear top down mandate. It is equally important that the role of the customer call center be communicated to both the target market or customer clearly and unambiguously. This is the place to call to obtain an answer to your request. Customers should understand this is the place to call to get an answer to their request. Spend as much time communicating to the "internal audience" as you do your external market. Clear recognition of the strategy and support by peers and peer organizations are key to successful reengineering of a customer contact and support process.

Take special care to ensure that the customer center personnel are impeccably trained, coordinate their activities and communicate with any other group that they could appear to conflict with. The obvious example is a field force of sales or support staff who are being refocused at larger opportunities. Unless due care is taken to integrate these organizations, the result is an ineffective customer call center and a field organization subverting the call center efforts and wasting time doing so.

5. A Focal Point For Customer Calls

It is important that this group recognizes they are the focal point for customer and prospect calls and service requests. They should understand this center is, or is about to become, the first point of contact for many of your company's prospects and customers.

It is important with all the correct attitudes, image and etiquette, that the agent or telephone representative, has access to the correct information. Well meaning, but ineffectual people are death to a customer call center. This is especially so if they are to wean the account management and support of the customer base away from a more traditional sales and support channel.

6. To The Point Of Customer Satisfaction

It is important the customer call center is adequately funded and equipped. This means funding, staffing and facilities. This book will be focusing on the actual systems and equipment required to manage these calls, satisfy and amaze customers.

When we talk of facilities, we talk of them in the broadest sense, this includes the physical housing, the telephone services or circuits that bring the calls to your building and allow you to make calls out. The actual equipment that calls are serviced by, whether it be a call sequencer, a call distributor or even voice response technologies that improve caller service and complement live agents also fall into the category of facilities.

The Applications Of A Call Center

The lists of enterprises that can use call distribution equipment is extensive. It is NOT TYPES of vertical businesses that have an application for call distribution equipment, but FUNCTIONS OR PROCESSES that cross businesses horizontally. Call center applications also run diagonally, across a corporation, from stockholder relations to bus fare and schedule information. See Figure 2.1 for an applications matrix.

FIG.2.1

CALL CENTER APPLICATION MATRIX

	Customer Service	Order Entry	Credit Authorization	Information	Reservations	Catalog Sales	Dispatch	Claims	Shareholder Service	Technical Services	Help Desks	Appointment Centers	Registration	Circulation	ClassifiedAds
Banking	☎		☎	☎					☎						
Travel Agents	☎	☎			☎						☎				
Airlines	☎			☎	☎		☎	☎							
Public Utilities	☎	☎		☎			☎			☎	☎	☎			
Newspapers		☎					☎							☎	☎
Hospitals	☎			☎			☎			☎		☎	☎		
Air Freight	☎	☎		☎		☎	☎								
Insurance Co.s	☎			☎				☎		☎	☎				
Cable TV Co.s	☎	☎		☎			☎			☎	☎	☎			
Public Transit				☎	☎		☎								
Gov't Info Agencies	☎			☎	☎	☎	☎	☎		☎	☎	☎			
Ticket Offices		☎	☎	☎	☎										
Railroads	☎			☎	☎		☎	☎							
Universities				☎	☎	☎						☎	☎		
Hotels					☎										
Telemarketing Co.s		☎	☎	☎		☎									
Credit Approval Co.s			☎	☎											
Distribution Co.s	☎	☎	☎	☎		☎	☎	☎		☎					
Manufacturers	☎	☎				☎		☎		☎	☎				
Department Stores	☎	☎	☎	☎		☎	☎			☎					

Courtesy Telcom Technologies

Customer Call Center Applications
Horizontals and Verticals

☐ Customer service and dispatch operations. Typically a reactive function with heavy interaction with computer aided dispatch and other outgoing communication systems. There is a growing need for integration with voice response, customer database profiles, paging and radio frequency communications.

☐ Order entry, or inside sales, where customers call in to place their orders for goods or services. This is also a reactive function that can be effectively coupled with account management strategies, order entry, fulfillment systems, and credit approval to change the speed and volume of calls and orders to favor the customer call center and center management.

☐ Credit authorization, where merchants call in to the authorization center as a substitute to use of automated point-of-sale credit authorization devices. Although voice-to-voice authorization is declining as a percentage of authorization activity, it is growing in total transaction volume.

☐ Information Provision. A growing field particularly with the 900 support and FAX back services, voice response technologies coupled with database systems and live operators.

☐ Reservations sales and service. The reason for the birth of this technology.

☐ Catalog sales. This is no longer an unusual application, particularly in business-to-business selling as most companies have discovered that coupling mail order, telephone sales and service works. A major computer company began an experiment 15 years ago to determine whether the sale of small items and consumable supplies was a viable revenue stream and business. Today the two customer call centers supply over 18% of this company's total revenue. Every major computer company is emulating this successful strategy driven by the high cost of sales and customer support in both business and consumer markets.. How many applications for a catalog and telephone sales strategy exist in your company?

❑ Dispatch. Generally coupled with a customer service function unless this is a staff scheduling and dispatch center. There are a number of applications in these centers for the integration of databases and voice response technologies.

❑ Claims processing for users who have experienced a loss of goods or services provided by your company. Again the cost of claims processing is a persuasive argument for using telephone for this function.

There is the obvious reason of turnaround time, but more critical are two demographic issues. First the aging of the population produces a concurrent reduction in mobility and therefore the ability and desire to travel.

Secondly a lowering in the literacy standards. These factors are encouraging an increase in the use of the telephone. Managed care (health insurance) is a compelling illustration of
this phenomenon.

❑ Stockholder relations. A recently automated function in many corporations caused by the upheavals in corporate ownership and control. American Transtech, a customer call center service agency is an AT&T unit that began life in the early 80's, "consoling the widows and orphans" who held stock in the-about-to-be dismembered AT&T. Transtech was so successful they have continued as a profitable strategic business unit within AT&T.

❑ Technical services or software support. Otherwise known as Help Desks. This application is particularly complex endeavor to manage due to the highly skilled personnel that man these support centers and the complex nature and length of the call. Here the call volume may not be high but the necessity to keep vital internal company applications running, account for service levels provided by the Help Desk and deliver productivity make it a particularly attractive application of ACD, desktop workflow technology and call management techniques.

❑ Appointment centers such as show up in modern health care delivery institutions.

❑ Registration, permit and license information applications occur in many hospital, college, state and municipal institutions.

☐   Circulation and customer service in newspapers and magazines. There are some particularly interesting phenomena that occur in the outbound aspects of circulation sales and service that allow smoothing of the inbound demand curve. These increase the flexibility for the circulation department.

☐   Advertising is typically the main source of revenue for any newspaper or magazine. The opportunities to better manage the capture and renewal of revenue from successful managing the running "advertising bank" is absolutely dependent on the effective management of the customer call center resources.

This is a generic list that crosses an even more extensive list of company types as illustrated in Figure 2.1.

Large users have generally recognized the advantages of ACD and related technology and have gone out and acquired the systems they need. These same companies are among the early users of computer telephony integration strategies.

Now smaller units both inside and outside those organizations want access to the benefits provided by these technologies yet were formerly unwilling or unable to pay the price of entry.

The greatest application of call distribution systems has just begun as the systems become less expensive to acquire. The largest markets fall under agent 40 positions. The same can be said for computer telephony applications which have now been embraced by vendors of PC client server solutions.

Chapter Three

The Call Center Structure
The Parts And The Principles

What is a customer call center and what are the physical elements involved in such a center? To receive telephone calls at a customer call center it must be connected to the outside world. There must be telephone circuits or trunks connecting the customer call center with the Central Office that is the local telephone company or "telco" exchange or the nearest long distance point-of-presence facility. These local loops may be digital or analog. They may be single channels or digital T spans of various sizes.

In turn, these links are connected or terminated on the switching equipment in the customer call center. This system is located on the customer premise, and termed customer premise equipment or CPE. It may be a key system, if the application is small. If the application is larger, a PBX may be used in a somewhat undemanding environment, or if it's a high volume application it will be a specific inbound call processing system, typically an Automatic Call Distributor (an ACD).

Attached to this switch are three types of devices other than the telephone trunks. They are the voice telephone instruments used by the customer call center representatives, the management information display devices such as cathode ray tubes (CRT, VDT, or supervisor screen) and printers. These devices are the ACD management tools and are provided with the switching system.

The last five years have seen significant deployment of voice response and automated attendant technology used for triage of callers or providing simple information. These voice devices are typically attached behind the switch so that they can be placed in the inbound call routing table and, so a caller upon request or scenario requirement, be transferred to a live agent on the ACD. This is increasing in significance as VRUs are used to request account and other caller identification for matching caller data with callers.

The individual agents or representatives also may work at a second CRT device where orders are entered or customer information inquiries made. These are typically attached to a "host" system that may be a mainframe computer, a minicomputer and more recently standalone or local area networked personal computers.

The telephone sales or service representative, (TSR) or agent does not perform their role in a vacuum and in turn must interact with the other aspects of the company that are responsible for meeting a prospect or customer need. Little or

no fulfillment of the customer request can be delivered on the telephone unless it is pure information, with no need of follow-up. The methods and speed in closing the fulfillment loop are critical to customer satisfaction and cashflow. A customer who has had their request satisfied quickly is much more inclined to pay promptly. What are these methods and how do they interact with the customer call center, represents another element in the customer call center?

There is a good example of why failure to integrate the whole customer response process from beginning to end can defeat the objective of the transaction from the outset. A company introduced a clever device that assured long distance service resellers the ability tell when a connected call was a billable call. This device "listened" to the call as it was set up. If there was human voice present, it was a billable call. This meant that many abnormally short calls, previously thought to be circuit overhead, and written off as there was doubt in the subscribers favor, could now be billed for. The economic rationale for buying this device was self evident as a reseller could now increase billings for previous lost calls. The company advertised and began a telemarketing program. They received substantial phone orders but didn't complete the sales cycle as they did not have a system to complete the cycle because they did not understand the fulfillment process. They assumed that once a customer said yes, and the "lead" was turned over to field sales, the deal would close and the equipment ship, invoice etc.

Just because an order is agreed to on the phone, the systems must be in place to close the cycle and satisfy the customer expectation created by the promotion and the call center representative. The fulfillment system interfaces must be thought through. These vary with the type of application. A catalog sales application may be simply satisfied with the use of an order entry package running on the company computer. This system probably would already have the fulfillment function as part of that system. A more complex interface may be that of a service dispatch system for the fixing malfunctioning computer equipment. Here the system may interface to a field service, manpower management system, telephone and radio dispatch facilities and response administration to ensure service is done in a timely and satisfactory fashion.

To summarize the customer call center elements are;

- ☐ the telephone circuits and services,
- ☐ the customer premise switching system,
- ☐ the telephone instruments,
- ☐ the customer call center management system tools,
- ☐ the staff at the workstations,
- ☐ the workstations, and
- ☐ fulfillment interfaces.

FIG. 3-1

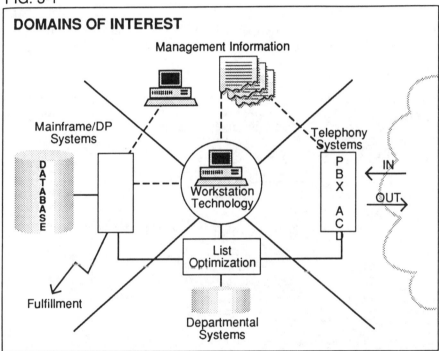

DOMAINS OF INTEREST

Management Information

Mainframe/DP Systems

Telephony Systems

DATABASE

Workstation Technology

P B X

A C D

IN

OUT

List Optimization

Fulfillment

Departmental Systems

Typical Call Center Structure. There are four domains of technical and administrative interest here. At the center of a call center is the individual telephone representative equipped with a phone and more often than not a computer terminal. If they are not happy and productive the system is nearly meaningless. Next (to your left) is the telephone system and network. To your right is the company computer system. At the *bottom of the picture is a departmental system often introduced because the mainframe can't keep up with all the needs of all the departments. At the top is the management information systems that measure and report on all the elements of the call center.*

System Elements And Responsibility

One of the first tasks a customer call center manager is determining who is responsible for critical customer call center elements. Then how to ensure the minimum of problems in having these elements interact as they should. Within each of the elements in Fig 3.1 there are subsets of responsibility as different entities may provide different parts of the puzzle or different services. For example the providers of information services in your company have evolved from the MIS department controlling the mainframe, terminal users and applications development, to include local area networks, desktop and data networks. Figure 3.2 illustrates the lines of demarcation and therefore responsibility. The point of this is that internally the interests of each of these departments affect the acquisition of the ACD. CTI deployment, unless done with a clear vision and driven by a very senior user, can devolve into a political slugfest.

FIG. 3-2

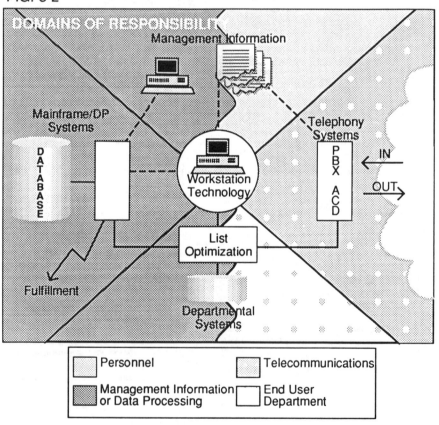

The Technology Is Straight Forward When You C
The Business Application
FIRST

One of the problems confronting a customer call center manager, and one of the reasons for this book, is that there are few sources of assistance through this minefield of opportunities. There appears to be a "mind boggling" array of technology and no one place to learn about this. The basic systems are relatively easy to understand when the pieces and their roles are explained. This is doubly complicated with the advent of computer telephony links and the many new companies that find themselves in this business.

The Telephone Circuits And Services

With telephone service, there are two basic parts to understand. Telephone circuits usually arrive at your business as wire circuits that may carry analog or digital service. Simply put, this is hardware and on this hardware telephone usage occurs, in the form of calls that are made. These represent the service that is delivered to a customer call center enabling the center to make or receive calls. It is important to recognize who has responsibility for the components associated with telephone circuits and usage services.

The telephone company is responsible for supplying local access to a central office or telephone exchange. Local service and connection is the function of the local telephone company, long distance that of AT&T or any alternate long distance service provider. This distinction continues to blur as MCI's recent and inevitable announcement of entry into providing local telephone service.

The Customer Premise Switching System

The telephone circuits are terminated on equipment at the customer call center location. Here things can get a little confusing unless we break them out a step at a time. There are five different combinations of equipment that could be used by a customer call center, again the responsibility of up to five different entities. These are;

> **a.** a single line instrument, that are frequently acquired in quantity. Attached to these instruments are the associated telephone lines that connect the instrument to the telephone exchange. These instruments are

unswitched, meaning that a call arriving on one instrument cannot be redirected to another. This may or may not be a handicap. This "phone banks" are typically used by temporary inbound or outbound operations such as fund raising or political campaigns.

Typically this type of circuit service is available from the local telephone company, who may or may not provide the instruments. Typically they will not.

b. Another arrangement, that looks a little like the above, also provides service to single line instruments at the customer call center, but provides features and switching (intercom, transfer, call the supervisor) by virtue of a switching service at the central office. This is called CO based switch service or CENTREX.

CO or CENTREX ACD service regained popularity as the major central office switch manufacturers deployed automatic call distribution services as part of their systems. However as is typical of this platform, the features are too truncated and too late compared with premised based solutions.

All CENTREX service is provided by the local telephone company. They take responsibility for the entire system except for the premise equipment such as instruments or any management information required by the user. This is a feature they sell heavily as an advantage CENTREX has over premise based ACD systems. The advantage to the customer being the allegedly reduced need to hire staff to support the switch. This argument gained disfavor in the early eighties, primarily because of the high price and the meager features offered by CO ACD products. The began to pendulum swing again as cost effective ACD features appeared to make their way back into CO based ACDs. These systems though promised a potentially painless transition path because of their instant ISDN compatibility.... ISDN! ISDN?... More later in Chapter Four.

c. There may be a system at the customer call center location, a portion of which is dedicated to switching incoming calls. These come in two flavors, a small implementation may occur on a key telephone system (KTS) or a small to medium sized customer call center may be accommodated on a private branch exchange (PBX) with integrated call distribution features.

Responsibility falls squarely on the constructive owner of that system. The use of the legal term "constructive" owner is to differentiate between the user and a "legal" owner such as a leasing company. Typically constructive owner is the primary end user who again, often subcontracts maintenance to system vendor or a qualified third party maintenance entity. In some large or specialized companies such as airlines or utilities, self maintenance may be the chosen support strategy.

d. To date the most sophisticated implementation of inbound call management capabilities occur on standalone purpose built automatic call distribution (ACD) systems. These can be found in all size applications. There have been many recent and aggressive developments in the ACD marketplace that benefit users greatly. The predictive dialer vendors are now claiming ACD functionality.

The responsibility for the ACD, like the previous alternative, falls on the owner and their chosen maintenance strategies.

e. A new entry into the ACD marketplace is the network based ACD system sold by a long distance carrier or designed to use a network or local telephone provider's ISDN availability as the control and call distribution mechanism. These systems are relatively new to marketplace and offer to deliver much of the promise offered by CO based systems, but on an inter exchange basis. These systems are ISDN compliant and involve little in the way of hardware other than the telephone "device" and a customer premise based "telephony server" which supplies the network control logic that effects switching of a call to the desired agent location. ISDN makes multiple circuits to an "at home" agent redundant.

f. Finally there is one combination that is made up of parts of other systems. These are inexpensive, management intense, and offer a viable entry level strategy for those customer call centers on a limited budget. These include outboard management systems that are microprocessor or personal computer based. These include call sequencers and staffing management systems. None of these include switches, but use either existing KTS, PBX or CENTREX based switches, deriving data from these to assist the customer call center management. Responsibilities in this last environment are a little more complex based on equipment a variety of vendors and service and support considerations.

The Telephone Instruments

Attached to each of the switching systems are the instruments that the telephone representatives work with. These instruments fall into four categories,

- ☐ the single line instrument,
- ☐ the KTS or PBX instrument,
- ☐ the specialized ACD instrument, and
- ☐ most recently, PC based intelligence (software) and telephone logic (inboard or outboard hardware) that place the telephony control on the PC screen.

Responsibility for maintenance lies with the provider of the device, the local telephone company or system provider. The infrequent exception may occur when the premise instrument is owned by the customer call center and directly attached to telco lines.

The Customer Call Center Management Tools

In most modern customer call centers there is little argument, there is a high need to manage the center. As a result, subsystems have been added to the call switching devices, CO, network or premise, to provide some level of reporting that in turn, allow management a superior level of control. These systems are typically limited to gathering quantitative or productivity data. How many calls are processed, not how well. This is rapidly changing as the ACD vendors search for differentiation in an increasingly crowded marketplace.

These systems may be integrated into the call switching and distribution devices or an adjunct or supplemental system. We will deal with these as we look at the different system strategies later in this book. Responsibility for support generally lies with the system provider.

And just when it appeared that ACD data gathering and reporting systems had matured extensively, a whole new era of call center administration, reporting and management server technology is making its way into use.

The Staff

Responsibility for hiring and maintaining staff rests directly upon the customer call center management unless the campaign is being subcontracted to a third party customer call center agency. Today there are several contract TSR staffing companies who will provide turnkey staffing.

The Workstations

Every TSR (telephone service representative) sits in a work space or at a position. At this position there are the usual accommodations such as a work surface, a chair and a telephone instrument. He or she also may have a computer workstation or CRT attached to a host computer system. Maintaining this is typically the responsibility of the person that provides the computer system or service. This could be an in-house data processing group or a remote data center or service bureau.

With the advent of screen based telephony and integrated desktop workstations, the system lines of demarcation and responsibility blur further as in a few leading cases, the telephone functionality is incorporated in the PC workstation.

The Fulfillment Interfaces

This is a good deal more complex as this may be a subset of the main company computer system described above or again a remote entity. This is the responsibility for promptly fulfilling the expectation begun by the marketing effort, confirmed by the customer call center, and is critical to profitably closing the transaction.

Customer Call Center Sizes

We have talked about customer call center sizing. There needs to be some frame of reference.

- ☐ Small - Less than 30 TSR positions
- ☐ Medium - 30 to 50 TSR positions.
- ☐ Large - 50 TSR positions and above.

There will be some that read this and take exception that I have termed 50 and above as large, when they are managing a customer call center with 300 positions or more. These centers are indeed very large. Often these are being recognized as less and less desirable because of the sheer effort needed to maintain the center. The tasks and disciplines needed to establish a center of 50 positions are comparable in variety and complexity to beginning a megacenter, though they may not be quite as economically intense.

A significant change has occurred since "The Inbound Call Center" was first written in 1987. Voice response technology has been widely deployed and the "port wars" discussed in the 1990 edition ended as expected. Voice response unit (VRU) or interactive voice response (IVR) vendors believed they would supplant most all ACD applications with voice technologies. This has not occurred to the extent that was predicted due to one thing. People like to be assured they can speak to a live agent, and that requires switching back to a live operator. Though the deployment of VRUs is ubiquitous and successful. A large California bank fields about 65,000,000 retail customer calls a year. Just 33% or 22,000,000 are ultimately served by a live operator proving the customer acceptance and cost containment worth of the technology.

Voice response vendors remained behind the ACD as switched resources for three reasons:

- ❑ an ACD port is still cheaper than most VRU ports,
- ❑ once behind a switch it can be "switched" from caller to caller based on demand. A dedicated VRU port cannot, and
- ❑ VRUs have generally provided poor reporting when compared with the more sophisticated ACD systems.

I would like to pose a question that I cannot find the answer to anywhere and the voice response industry provides a perfect illustration. "Why is it when a new industry is born, even though it is a minor register shift from a previous technology (PBXs and ACDs,) they forget all the lessons of the previous business?" In this case, a call center cannot get enough information about performance, yet the IVR business generally provides minimal reporting which has significant implications when integrated customer experience reporting is requirement of the customer call center.

Customer Call Center Location

Customer call center sizing often influences the location of a customer call center and becomes an important issue in choosing a location. More on this later.

Customer Call Centers vs. Normal Telecom Tasks

Customer call centers are unlike most telecommunications applications your in-house telecommunications departments have ever encountered. In an early ACD book, "A Management Guide to ACDs," the author, Steven Grant, best

describes the philosophic differences of a customer call center to any other telecommunications application....

> *" An ACD (read inbound customer call center) is more complicated to manage than other communications devices (read applications) because its operation must be tuned in response to even short variations in staffing and call volumes. These fluctuations profoundly affect so many different aspects of an ACD-based business, it requires day-by-day, hour-by-hour analysis and management judgment to operate at an optimal level. It is never adequate to staff an ACD only for a peak period like a PABX, or to configure the number of trunks simply based on the average hours of highest traffic load like a tandem switch. The ACD's proper role is not to offer an arbitrary service level at random, but to perform consistently at a service level that will generate profit or save money for the profit center"....*

These are the statements of a person whose professional endeavors began as a telecommunications manager. Here is recognition from an enlightened telecommunications manager that the core philosophies driving traditional (read administrative) telecommunications, planning do not apply to customer call center engineering, planning and management.

When reconciling the higher costs of establishing and operating a customer call center remember the value of the transaction, represented by the call generally far outstrips the cost of the call. Not untypically, up to a hundredfold. We discussed the marketing and sales effort costs of customer acquisition and keeping the phones ringing, yet the value of the transaction conducted on the phone is also of real value, and a separate opportunity.

When visiting large mail order catalog companies, so often there are rows and rows of empty telephone representative positions, ready to be used at the slightest uptick in business. Expensive telephone lines and switching facilities lie almost idle waiting for the next catalog mailing drop or the onset of the Christmas buying season. This idleness and under-utilization is an absolute aberration to the average telecommunications manager or accountant. Yet it is a way of life of the customer call center manager. No call center, reflecting the market dynamics of advertising, buying and fashion seasons, can ever afford to be equipped at average capacity.

In the words of Steven Grant,

> *"the...customer call center...role is not to offer and arbitrary level selected at random, but to perform consistently at a....level.. which will generate a profit or save money....!"*

Overcapacity is therefore a fact of life in customer call center planning. You need to recognize this early while developing your operating plan.

Ordinary And Extraordinary Growth Issues

Customer call centers that are begun intelligently and well integrated into the corporate structure, grow beyond expectations, at unanticipated rates.

Customer call centers live in the world of "real-time marketing." While talking to your customers and prospects you get real-time market feedback. The best illustration of this is the restaurant business. If a customer is happy, you are promptly paid, accolades accompany the payment and the waiter is presented with a generous gratuity. Great food is seldom badly served. This is good real-time market feedback and, as a result, the restaurant management can make timely changes based on the diners' responses.

Until they introduce a customer call center, few traditional companies have this consistent amount of real-time contact with their markets. Field feedback is spotty at best. Provided the customer call center is managed and well integrated into informal internal communications networks, this feedback becomes an important part of judging market conditions and adjusting to them.

Also significant is that this data gathering can be done at a lower cost than most other research techniques. It can be done impromptually, quickly and relatively informally. A huge process does not have to be set up to deal with a field organization or distribution network. The research also can be focused at small market segments. Simply ask questions on the phone.

Because all the reps are under one set of managers who require answers to a simple script, the data gathered is much more consistent.

With this potential for success and the recognition that this real-time market intelligence medium exists in the customer call center, new tasks and projects are suddenly found. Test projects are created. Questions are created to ask prospect

and customer as they call in. This further expands the workload of the center. All the traditional growth planning is out the proverbial window.

Customer call centers are often begun as pilot projects to figure out whether they will work in the company marketing, distribution and customer support plan. If planned and supported properly, they nearly always exceed expectation and are given expanded roles with larger projects and newly discovered ones.

Be aware this can happen to you. Congratulations, this success can kill your customer call center!

Planning around this is difficult from a factual and a political point of view. First you're too optimistic. Second you're unrealistic about the corporate budgeting system. There are no simple answers other than to operate and plan around this potential for sudden success. Educating direct management to the potential of the customer call center and these unusual dynamics can avert unwelcome surprises. In short, prepare for growth.

Computer Telephony Integration

By any other name this is process reengineering of the customer call center. Consequently there are three schools of promotional thought; telecentric, datacentric and workflow reengineering. The Telecentrics; the PBX and ACD systems vendors generally promote CTI as a tool to save money based on circuit savings and labor reduction. The datacentrics or computer vendors believe that the justification for CTI lies in cost savings and the efficiency driven by intermachine "plumbing." Both are right for very superficial reasons. The folks that grasp the vision and long term implications of CTI understand that the real success of CTI is the fact it is a platform for workflow changes. Reengineering of any workflow process is fundamental, disruptive and downright scary. To grasp this and limit CTI to the realm of "plumbing" is to miss the entire point.

The real opportunity in reengineering the customer call center is typically addressed at two levels:

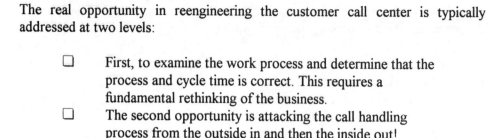

- ☐ First, to examine the work process and determine that the process and cycle time is correct. This requires a fundamental rethinking of the business.
- ☐ The second opportunity is attacking the call handling process from the outside in and then the inside out!

First optimize agent availability to serve customers for the highest possible work time per day. That is optimizing the agent occupancy. That is outside in. The second aspect is to ensure that the agent then is positioned and supported to work at the most productively as possible. Ensure the agent has the best tools possible to satisfy that customer. That is the inside out. Examine the call types (and those are not the only means of customer contact!) Determine the steps and process required to satisfy a customer (within the call or with subsequent follow up.) Determine is there is time to be saved in the entire process of meeting that request and DO NOT limit your thinking to the actual duration of the call. Now you looking beyond the call at the fundamentals of workflow and the real opportunities to improve process.

Chapter Four

Service And Traffic Issues:

The Parts And The Principles

To receive telephone calls at a customer call center, the center must be connected to the outside world. Calls arrive on trunks that are connected (the telephone term is "terminated") on the customer call center switching equipment. More frequently than not, this customer call center system is located on the customer premise. This equipment is termed customer premise equipment or CPE. It may be a key system, if the application is relatively small. If the application is larger, a private branch exchange (PBX) or switchboard may be used in a relatively undemanding environment. For a high volume application, a sophisticated inbound call processing system, typically a standalone automatic call distributor (ACD) may be used.

An alternative to buying a telephone switching system is now being offered as automatic call distribution service by your local telephone company. Central office based ACD services can provide a similar range of features to the ACDs based on PBX systems. The key difference is there is no equipment, other than the agent station equipment, located at the customer's call center.

This has also expanded to include most the long distance network providers who have begun offering basic call routing and distribution. These network based services offer significant potential in far flung enterprise wide call distribution where small centers and "at home" agents are used.

Telephone circuits or trunks connect the customer call center switching equipment with the Central Office. These trunks and the central office, (the "CO") belong to the local serving telephone company or "telco."

For a CO-ACD or a network based service these circuits are station lines from the CO to your premises and/or the individual agent stations. This central office is then connected to other central offices and the long distance networks that are available to carry inbound calls to and from call center.

This chapter is not meant to be a comprehensive explanation of the workings of the telephone network, but an explanation of a few parts and principles that affect the customer call center manager. (You can acquire more knowledge from the many fine books available from the Telcom Library. 1-800-LIBRARY. Ask for a free catalog.)

The Network Hierarchy

To understand how all this fits together, a review of post-Divestiture network structure is helpful. Imagine the overall telephone network as a connected hierarchy elements -- sort of like an "army-style" organization chart. At the highest level, the telephone on the desk in front of you is the most rudimentary and ubiquitous element representing this network. This telephone instrument is connected to all other telephones by many central office switches assembled together in hierarchical importance. They fall into two categories;

a.) **local service or distribution switches serving local telephone subscribers, and,**

b.) **those switches that allow connection between these switches and the switches of the regional and long distance carriers.**

This latter category are primarily long distance transmission switches. These levels are all connected by local cable and elements of the public switched network(s). Beginning at the highest level, or man/machine interface, (phone or voice terminal), the list and order of the elements making up a long distance call look like this;

The Telephone Number

Everybody that subscribes to telephone has a unique and unambiguous telephone identity or "address." This is a telephone number. The only exception to the unique numbering rule is a party line. Here several subscribers share the use of a line. This occurs when equipment is in short supply. Or it's expensive to get to the person (out in the boonies). Party lines are becoming less and less common.

Numbers are assigned to subscribers under an orderly numbering plan. Telephone numbers follow an orderly arrangement and in doing so, reflect the switching hierarchy we have been discussing.

FIG. 4-1

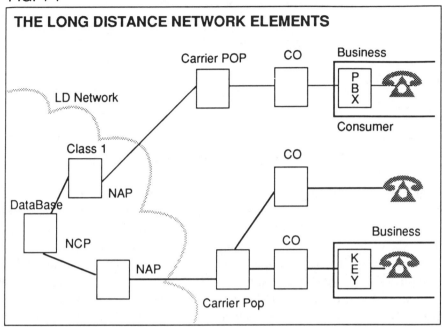

THE LONG DISTANCE NETWORK ELEMENTS

Key to acronyms and explanations:
LD Network = dial-up public long distance network, any carrier.
Carrier POP = Long distance carrier point of presence in the local telephone companies franchise.
CO = Local telephone company central office or phone exchange
Class 1 = Major long distance switching center
NAP = Network Action Point is a long distance switching point
NCP = Network Control Point is the source of control for the NAP
D/Base = Network control database

MAKING A CALL

When a call is placed to your customer call center the caller raises the handset on the telephone, (identified in Figure 4.4 as element 1,) and upon receiving dial tone from the telco CO, (2,) begins to dial your directory number. As this occurs (2 through 9) receive the instructions necessary, in the form of the request for dial tone, then the dialed digits (pulses or tones) that indicate the intended party to be called. The call is carried into the network. This is the path the call follows "into" the network. Other elements identified as 7 through 1 must be used "leaving" the network to reach the intended callee, or your customer call center.

FIG. 4-2

NORTH AMERICAN NUMBERING PLAN

TIME FRAME	NUMBERING PLAN AREA AREA CODE	LISTED DIRECTORY NUMBER SUBSCRIBER NUMBER	
		OFFICE CODE	LINE NUMBER
TODAY	N∅ or 1 X	NNX	XXXX
1990s	NXX	NXX	XXXX

Key X = 0-9, N = 2- 9, 0 or 1 - 0 or 1

By using these numbering plans certain subscriber capacities are attainable. There used to be a rule that only area codes could contain a 0 or a 1 as the center digit, 212, 203 etc. More recently exchange office codes are showing up with 0 or 1 as the second digit. The reason is the phone companies are running out of numbering codes. Today, to dial long distance, the subscriber must dial 1 (one) before dialing the long distance number. Now this is been implemented across the country there is no longer confusion between dialing an area code and a local exchange code with the same leading digits.   As a result there are some unfamiliar looking telephone numbers.

FIG. 4-3

NUMBERING PLAN CAPACITIES

CODE	CAPACITY
XXX	10,000 CODES
N 0 or 1	152 "
	640 "
NNX	800 "

FIG. 4-4

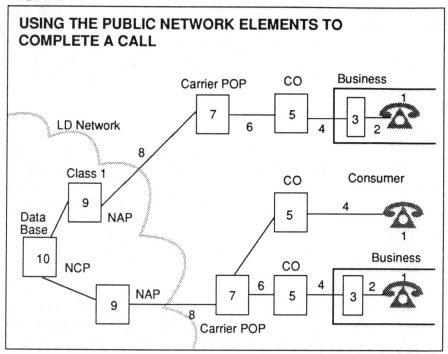

USING THE PUBLIC NETWORK ELEMENTS TO COMPLETE A CALL

1. This is the customer switching system.
2. This is the local telephone line to the telco exchange or central office.
3. The central office or CO.
4. The inter-exchange circuit to the long distance carrier point of presence in or near the local telephone company exchange.
5. The long distance carrier "point of presence" or POP — the long distance exchange.
6. The carrier long distance network.
7. The major long distance switching hubs or Class 1 network offices.
8. The centralized network database where number translations and routing instructions reside.

To place a call, the caller must have a clear knowledge of the number of the entity they wish to call, and there are a whole series of dialing plans to achieve this. We need not deal with this detail here, however there is one exception that needs to be explained, as it effects toll-free or 800 service (as it is designated in North America).

We have described a typical telephone network as it operates today. The "addressing and routing" signals (the dialed digits) travel on the same circuits the call will be conducted upon. This is called "inband" signaling because it travels in the same signal bandwidth of the voice telephone call.

This same hardware and circuit structure is also used in an ISDN (Integrated Services Digital Network) network but differs in that the signaling and routing data travels on a separate parallel circuit dedicated to this function. This is called out-of-band signaling. To run an ISDN network a parallel signaling network called a Signaling System 7 (SS7) must exist between the local and long distance telephone exchanges.

The call is now separated into two basic aspects; the actual voice call, albeit digitized and the data packet that describes the call and ensures it is routed to the intended party. There are two types of ISDN circuit that the average customer call center will encounter. Basic Rate and Primary Rate service. Basic rate is the service that is delivered to a residential subscriber. This is described as 2 B + D, that is the equivalent of two voice grade circuits and a data path. As volume grows or a business demands it, T1 capacity circuits or 23 B + D are typical. These as expected are the capacity equivalent of 23 voice grade lines and a data channel.

The voice signal is digitized voice and requires ISDN compliant connections either as part of the equipment or an outboard adapter. The messages carried on the data channel allow a number of value added services that allow a customer call center to really personalize the service they are offering to their customers. Among the various services are Automatic Number Identification and Dialed Number Identification. These two services will be described later in the context of customer call center applications.

Physical And Logical

800 numbers have no "physical" or hardware addresses. An 800 number is a "software defined" or logical address. When you dial an 800 number, the number is translated into a "physical" address identified as an area, exchange and subscriber code. Just like your residential telephone number. This is a physical address. This is an important idea. It is important to realize the number of times software - number translation software - effects customer call centers. Here is a identifiable number, 800-LIBRARY, (800-542-7279) (TELCOM LIBRARY.) It is published and calls are placed to it by Telcom Library book customers, and Telcom is billed for usage. But unlike a regular subscriber directory number, there are no physical trunks identified as 800-542-7279. What is assigned to this number is a translation target directory number. The 800 number is a "logical" facility, while the subscriber number and the trunks are a "physical" facility. The 800 entity exists because of software, not hardware.

The "real" 800-LIBRARY phone number is 212-206-6870. A caller ultimately reaches this number in New York when they dial 800-542-7279 from California, Florida or anywhere in the U.S. Before the call proceeds through the network, the 800 database translates the called number (800-542-7279) to the final 212 number in New York City that we answer.

This translation ability means we can not only translate logical 800 numbers into one other physical target number, but we can use different number based on different conditions. These conditions may be time-of-day, day-of-week or year or when certain other things happen. These other circumstances could be based on service levels at, or calls offered to, a regional customer call center. Or a center outage and invoking of a backup strategy.

Once a certain parameter (e.g. exceeding a call count threshold or intentional switch over to a backup strategy,) the next calls can be rerouted to another (customer call center) number. Incoming call services are expanding at a great rate. Some carriers are experimenting with forwarding incoming calls to a local dealer based on knowing the number called and the number the call is originating from. New call distribution capabilities are being imbedded in the network all with the intention of making one 800 service provider more competitive with another.

Toll-Free Calls

Deep in the network, (element 10 in Figure 4.4,) is a large network control database. This is called a Network Control Point or NCP. Here resides a master table that cross references the advertised (logical) 800 number with a regular subscriber directory (physical) number. When the 800 number is dialed, the receiving CO (element 5) communicates with this master database (element 10). A "look up" of the master cross reference listing occurs. The destination subscriber directory number is sent back to the originating CO. This physical address follows the area/exchange/subscriber code rules so orderly call routing happens within the long distance network. This is called "number translation." This is translating the 800 number to an actual subscriber number. The CO point where the call originated and each switching step of the routing process are called Network Action Points or NAPs. The role of the NAP is determined by the rout sent on a per call basis from the NCP database.

Signaling

Underneath the telephone call there is a whole subset of housekeeping controls that allow the call to be made, billed for and then return the circuit path to idle for reuse by the next caller. It is important to understand this control system as it effects a customer call center. There are some billing and circuit maintenance issues that are key to a customer call center's cost of operation and effective circuit use. A telephone call occurs at two levels, the actual communication (voice or data) and the underlying housekeeping or "supervision" signaling. This signaling information falls into four categories;

1.   **Supervisory signals,**
- control; transmitted forward as requests for service,
- status; transmitted backward as answers to these requests.

Supervision can be compared to "handshake" and acknowledgment that occurs between communicating computers. "Are you there?" "Yes." "How do you wish to proceed?" "Etc."

2.   **Address signals, or the requested telephone number;**
- in digital (numerals,) or
- analog (tone (DTMF) or pulse) format.

3.   **Call Service Signals (audible tones, announcements, etc.)**
- dial tone,
- busy signal,
- reorder tone,
- receiver off hook,
- recorded announcement, or
- system intercept tones.

4.   **Network Management Data.**

Every telephone call is made through this established and orderly set of control signals. It is important to understand that the entire network control system begins with a request for service by the person INITIATING the call. It seems pedantic to emphasize this as it seems obvious. The person wishing to make the call has the responsibility for it and with the ability to use the phone, the obligation to pay for that use.

This is fine until the concept of toll free calling is introduced. Here we appear to subvert the whole notion of "user pays" and upset the physical addressing system by introducing a "fictitious" or logical number. What we do not upset however, is the way calls are set up and the principle of the caller controlling the supervisory signaling. The significant difference is that the payment responsibility is shifted to the receiving party.

Billing Responsibility

As you would expect the notion of "user pays" is an underlying principle in the establishing of telephone service. With the introduction of toll-free service there was clear recognition by sellers and buyers of 800 numbers that the market for offering free service to a caller was attractive for a much broader reason -- serving prospects and customers by phone. It is no accident that today the 800 business produces over $15 billion dollars for AT&T and the other common carriers providing 800 services. AT&T, MCI and SPRINT are offering new and innovative services with 800 service, some of which we will discuss later.

FIG. 4-5

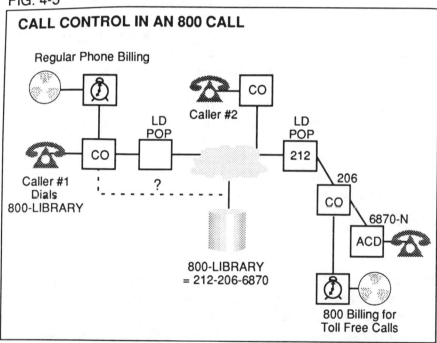

CALL CONTROL IN AN 800 CALL

Regular Phone Billing

Caller #2

Caller #1
Dials
800-LIBRARY

?

LD POP

212

206

CO

6870-N

ACD

800-LIBRARY
= 212-206-6870

800 Billing for
Toll Free Calls

Shows the signaling originating with the caller lifting the handset and beginning to call the call center. The call ends with that same caller hanging up the phone. Once the phone is returned to idle a set of control signals are sent to the receiving party ending the call. This allows the call to be "broken down." This means all the links and the switches that carried this call from the callers phone to the call center are released to new callers.

As noted, the significant change to the call set up procedure on an 800 call is that the billing responsibility is shifted to the receiving party. All the control and supervisory signal still originate and terminate with the caller. This is significant when we discuss call set up and breakdown control on ACD systems in Chapter Eight because the caller "owns" the link until they hang up and the disconnect signal is received by your customer call center.

Integrated Systems Digital Services (ISDN)

ISDN is a plan of how the world's telephone network should be. There are distinct shortcomings in the way the analog telephone network behaves. This is brought about by the principles, rules and media that have evolved into the network. The limitations occur in the area of circuit capacity, supervision overhead on the network, undesirable redundancy in voice and data networks and the explosion of incompatible devices and standards. To date, digitizing this network has merely reduced analog circuits and increased circuit capacity. Digitization of the analog networks and their signaling standards has not reduced supervision overhead, introduced universal standards or reduced the redundancy in voice or data networks as it remains a digital replica of an analog network.

ISDN is the vision to overcome this. It is such a sweeping revision of the existent network standards and systems investments that it has been slow to arrive in the public network. Much of the hand waving that has occurred has been primarily marketing hype. That is until now. ISDN equipped services are clearly a significant service targeted at the call center as a primary beneficiary of this technology as calls have a definitive value, that is a sale or customers service implications.

What is ISDN?

ISDN is based upon T-1 formats. For many years, computer telephony system developers have been enjoying the benefits of T-1 digital trunk access to their service provider. T-1 provides simpler cabling, good voice quality, lower cost, and in many cases, convenient access to Automatic Number Identification, or ANI (the calling party's number) and Dialed Number Identification Service, or DNIS (what number did they call) information.

When conventional digital T-1 trunks place outbound calls or receive inbound calls, they rely on a combination of in-band DTMF/MF tones, an also by robbing bits from the voice channels (you cannot hear the bits being stolen - it happens quietly and too infrequently) to accomplish the call control signaling. These methods work, but are slow and have limited possibility for growth. ISDN adds sophistication, accuracy and speed to the network. ISDN is a communications protocol that layers on top of T-1. ISDN robs an entire voice channel (in the case of Basic Rate Interface, 2B+D for home use or, Primary Rate, 23B+D, for business use) and uses it for communicating the signaling information by using a standard packet protocol. For example, to place a call, the ISDN customer premise equipment would send a packetized message containing the number being called directly to the telephone network's computer. Because it is peer-to-peer digital signals, versus DTMF/MF telephone terminal emulation, the call is routed and placed much faster.

On an inbound call, the ANI and DNIS information is received via similar message packets. This method is again much faster than the several seconds required by T-1's combination of winking and tone transmission.

Who needs ISDN?

ANI and DNIS information, critical to the customer call center, is not always offered on conventional T-1. AT&T, many local RBOCs and Bell Canada require ISDN for access to ANI and DNIS information.

Even if a customer call center is able to obtain ANI and DNIS information today from their T-1 carrier, ISDN can offer the immediate benefits of higher accuracy and speed by virtual of the digital signal packets. Outbound calls, as well as ANI and DNIS information collection, happens virtually in an instant. This enables the customer call center to handle more traffic.

Future ISDN features will enable the call center to quickly transfer and reroute calls to other customer call centers in different geographic locations by allowing the caller's ANI and DNIS, and account information to be passed through the network along with the call! For the enterprise, ISDN will enable high speed data, fax and video to be transmitted to other enterprises without dedicated tie lines.

ISDN Features

Primary Rate vs. Basic Rate

A T-1 trunk carries 24 time slots. ISDN based on T-1 rates is referred to as Primary Rate Interface (PRI). There are two types of time slots on ISDN. The first type carries voice or data information, and is called the "Bearer" or "B" channel. The second type carries signaling information and is called the "D" channel. For Primary Rate ISDN, 24 time slots are typically allocated as 23 B channels and 1 D channel. For residential services that require less channels, a Basic Rate Interface is defined. BRI consists of two B channels and one D channel.

ANI & DNIS

Many customer call centers of today rely on obtaining ANI and DNIS for efficient call handling. ISDN offers the fastest and most effective means for obtaining this information from the network. Outbound call centers enjoy ISDN's fast call setup to increase outbound calling productivity. Distributed call centers utilize ISDN for its intelligent call routing capabilities. With standard offerings from companies like Dialogic's and the onboard PRI firmware, all of these benefits and more are accessible in PC-based computer telephony systems.

Vari-A-Bill

With AT&T's Vari-A-Bill service, a bureau can vary the billing rate of a 900 call at any time during the call. Callers typically select services from a voice-automated menu, with each service individually priced.

Call by Call Service Selection

Today's modems are limited to about 28.8 kbps transmission rates because they must treat the network as an analog trunk. Faster when a permanent circuit or tie line is used. ISDN enables data to take full advantage of the speed of the digital telephone network. When placing a call, an ISDN user can specify that the call is data, not voice. The network will ensure an end-to-end digital connection is established - enabling high speed data transmission. This scheme is especially popular for video conferencing applications. Call-by-Call Service Selection allows applications to specify the type of call, be it voice or data, on a dynamic basis as the call is placed.

Non-Facility Associated Signaling

Non-Facility Associated Signaling (NFAS) is a feature which enables savings on access charges. In North America, carriers typically charge a premium rate for the D channel, as much as $400 per month over and above the T-1 span charges, plus a several thousand dollar installation fee. However, this D channel is capable of handling additional signaling than is required by the 23B (bearer) channels also contained on the same span or "facility." NFAS allows a single D channel to support up to eight ISDN T-1 spans (24B). The result is overall lower access costs by efficient use of this D channel.

Sub-Addressing & User to User Information

Sub-addressing allows multiple devices or extensions to share the same phone number. This allows for efficient and direct communication between multiple ISDN equipped sites. For example, Sub-addressing allows an ISDN caller to call directly to an extension behind an ISDN PBX. User-to-User Information allows the application to send proprietary information along with a call to another ISDN-equipped site. A popular application for both Sub-addressing and User-to-User Information is transferring calls within a geographically dispersed call center. Suppose a customer call arrives at one call center and, after collecting information on the caller, it is determined that the customer will best be handled by a particular agent at another location. The call can be transferred to the other location with the caller's account identification included in the User-to-User Information field, and the agents extension number in the Subaddressing field.

<u>ISDN is not exactly a standard</u>

ISDN is slightly different in each location, depending on the CO switch being used. The user must be aware of what type of switch, and subsequently what type of protocol is available to them. There are some emerging standards, though. In Europe, the standard is called Euro-ISDN. In North America, it is called National ISDN. Today, switch based protocols are in abundance.

Switch Protocol	Country
AT&T 4ESS, 5ESS	USA
NT DMS 100 / 250	Canada
INS1500	Japan
VN3	France
1TR6	Germany
DASS2	UK

Here we must move into some basic technical concepts. They will make your life as a customer call center manager much simpler. Engineers will not be so quick to blind you with technical mumbo jumbo.

Transmission Concepts

There are two primary types of transmission signaling that a customer call center manager will encounter: analog and digital.

Analog Transmission And Switching

This term is not meaningful in correct English usage however as it is a derivative of the word "analogous" or "similar to." In telephone transmission the signal that is being transmitted is analogous to the original. In technical terms it is a wave

form of continuously varying quantity (amplitude, or loudness and frequency, tonal pitch) reflecting changes of signal source (typically your voice) in time. In other words if you were to speak into a microphone and see your voice on an oscilloscope there would be an image of a wave form. The vertical or X coordinate expresses amplitude while the horizontal or Y coordinate expresses time. The same wave form is transmitted on a telephone line although as it is electrically transmitted on a telephone line, the frequency is higher.

FIG. 4-6

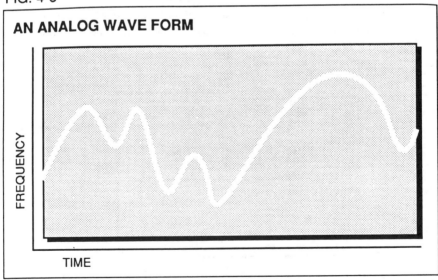

AN ANALOG WAVE FORM

FREQUENCY

TIME

In an analog switching system there is a physical switch matrix. These are a matrix of switches. They are either physical switch relays or solid state switches that represent these physical relays. These switches are arranged in a square matrix with X and Y coordinates. Each on of the ports on the X/Y matrix have an address and a physical path to a second X/Y port. Connections are made between these ports (for example an incoming trunk and an agent instrument) by directing the switchpoint that allows X 14 to connect to Y 12. X 14 could be a trunk, whereas Y 12 an agent station. To connect between X 14 and Y 12, there must be an available physical path (unsurprisingly called a talk path) through the network matrix. If not, the call is blocked.

FIG. 4-7

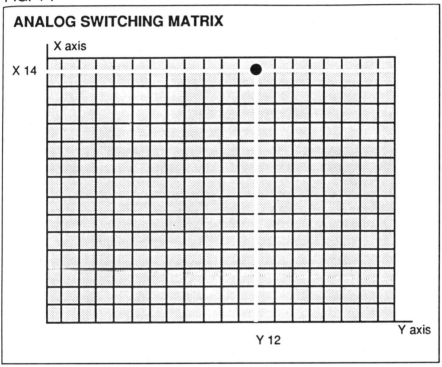

Digital Transmission And Switching

Digital technology is a more recent transmission and switching technology that was brought about to economically increase the capacity and speed of switching and transmission systems and facilities. Digital systems are less expensive and smaller to build. They are infinitely more complex and software intense and require absolutely stable power environments to maintain orderly operation.

Digital transmission and switching technologies take the analog wave form we discussed above, and plot it on an imaginary grid. Each point on this grid has a distinct numeric or digital value. This is then transmitted in order of occurrence in the wave form and then reassembled at the end of the transmission. This feat is accomplished by coding and decoding (of analog to digital and back to analog).

The device that performs this is called a CODEC. The most common method of coding and decoding is called "pulse code modulation or PCM. PCM coding and decoding occurs at 8000 samples a second. This means the analog wave is sampled 8000 times a second and a digital expression in that point of the waveform is generated and transmitted to a corresponding CODEC which decodes this to analog sound capable of being heard by a human.

To transmit these across a digital network, tiny time slices or slots are assigned on a transmission buss to each of the samples. Attached to each of these digital samples is a destination port address so that the digital packet ends up at the right destination for decoding into the voice of the person calling this destination. The capacity test of a switch or transmission facility is the number of time slots the device will support. Divide this by two as each time slot is one way and two are required for a conversation. One is dedicated to the caller and the other to the called party. This is analogous to the capacity of a single talk path in an analog switch which is two way per talkpath. The connection between two ports in an analog switch equal the capacity of two time slots in a digital switch. A manufacturer may talk about time slots, simultaneous conversations or highways. The trick is to ask what it takes to carry one conversation between two parties, then how many simultaneous conversations can be carried within the device.

You now have the information to ask about the conversation capacity of a switch and understand the answer.

This capacity issue may also find some other limitations when you are building a screen pop application where not only voice connections are important but also the capacity of the host to deliver screens with calls in a timely fashion. One of the greatest tests of computer systems and applications in a customer call center is the ability to keep up with the pace of the conversation.

FIG. 4-8

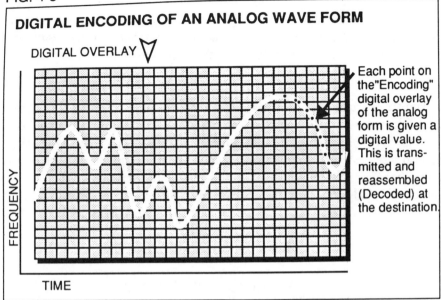

DIGITAL ENCODING OF AN ANALOG WAVE FORM

DIGITAL OVERLAY ▽

Each point on the"Encoding" digital overlay of the analog form is given a digital value. This is transmitted and reassembled (Decoded) at the destination.

FREQUENCY

TIME

Analog Versus Digital

Although the world has almost completely moved to digital transmission and switching systems, analog transmission techniques have served us well since the beginning of the telephone industry and will continue to serve much of the world for many years to come. The reason? Analog works and technologies that have been developed to support analog transmission are extremely reliable.

Analog has built in signal redundancy. It is not a simple digital signal of an analog form, rather the actual sound energy. A replication of the analog wave. If you "drop" (lose) digital bits, the message is lost. Analog signals are therefore more robust. A little noise momentarily interferes with the clarity of the signal but the signal is still present. More noise, less signal, but it still goes through until the ""signal to noise ratio" overwhelms the signal.

Digital switching and transmission systems are much more economical to design and build as they take up less space, power and therefore allow much larger capacity at a lower cost than their analog equivalents. Digital signals also have a much lower susceptibility to interference from noise over distance. Conversely a digital signal needs a much "cleaner" electronic environment to travel in otherwise the signal can be interrupted. Most readers will have experienced a faxed being "knocked off" the line when some sort of electronic interference is encountered on the circuit. Although the fax may be being transmitted on an analog line, a modem is converting digital signals into very precise analog signals. The slightest interruption drops a bit (analog representation) and can blow up the message.

All signals degrade over distance. An analog signal is "boosted" or "amplified" when it gets weak. This means any circuit noise is picked up and amplified also. Contrast this with a digital signal that is regenerated. The digital signal is reconstructed. A simple circuit makes a judgment: is this signal a one or a zero? It then reconstructs the signal, boosts it and retransmits it. When no one is speaking, digital signals can be so quiet some phone systems actually inject "side tone" or noise -- just to make the users feel something is happening.

Transmission Media

The most common transmission medium is (a) twisted pair (of wires). These are used both in premise (inside the building) and outside (the building, in the street) cable plant. Twisted pair is usually copper wire and is used extensively. It is inexpensive. There is a vast investment in local loops and metropolitan switch to switch trunks (metro trunks) already in use. This medium can be a single pair or occur in multiples of up to 3600 pair per cable. The transmission characteristics of this medium are good although can be susceptible to noise in the form of electromagnetic impulses (hum) and crosstalk. "Crosstalk" is where you encounter another conversation on the connection you have just had set-up. The intra-switch connection can be plain old voice service or digital T-1 carrier of 24 voice channels per T-1 span on two pairs of twisted wire.

Less frequently encountered by end users is coaxial cable, microwave radio and optical fiber. Although these media are frequently used by telcos, long distance carriers and bypass media to large customer call centers. Up until recently understanding of their use and characteristics have not of been great importance to the customer call center manager, and in many cases are still beyond the average user. If you need to understand nothing else, it is vital these operate flawlessly when they are carrying that ever so important inbound customer call.

T-1 is of increased importance to customer call centers especially with the increasing availability of cost effective T-1 facilities and carrier services such as AT&T Megacom, sold with a preferred local T-1 loop. There are pros and cons in buying telephone service on T-1 loops that deal with reliability, cost effective circuit sizes justifying T-1 and interconnection issues. For a full explanation of T-1 see a companion volume by Bill Flanagan, The Teleconnect Guide to T-1 Networking. Call 1-800-LIBRARY for your copy.

The Players

There are a minimum of three players in the provision of telephone services to a customer call center. They fall into three categories;

- ☐ The provider of the switching system (KTS, PBX, PBX/ACD or ACD),
- ☐ The provider of local telephone service and access to long distance services. The telephone company or telco may also own the provider of the premise equipment or as an alternative to premise equipment may provide CO based premise switch services called CENTREX.
- ☐ The long distance carriers.

Now this distinction is increasingly blurred as the long distance carrier attempt to get into local services and the local service providers begin to provide long distance services. If history is a teacher, it will only take a few years for the various enterprises to realize that their real skills are based in their traditional businesses and to degree, return their focus to these familiar and profitable markets. In the mean time, take advantage of the user discounts that inevitably accompany "marketshare wars."

FIG. 4-9

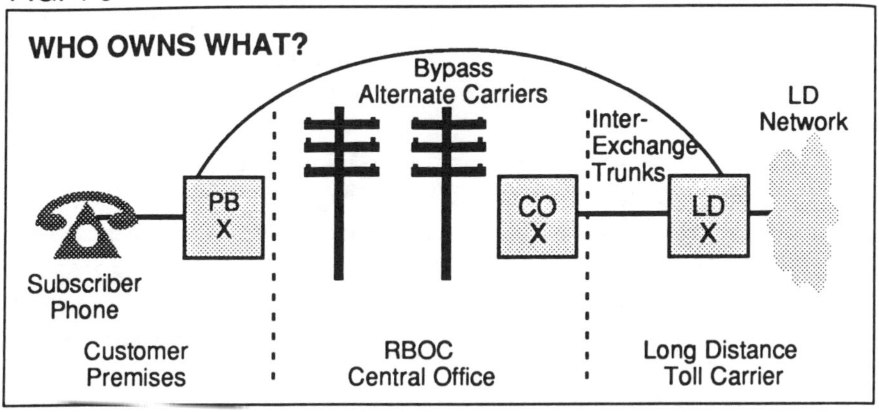

WHO OWNS WHAT?

Dealing with the local telephone company is typically the responsibility of the customer call center manager in a small to medium sized company. In a larger organization this is normally the role of telecommunications department. The telephone company is capable of everything from absolute stupidity to sheer miracles. Your relationship with them, and understanding of what they do, is vital to your sanity and important to achieving your goals.

Long distance carriers are changing services and tariffs at an ever accelerating rate. There is no substitute for up to date information from the individual carriers that serve your location. There are a few basic traffic principles we will examine in a moment that are necessary to use when you interpret this data.

Telephone Traffic

As we have discussed there are three economic realities associated with a telephone call to your center;

☐   The cost of inducing the caller to call,

☐   the potential value in the revenue opportunity offered by the call, or protection of future revenue in the case of a service call, and then,

☐   the actual cost of processing the call.

A simple telephone call to your center is not just a simple event. First there are two types of call;

■ a simple single dimensional transaction. A call for rock concert tickets. You get your seat reservation, make payment arrangements and receive ticket pickup instructions. That's it.

■ Then there is a compound transaction that continues over time. An ideal example is a business-to-business account management or a mail order catalog/consumer relationship.

A call represents a single call event. This is made up of telephony "milestones" marked by status changes and events that comprise the customer call. These are;

The call begins by a caller lifting the phone or going "off hook",

- Dialing the number,
- The network receiving the dialed digits, interpreting and "setting up" the call to the receiving central office,
- The receiving central office receiving the call and "seizing" a local trunk to the customer call center and sending a request for service,
- The customer call center equipment responds and receives the call,
- The call is answered with a call processing method that is transparent to the caller. That process may include an announcement, a live person and more frequently an automated attendant offering the caller treatment options.
- The call is processed by the telephone service or sales representative,
- The call ended and the customer call center "hangs up" or terminates the call,
- The breakdown signal from the originating party makes its way (at electronic speed) through the network,
- Returning the receiving end facilities, the CO, local loop or trunk and receiving customer call center equipment to idle, for the next call, when all this is repeated again. All of these events represent a call that takes time to process and during that time occupies various expensive facilities at the expense of other competing calls.

It is key to understand the value of a call, what it takes to process it, and then to ensure the customer call center has enough circuit, equipment and staff capacity at the time the traffic or call volume occurs. This so the objectives of encouraging your prospects or customers to call, is achieved.

NOTE WELL: As we first pointed out, we believe the customer call center business is undergoing dramatic change. Even though we are dissecting this call transaction on a very basic level, we are not negating our original message.

Forecasting Caller Behavior

Difficult as this may sound, inbound call traffic prediction is a very stable science. The only problems occur when reality deviates from theory. An example of this is and when the marketing department finds a great spot buy in cable or TV advertising time for a direct response ad, and executes the buy without warning to the customer call center. Oh yes it happens all the time!

Understanding that every telephone call represents an event in time, that occupies unique and finite facilities is a key issue. Only one call can be conducted on one line, talk path or two time slots, at a one time. Every call has two parties to it, particularly when a conversation begins. When a call arrives it occupies an inbound trunk port. While it is in queue, it is connected to an announcement or music source port, therefore occupying two ports and a talk path or two time slots. Even if the call is not completed because the caller hangs up and abandons the call, that call occupied customer call center resources at the expense of other callers, while it was connected to ringing, announcements, music or "dead air." Another caller could not access the same facilities, period! All this is critical to understanding telephone call traffic and the capacity and resources required to serve caller demand. We will discuss forecasting demand in Chapter Five.

FIG. 4-10

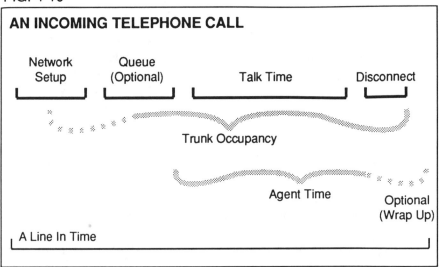

AN INCOMING TELEPHONE CALL

Network Setup

Queue (Optional)

Talk Time

Disconnect

Trunk Occupancy

Agent Time

Optional (Wrap Up)

A Line In Time

In this illustration we are looking at the call from the point of view of the receiving end and the various gross states the call can be in. We are ignoring the minute signaling and status changes associated with this. The call occupies facilities and this amounts to "occupancy time". This is not however the entire length of the actual call transaction, as we are not recognizing any "after call work" or "wrap-up" time. This is an issue that needs to be considered in telephone traffic engineering and particularly staff scheduling. While agents are in a wrap-up state, they are unavailable to answer calls, therefore calls are in queue, occupying line and switch resources.

As we add computer telephony connections to the mix of customer call center services, we also demand higher performance and reliability from computers that support this mission critical customer application. There are a number of key issues in system latency, response and redundancy. A key difference between the way typical applications computers are built and those that are found in telephone systems is operating speed. The computers found driving telephone systems are designed to operate in "ultra-realtime." That is typically not the case in the computers driving most applications.

When CTI workflow applications are considered this whole process needs to be considered carefully as the original baseline argument of reducing call length may be called in to doubt. The reason being that keeping the caller on hold longer and completing the transaction or gaining more data may eliminate a subsequent call or customer research. However this can only be determined when you begin to define individual desktop processes as these relate to customer call type and the desired objectives of your enterprise.

As we recognized earlier in this chapter, ACD traffic engineering does not share the luxury of engineering for the "average usage" of administrative PBX design and engineering. Having enough resources, network services (lines), a large enough switch and sufficient staff at that critical point in time when callers wish to reach you, is a decisive measurement of customer call center success.

Fortunately in most cases a strong case can be made for protecting the high marketing investment in inducing the caller to call and maximizing the revenue opportunity represented by the call. This brings us back to satisfying the reason the customer call exists.

Incoming Customer Call Center Traffic Engineering

At this point recommended reading is The TELECONNECT GUIDE TO ACDS, where twenty pages are spent on rudimentary telephone traffic engineering for the customer call center manager. Here issues such as offered call load versus actual call handled are explored in depth. All the well known traffic tables assume all calls are handled. Typically, call abandonment rates are not included in these calculations, so over staffing occurs if these tables are blindly adhered to. Alternatives and solutions to this dilemma are discussed. customer call center traffic patterns are also explored in depth, well beyond what can be accomplished here.

A short cut:
"Rule of Thumb" Traffic Engineering for the Customer Call Center Manager

Despite all of the technical skills required to build and operate large customer call centers, a number of "rules of thumb" seem to apply over and over again.

- ☐ The average month is 22.2 days.
- ☐ The average operating hours for a regional business customer call center is 9 hours per day.
- ☐ Typically the busiest hour occurs between 10 a.m. and 11 a.m. or 1.00 p.m. and 2 p.m.
- ☐ During this "busy hour," the call traffic will represent 17% of your total calls or business.
- ☐ If your daily hours are longer than 9, say 12 or 24, the busiest hour will represent 12% of your total calls.

Using this data, you can get 90% of the way to solving most demand questions, required staff or circuit numbers.

Chapter Five

Staffing Issues

This chapter touches on the importance of adequate labor pools in the location you have chosen to operate your customer call center.

Labor Supply

When you have over 150 agent positions, a customer call center becomes unwieldy to manage, hard to maintain a full complement of staff, vulnerable to adverse weather conditions, utility problems and natural disasters. Further, with this many "pink collar" employees in a single location, you become an ideal candidate for union organization attention.

In 1985 an article in a May issue of U.S. News and World Report noted that 8,000,000 new jobs were going to be created in the telemarketing or call center business by the 90's. In 1995 the customer call center has become the icon of the Information Age, just as the assembly line was the icon of the Industrial Age.

Many of these new jobs are however being created at the expense of more labor intense support jobs such as field service. An effective help desk, remote diagnostics and depot maintenance have reduced many field service forces dramatically.

Staffing has become extremely critical in certain North Eastern states and other areas where high employment is the norm. This situation is worsening as the demographics of the 90s run into the labor demands of a service economy. Hence the increasing deployment of interactive voice response and the searching for productivity leverage such as CTI.

Already a number of large customer call centers in the North East are accepting high abandonment rates due to a lack of staff and are looking to establish secondary centers in other parts of the country. These, by necessity, are outside their current operating areas. There centers have embraced technology in the form of networking the customer call centers so that they work in concert and can be managed centrally.

Great care needs to be taken to ensure that the customer call center location does indeed have an abundant supply of labor that is willing to work in a call center.

True Story. A large hospitality corporation opened a showcase reservation center near a concentration of middle class neighborhoods in a large Southern city. The assumption was that light full and part time customer call center employment would be desirable to the residents of these surrounding suburbs. No one asked the target workforce candidates if this was a valid assumption. No market research. Two years after this customer call center was opened, finding adequate staff is still difficult. And they have never received a job application or even inquiry from the "model" employee they assumed would find this work desirable.

Part time employees are an extremely important strategy for the customer call center manager. By introducing part timers additional location issues come into play. It is nearly impossible to ask a part time employee to commute an hour each way to a four hour shift. It then becomes almost a full time job.

Decentralized centers make increased sense. The current generation of standalone ACD and PBX based ACD systems allow distributed operation by duplication of switching facilities or remote shelves at the second and subsequent customer call center sites. There are costs to this but again it is a matter of payback calculations based on the business represented by successfully processing these calls. One example can be seen at a major California health plan. After the LA Earthquake of 1994, they decided to expand a remote service site in a remote town in LA county. Lancaster is nearly an 80 mile one way trip to the headquarters member call center. They placed a remote shelf tied to the central ACD at the Lancaster site and employed 33 customer center employees serving local and overflow member calls. By doing this they reduced travel by these 33 employees 24,000 miles a week, reduced gasoline consumption by 1200 gallons a week while saving each employ $200 in gas costs, and giving each employee 12 more hours of personal time a week! Productivity and morale rose, average tenure increased while the actual costs of operation rose marginally.

The new generation of central office based ACD systems from the two vendors of CO based ACD systems have been aggressively sold to the telephone companies. Both have embraced basic ACD features by enriching the CO to support user features, management reports and a breakthrough feature called at-home agents.

Now the long distance providers have gotten into this act by imbedding apparent ACD features in their networks. Their strong suite is nationwide distribution and load balancing. The lighter part of their offerings occur in user controlled features and reporting. Another type of offering is premises telephony server based call distribution that can "talk" to ISDN compatible COs and ISDN services allowing economical call distribution down to a single ISDN line. This is truly a breakthrough in at-home agents. The one ISDN 2B + D line allows cost effective delivery of both voice and terminal data transactions on one link.

Beware though, small groups of remotely located agents and at-home agents need to managed especially carefully with a view to self motivation, morale and their loss of the daily camaraderie of working with a larger group of co-workers. It seems the best strategies with these types of employees combine flexible locations (for example, two days at the customer call center, three at home.)

A Great Recruitment Idea

One of the best staffing and motivation consultants in the customer call center business is George Walther, Seattle, Washington has a great interviewing idea. Don't run a help wanted ad in the local paper, look at resumes and set personal appointments. You'll hire people with a great "interview" face. What you are after is a great phone presence. Use your answering machine as the interview tool. Set up a separate telephone number and equip it with an answering machine. Tell the job candidate to call for more information. Tell them they will encounter a machine and be prepared to leave an "audio" resume.

By using this approach you hear people with great phone presence that you

Staffing To Caller Demand

There are inexpensive telephone customer call center staff and management optimization software packages that allow the customer call center manager to better match the staff needed to meet caller demand.

These packages are designed to assist in solving the major challenge faced by every customer call center. How do you offer your customer base access to your center every time they call to place an order or ask for help, fulfill the callers expectation to a point of customer satisfaction and do this in a profitable manner.

These packages are modular in structure. It is designed to flexible and easy to use by non-technical customer call center management. You can buy these packages for entry level prices of less than $4,000. The benefit of these systems is simple. They reduce operating costs and increase service to the caller.

All calls presented to your telephone customer call center fall in to two categories. They offer revenue in the case of a direct response call or future revenue where this is a call for help, support or service.

Failure to adequately service this incoming customer call costs your company.

- immediate revenue,
- goodwill and long term revenue potential,
- the marketing expense invested in encouraging the caller to call, and
- the operating costs of carrying this call only to fail to provide service.

The major challenge in establishing an inbound telephone call service center is matching your caller demand with the correct supply of telephone service or sales agents. To miscalculate the balance of staff to caller demand does one of two things:

1. With too few agents, the worst possible thing happening is your callers call and don't receive the service you advertised they would receive.

   First, the marketing investment made to induce the call is wasted.

Second, the caller is given a potentially damaging impression of your lack of care and attention to customer service.

Third, any revenue potential represented by this call transaction is lost unless this prospect or customer calls back.

2. Alternatively, providing perfect service and having more staff available than is necessary to serve the inbound callers, is expensive unless the value represented by the callers and their reason for calling far outweighs the cost of over staffing.

These demand forecasting and staff scheduling packages are designed to help in solve this dilemma. The immediate benefits are to;

■ **Reduced operating costs.** It is recognized by the customer call center industry that a staff forecasting and scheduling system will reduce staffing costs by up to 15% by better matching staff to caller demand.

■ **Better staff use.** If you run a center with 20 full time agents you can potentially reduce you staff head count by as many as two agents. You may wish to redeploy these staff members to better match caller demand, extend call center hours, delay asking for additional headcount or take on new projects without additional staff.

■ **Better customer service.** It is also recognized staff forecasting and scheduling allows management to reduce the number of lost calls by better matching the staff complement to caller demand thus providing better service to your callers.

■ **Increased revenue potential.** If you give better service to more callers you have a greater opportunity to capture any immediate or future revenue offered by these caller transactions.

■ **Reduce management time and cost to prepare staff schedules.** Most customer call center service level analysis, forecasting and scheduling is done manually. This requires specialized staff and/or substantial time away from active customer call center management by supervisory staff to do this. It is time consuming to gather the data, and is cumbersome as it requires managing many details. This leads to inaccuracy and less frequent forecasting and scheduling to match staffing to caller demand.

- **Increase the convenience and frequency of preparing optimum staff to service plans.** If these tasks are performed manually they are not performed as frequently as the dynamics of a typical customer call center demands. If they are performed on a mainframe system, again these tasks are not performed as frequently as call center reality demands. If you are among the few customer call centers already enjoying the benefits of a PC forecasting based system you are already using less staff time to data collection and analysis.

- **Position the company customer call center more cost effectively and the company more competitively.**

Large companies with large customer call centers use forecasting and scheduling systems to ensure they are cost competitive in selling and serving their customers. Managing the customer call center to build sales and deliver customer service cost effectively is vital in a competitive market.

This task is an ideal task for a personal computer. These systems typically begin at $15,000 and when fully equipped with all the scheduling, bidding and payroll reporting features approach $30,000. This price is well within the reach of most customer call centers. These systems consist of a FORECAST module to forecast caller demand, match REQUIRED STAFF headcount to forecasted demand, SCHEDULE STAFF and allow for any necessary SHIFT BIDDING to accommodate individual staff preferences.

Historic performance files are built of the customer call center call volume. This is the basis for all forecasting of future calling activity. This data is typically gathered for monthly, daily and half-hour increments and is presented in the same way by the forecasting module.

This file may be developed in two ways. First by loading actual historic data gathered by management from the customer call center switching system or other source. These systems should provide data entry templates or forms to aid the new user in identifying and loading key data.

If the center is a new installation and no history exists these systems should include a number of generalized models of typical customer call center size and performance so the management can begin from some performance base.

Where historic data exists these systems typically provide an on line guide for gathering and loading basic data. These systems provide key form fields by months, weeks, days and half hour increments. They also allow for exception days. These account for holidays or other exceptional days brought about inclement weather, unusual labor conditions and other unprecedented developments.

Customer Call Center Database Profile

These systems typically provide for the building of a comprehensive customer call center database. This database consists of information arranged hierarchically by customer call center element. These consist of;

- employee,
- supervisor,
- team,
- group, and
- customer call center.

The basic employee information includes;

- Proper name,
- Social security or employee number,
- Hire or seniority date,
- Other seniority considerations such as skill level and training classes attended,
- Birth date,
- Employee type such as, full time, part time, relief or floater,
- ACD position or log in identity number,
- any fixed team, group and supervisor assignment,
- any shift preference,
- any lunch break schedule preference,
- agent skill set and training matrix,
- weighted pay rate, and
- other basic data.

In some ACD systems no allowance is made for personal log on identification. It is necessary to maintain a separate record of who was assigned to which ACD station to track agent work and productivity. Ideally these systems provide a way to track agent to position assignment thus produce meaningful reports by individual even though no ACD agent sign on is available. The basic customer call center database profile includes;

- Company name,
- Department names,
- Group names,
- Team names,
- Assigned supervisor name,
- Hours of operation for each customer call center element,
- Actual or assigned value of the typical call received by each team or group, and
- If revenue calls, the typical conversion rate.

The Forecast

Once there is an office and employee database this is merged with the call center historic performance data to provide the forecast. Forecasting future customer call center performance is only possible with some historic experience. If you are beginning with no history, you can use broad estimates from similar experiences elsewhere in similar customer call centers, then modify this as you gain experience.

Forecasts can be produced by year, month, day or half hour increment. These are prepared and presented based on the available historical database. In the case of a new customer call center or an existing center where poor records have been kept it is a chore to gather effective historic data.

The user may modify certain parameters to reflect expected changes based on anticipated growth brought about by an expanding business or introduction of addition sales or service campaigns. The effect of an other than usual day such as a statutory holiday, calendar or special business event are automatically factored into the forecast. Special and unusual events can be forecast. All data is presented in columnar and graphical form, as a screen display or printed report.

Match Required Staff Headcount To Caller Demand

Once the forecast is built by half hour, by day of week, week of month, it is necessary to match the supply of available staff headcount hours to caller demand.

This module converts the forecasted half hourly call activity into the staff required for each half hourly period. This can be done to meet a predetermined service level or may be balanced against expected customer call center revenue and costs. With this calculation various staffing level costs, telephone trunk and usage charges, and overhead items are balanced against expected revenue to determine maximum revenue and if and what abandoned call rate is tolerable.

Because this is an onerous task at most companies assumptions are made which attempt to normalize data. Week One and subsequent weeks of a month look alike. In many cases this is an erroneous assumption due to invoice, collection and other business cycles distort weeks and even days of a particular week. Statistical normalization and rounding ignores staffing subtleties, increases customer call center staff costs, erodes service and retards revenue opportunities. By applying system these subtleties and nuances are recorded as a baseline and recognized as key data in all subsequent forecasts and explanation of the required staff headcount to meet desired service levels.

Service Levels

A service level is very much a function of what level of service a company wishes to provide callers. The received wisdom of the customer call center industry is 80% of all callers will be answered by a live operator in 20 seconds. This may be adequate or conversely totally unrealistic. The issue is what your company will accept. This is based on the tolerance your callers have for being queued or delayed with announcements and music before they speak to a live operator or voice response device. This is considered from an economic perspective.

It is very necessary to allow the customer call center user to experiment with a variety of service levels and determine any points of diminishing returns by pursuing completion of every possible offered transaction. If a transaction produces X revenue and costs Y marketing expense how many staff can I employ to provide potentially perfect service without it negating potential profit.

Schedule Required Staff Head Count
Into Correct Shift Slots

Once the expected call load is spread across the time frame which callers typically call this is then converted to represent typical employee work schedules. It is now necessary to match the available individuals to the available shift slots. Simplistically this compares with manually sorting incoming mail (demand) with mail slots (supply) in a timely fashion. No available staff, less service. Too many staff, over capacity.

Customer call centers fall into three categories when you consider the hours they work.

1.   They may be open during typical business hours as they deal with other businesses in their local time zone. Typical hours of work are nine to five.

2.   Second example is a business to business customer call center that works extended hours to cover the extended business day worked by national customer base. Here a number of staggered and overlapping nine hour shifts are necessary to cover expected customer calls.

3.   Then there are those centers that serve consumers for extended periods up to 24 hours a day, 7 days a week, 365 days a year.

The scheduling component produces a set of shifts that need to individual staff members to fulfill. It is necessary now to match the names with the available shift slots. This may be done by simple ASSIGNMENT of shifts to the available employees or may be done according to some plan dictated by staff seniority or union contract.

Shift Bidding And The Staffed Schedule

In some cases SHIFT BIDDING is necessary to accommodate individual staff preferences. Here the SCHEDULE is published showing the shifts required to be filled by the customer call center staff. They are then given the option to bid on their desired shifts. Beginning with the staff member with the oldest employment date or other accepted priority. Upon completion of the bidding process each individual shift is assigned the name of the successful candidate.

Adherence

Adherence is an additional module in a number of these offerings that allows an interface to the ACD data gathering function. The ACD automatically downloads information to the forecasting and scheduling program to enable it to track agent sign on and sign off. The adherence portion of the program then provides a report that shows how closely staffing reality matched the scheduled plan.

Payroll Interfaces

There is a rather different approach that has been taken by some customer call centers, particularly those who are determined to get the most from their employees. Southwest Airlines, arguably the most successful airline in the world, has taken this to the furthest extent and pays their agents from the ACD sign on/sign off reports. Agents do not get paid for being idle.

The interesting shift here is really philosophy and not simply the technical interface of the ACD time keeping to the company payroll system. The company has made it known that to work there, the agents do not "sign in" on traditional attendance sheets or punch a time clock. Rather they are paid from the accumulated ACD sign on time. This subtly shifts the management of personnel presence to each agent.

The significant philosophy is that Southwest believes in the average employee and their personal motivation to do a good job and deliver the effort they are being paid for. They have moved management responsibility for individual agent attendance and effort to each and every reservation center employee. This reduces supervisor time and involvement in all but exceptional situations and has proved to recover an average of 30 minutes worth of agent "time shrinkage" per day! Instead of hitting the time clock and then the coffee pot, agents go straight to work with the preliminaries attended to before they go on the company payroll. Powerful and effective stuff.

Quality Monitoring Interfaces

With the addition of automated quality monitoring tools in customer call centers that share database requirements such as staff schedules, it is important that the staff schedule software can automatically download these staff schedules to the quality monitoring recording machine. This eliminates an additional level of database maintenance in a device that needs to the same schedule data for the recording of review sessions (calls) for each agent.

New Performance Pressures

A new trend first experienced in the managed care business (health insurance) is "performance guarantees." The marketing departments of some health insurers have decided that offering an employer group a guaranteed response level for their employees offers a competitive edge in a fiercely competitive market. The health insurer simply arbitrages the demand (patients) against supply (medical

service providers,) then optimizes the cost and administration of the service as best they can. Service levels provided to the members become extremely important differentiation point. Marketers have decided that guaranteeing service, such as all calls answered for a certain group, and even products within that group (primary versus dental as an example.) This not only effects calls but all correspondence. The standard may be all calls within 20 seconds of arriving at the call center or all correspondence within 48 hours of receipt. If these standards are not met, the employer group is refunded a portion of their premium, which could amount to millions of dollars.

This creates a powerful precedent that every call or written inquiry needs to be tracked at the lowest possible data element and all but limits a call center to such sophisticated standalone ACD systems, as these are the only machines that collect the call detail essential to building call/inquiry tracking data essential to building the information to prove performance guarantee reporting and introduces an additional and compelling argument for sophisticated staff scheduling software.

Chapter Six

Strategic Buying

A typical comment following a presentation on the technologies and techniques of customer call center management goes like this. "I really enjoyed the presentation, but we are just beginning our customer call center. Management wants to try the concept out before they spend any money."

The problem here is not the lack of budget, but the lack of management commitment to the strategy. More important than money, is the belief in the customer call center as a key part of a companies sales or service strategy. Management is not committed to the belief that the customer call center can provide immense leverage to traditional sales, support distribution and market administration techniques. Despite all the remonstrations we could indulge in here, lack of budget, limited management commitment and vision, are handicaps that are there to be overcome.

Overcoming traditional delivery philosophy is coming in the form of corporate reengineering. Cost of sales and servicing customers are expanding in most companies as products and services get more complex and competition for market niches become more intense. There is a real hope that process reengineering will challenge bottlenecks in the customer satisfaction delivery process.

Confronting Budget Limits

Despite your limited budget, as customer call center manager, you are expected to perform to the management expectations for the customer call center. What are the options?

The first option open to the customer call center manager, confronted with limited vision is challenging the perception the customer call center is unimportant. Overcoming limited vision on the part of immediate management can be an impossible task if you are not equipped with the tools needed to convince them more of their support is needed.

Putting Costs In Perspective

We first began this book by talking about the cost of acquiring a new customer, and the value each call represented. We will revisit a diagram we used in Chapter One, but with more context added. From this you can develop an argument to assist in you developing rational and convincing budget requests.

The first question to ask is one of size. There is no such thing as an unimportant customer call center, so size is of little significance. Costs are large...20 people in a customer call center cost roughly a million dollars a year. And that is only the direct costs. We have ignored the marketing investment to drive the callers to call and any revenue that may flow from successfully completing any transaction.

Second, how big is this project likely to become, and therefore how big will the customer call center have to be to serve the application. This is important from a facilities and funding point of view. This may be a difficult question to answer at the start of a project. Customer call center sizes are based on call volumes and the number of calls an agent force can effectively process in a given work period. These calculations are call length dependent and vary based on the type of transaction to be conducted. A "Help" desk transaction may average 20 minutes per call as the software analyst assists the caller through a complex sequence of events. A directory assistance call to the telephone company may be over in less than 25 seconds. Understanding the average call length and the anticipated volume of call allows calculations to be made that will allow customer call center management to roughly estimate the size the center.

A small customer call center may never anticipate growing larger than 30 telephone representatives, yet their mission may be just as critical to their company as the reservation center of the giant airlines. Relate the revenue potential as a percentage of the company or business unit revenue volume. Do this by polling similar center managers. You can find these types of people as members of the American Telemarketing Association (Van Nuys CA.) or the Direct Marketing Association (Telephone Chapter, New York, NY.)

Understanding the value and the costs of the customer call center opportunity is vital to being able to present your budget case to management. Let's examine these customer call center cost elements in detail.

Customer Call Center Costs

The customer call center will need staff, circuits and some sort of system to switch the incoming calls.

PERSONNEL STAFFING, 30 telephone reps.

40 hour week at $7.00 at hour	=	$ 280
(This assumes a minimum wage and some sort of commission or bonus)		
4.2 weeks per month,		
+ benefits and salary burden of 30%	=	$ 1,529
30 representatives, per month	=	$ 45,870
12 month total	=	**$ 550,440**

Supervision;
2 Supervisors.

40 hour week at $9.00 an hour	=	$ 360
4.2 weeks per month,		
+ benefits and burden of 30%		$ 1,966
2 supervisors, per month	=	$ 3,932
12 month total	=	**$ 47,184**

Management and support staff beyond the actual center staff are in addition to the basic customer call center staff. The variables become less predictable at these levels so estimating costs are not as simple. Understand they are both essential and are in addition to basic staffing costs adds to center overhead.

TELEPHONE CIRCUITS AND SERVICE

Conservatively, the average cost per hour for national 800 service is about $16.00. This can be higher if all of the customer call center business occurs during the local business day. Given our model customer call center has a complement of 30 telephone representatives, there is probably enough work to keep them employed constantly on the telephone, for at least 80% of the day, or 192 available man hours a day.

192 hours x $ 16.00 per hour	=	$ 3,072
5 days per week	=	$ 15,360
4.2 weeks per month	=	$ 64,512
12 months per year. Total	=	**$ 774,144**

Your customer center may not be positioned to serve a national customer base so may not need 800 service, therefore this part of the calculation need not apply. Nevertheless do not avoid including trunk access and any usage charges associated with calls arriving on these trunks.

THE TELEPHONE SUPPORT SYSTEM

A well equipped inbound call management system, with support for 30 telephone representatives, two or three supervisor positions, the requisite trunk capacity, and reporting capability, can be acquired for about $ 3500 a position. There are systems that are more or less expensive than this but as expected, offer greater or lesser feature sets to address the customer call center application.
Much of this book is about buying this type of automatic call distribution equipment and argues for more features, not less. A well equipped automatic call distributor is a vital tool. Call center performance and business results are enhanced with the right machine, handicapped with the wrong one.

Since the original writing in 1987, PBX manufacturers have attempted to close the gap by providing more user control and greater reporting via outboard call management reporting strategies. The author has recently been involved in the adaptation of sophisticated call management technology to some of the most popular PBX based ACD's. The most striking discovery is the horrendous inaccuracy and cavalier vendor attitude to agent data gathering. In one case, there is no guarantee the data being gathered about one agent is indeed that agent.

Don't tell your human resources department. They would go apoplectic! Then force you to buy an application specific customer call center switch.

There is a large bank in California that has never challenged an unemployment compensation hearing until recently because they knew how flawed their agent data gathering and review process was. The agents knew this and even those who were fired for cause who request unemployment and receive it. Since buying application specific ACD systems and sophisticated monitoring and review technology, they have challenged and won every agent unemployment hearing where the employee claims unlawful dismissal and a biased management review strategy.

This is no longer the case and represents a significant bottom line saving to this teleservice operation.

FIRST YEAR CUSTOMER CALL CENTER COST SUMMARY

PERSONNEL COSTS	$ 597,624
CIRCUIT COSTS	$ 774,144
TELEPHONE EQUIPMENT	$ 105,000
FIRST YEAR TOTAL	**$ 1,476,768**

FIG. 6-1

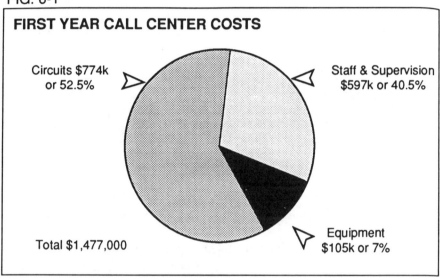

FIRST YEAR CALL CENTER COSTS

Circuits $774k or 52.5%

Staff & Supervision $597k or 40.5%

Total $1,477,000

Equipment $105k or 7%

This is not a minor investment for a start up customer call center. You can adjust your numbers around these to get a feel for your particular customer call center costs.

Repeating an earlier statement, the value of the call and the cost of acquiring the customer were important calculations, allowing the cost of the customer call center to be put into perspective. Lets look at the cost dynamics of serving that call.

FIG. 6-2

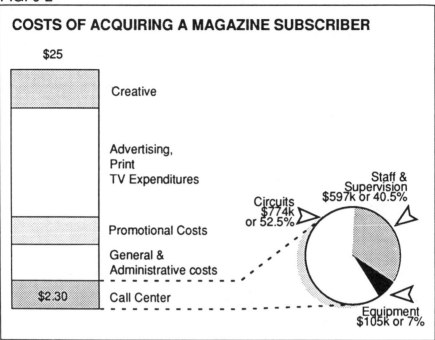

COSTS OF ACQUIRING A MAGAZINE SUBSCRIBER

$25 — Creative

Advertising, Print TV Expenditures

Circuits $774k or 52.5%

Staff & Supervision $597k or 40.5%

Promotional Costs

General & Administrative costs

$2.30 — Call Center

Equipment $105k or 7%

What is apparent here is that the actual call handling cost is about $2.30 a call or less than 10% of the entire cost of sale for this particular paid subscriber.

As an aside, obviously given the annual subscription rate, the actual subscriber, although extremely important, is not the primary sale. The primary sale is advertising space, yet the space rate cannot be achieved without a substantial subscriber count. The magazine has spent $22.50 in inducing the potential subscriber to call, only to inadequately process the call and subvert the sale because the last 10% of the call handling costs were misunderstood and inadequately invested and managed. When the ripple effect of this is examined, additional unexpected though predictable impact occurs.

OTHER PREDICTABLE SIDE EFFECTS

As a side note, it is important to note that deteriorating service levels cause more than disgruntled customers. Disgruntled customers complain more, then without satisfaction, go silent. That is to your company, however, they can be expected to tell up to 25 other prospective customers of the bad experience they have had with you. More complaints by phone displace genuinely productive calls, revenue and positive business. There is also the effect of lowering morale for your existing agent force who consciously or unconsciously, impart that to the next caller, their coworkers or others leading to an overall deterioration in attitude.

Back to the customer call center math. What is clear here, is the amount of money that has been invested to create the demand that causes these prospects to call. With 192 hours of inbound WATS time being used per day by our fictitious customer call center, there is obviously a way to back into the number of calls being received and the marketing expense being incurred to achieve this caller demand. If a call averages 4.0 minutes, which is not untypical, and 11,520 minutes (192 hours) of call traffic is offered to the customer call center, this amounts to 2,880 calls per day. Not all calls are sales so it is necessary to discount a certain (known?) percentage of inquiry or overhead calls. Assuming 15% do not convert to sales, 2,448 subscriptions are sold per day at an average cost per sale of $ 25. The marketing investment for that day is in excess of $ 61,000! The revenue potential to be gained from these potential subscribers is another opportunity again.

Using the magazine subscription example, where the annual subscription rate is $ 37.95, the 2,448 callers converted to one year subscribers produce $ 92,902 in revenue. If they convert to two or three year subscriptions, the revenue potential is even larger.

To place the customer call center cost in context suddenly takes on a whole new complexion.

Average daily marketing investment	$	61,000
Average daily revenue potential	$	92,902
Average daily customer call center cost (1st year)	$	5,594 !

Annualizing this simple example is even more graphic;

Average annual marketing investment	$ 16,104,000
Average annual revenue potential	$ 24,526,128
Average annual customer call center cost (1st. year)	$ 1,476,768

This calculation assumes 12 months of operation with 22 day months.

FIG. 6-3

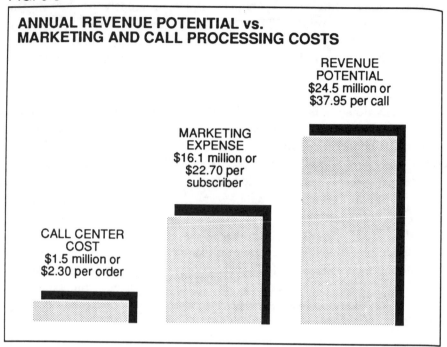

**ANNUAL REVENUE POTENTIAL vs.
MARKETING AND CALL PROCESSING COSTS**

REVENUE
POTENTIAL
$24.5 million or
$37.95 per call

MARKETING
EXPENSE
$16.1 million or
$22.70 per
subscriber

CALL CENTER
COST
$1.5 million or
$2.30 per order

Caution With The Numbers

When you do these types of illustrations be careful to use "shoulder" months and don't overstate the numbers. If they appear too dramatic, despite their validity, they are harder for management to accept. There is also the veiled suggestion that this project should have been understood and begun lots earlier. Should "heads roll" for a neglected opportunity?

What About A Pure Service Application?

When the customer call center is a pure service application and there is no apparent revenue associated with these calls, look to the lifetime value of maintaining the caller as a customer. We discussed the cost of acquiring a new customer, but we need to be reminded that keeping that customer into the second and subsequent years of the relationship is much more profitable that initial relationship. In the world of circulation management it is generally accepted it costs five times as much to capture a new subscriber than to maintain an existing subscriber.

With the cost to acquire a new subscriber at $ 25, and the first year revenue being $37.75, there is only $12.75 left to fulfill the subscription over the next year. Year 2 of the relationship may be initiate by a mailed subscription renewal reminder or invoice. It may be a follow-up telephone call. Whatever method is used it is targeted at a known subscriber and the focused marketing cost is less than $ 5. This is because this particular renewal sale does not carry the cost burden of the initial marketing expense. Protecting goodwill and subscriber satisfaction is vital to holding the line on marketing expenses.

Consider for a moment the subscriber has a problem with his subscription, needs to change his address or called to renew and was unable to reach the magazine customer call center, then is inadequately served. This could be enough to place the renewal in jeopardy. In the context of your business is this something you wish to consider.

There is the story of a California telephone utility company whom in the late Seventies and early Eighties was besieged with customer complaints. They had gone to the Public Utility Commission to petition for rate increases to improve service. The PUC denied these billion dollars rate requests as they did not deem the most visible service provision (customer call centers) to be delivering adequate service! Simply the customer complaint of poor customer service gained more attention and until that was fixed, the PUC was unwilling to allow the utility more revenue to fix the core problem, overall service.

In addition, do not ignore the fact a service or response center can gather strategic market information so the traditional sellers of the company are better positioned to sell upgrades and add-ons. This is a valuable bonus positioning potential for the customer call center.

Investing Where It Counts

If the cost processing the call amounts to less than 10% the cost of acquiring the customer, the switching equipment costs less that 10% of the ongoing call center costs. Understanding these cost dynamics and your corporate cost justification process are necessary to your success in arguing for an appropriate budget for customer call center equipment.

This is key to establishing the perspective necessary to challenge limited thinking as customer call center start up budgets are drawn up. Communicating these relative costs and the investment necessary, to ensure upper management expectations are met, is up to customer call center management.

Typically expenses will be examined and those that are perceived to be more finite will be considered targets for budget restraint. Here is where equipment comes under scrutiny, and a target for expenditure control, while the management of operating costs take a back seat.

Capital Investments versus Operating Costs

There are two portions to any customer call center expenditure: Capital costs and operating costs. Oil field accounting logic applies...if you can paint it, it's capital goods and can be depreciated, if you can't paint it, its operating costs and can only be expensed. In many peoples minds, tangibles are more easily subject to budget and price restrictions. Operating costs are less predictable, thus more conceptual. Things like labor and circuit usage are subject to demand and usage, therefore tougher to control. They also continue for the life of the call center as opposed to capital expenditures which are typically one time costs, plus ongoing maintenance and upgrades.

Other parties to the customer call center purchasing process, such as telecom and MIS management, purchasing and finance, are often only judged on the set up costs, not ongoing operation. They are judged on how much they can preserve company capital assets. These parties are typically the economic and technical forces in a company. customer call center hardware seems easy to skimp on. "Why go with a Cadillac, when a Chevrolet will do?"

Conversely, the customer call center manager is going to be judged over the life of the center, or his tenure as manager of this center, whichever be shorter. There are other vital accounting dynamics that come into play also.

"Mission Critical" vs. Technical And Administrative Roles

A customer call center more often than not plays a "mission critical" role in revenue or customer satisfaction. Emotion is high. So is the ability to measure customer call center performance.

First, the customer call center is typically a very visible customer contact point. It is in either a primary sales or sales support role and therefore carries a sales revenue quota. This quota is reviewed on at least a quarterly or more frequent basis. The results and the success of the center is eminently measurable. There is great emotion surrounding the mission and making the numbers.

Secondly, if your customer call center is a source of service or customer support, the measurement of customer satisfaction is measured in two ways. One more quantifiable than the other, while the other carries enormous visibility.

1. Ensuring customer satisfaction begins way "upstream" of the customer call center, but the customer call center is expected to be ombudsman and resolver of problems for existing customers. Most of these problems are not of the customer call centers making. If satisfaction is not achieved, customers are lost and the customer call center is often considered as part of the problem. If not the problem, they had knowledge of it and did not communicate the product or service shortfall to the responsible departments so they in turn could remedy these. It is hard to be right.

2. The other source of judgment comes from the president's office. It comes in the form of a letter or call from a disgruntled customer (maybe a stockholder?) who rightly or wrongly feels they are not being served well. Down comes dicta, "fix the problem, no matter what the cost." It comes as no surprise that lots of "emotion" is attached to the transactions processed by a customer call center.

These issues, system feature nuances and the management of same are often lost on technical and financial buyers as they help select the most appropriate system for your customer call center.

Customer Call Center Mission Choke Points

A customer call center can fail in its mission at one or more of five points in the call process:

1. An inadequate telephone network, by being under-equipped with too few and/or poor quality telephone circuits.
2. Too few local loops between the telephone company central office or long distance service and the customer call center.
3. An inadequate or unreliable customer premise switching system.

4. Lack of understanding the proper staff required to serve the inbound call volume.
5. Poorly trained and motivated telephone representatives, who have little or no stake in effectively completing the call.

An additional reason for failing at the mission can be failing to fulfill the expectation created by the call, but this moves us into a region of motivation, training and marketing that this book is not trying to address. There are already many great books on these subjects.

A Realtime Business Window

A sophisticated ACD system provides customer call center management with a window into all the information necessary to monitor the network, local loops, business character, staff performance and achieving the goals set for the center.

Be aware, many ACD systems do not provide the depth of data gathering and reporting to understand real performance of these customer call center elements. Despite what the vendors will say! Understanding these elements and the tools necessary to manage them is vital to arguing the significance of acquiring an appropriate application specific switching system. What the vendors don't tell you can cost a customer call center additional and needless operating expenses.

Strategic Buying

Typically three corporate interest groups are involved in acquiring call center equipment and services;

- □ **the technical buyer,**
- □ **the economic buyer, and**
- □ **the user buyer.**

This committee or group, formally or informally assembled, have different individual objectives. All ostensibly have the same overall goal, serving the profitability of the corporation, by buying the most cost effective system. But even that is relative based on the discipline and agenda of the committee member.

The technical buyer is a telecommunications or data processing professional, who has little opportunity for gaining experience in establishing a call center. This is because this is not a frequent exercise for most corporations. Understandably, technologists are typically more fascinated by the technology of the machine. What a device is, rather than what it can do for the business.

Since first writing the predecessor text in 1987, the author is happy to report that there is a significant improvement in telecom and data management view of the user and their requirements. However in many companies, the battle is not over. Another interesting phenomenon is that in many corporations the MIS management juggernaut has slowed due to the arrival of the PC which has had two effects: democratizing of computing and stripping away of much of the MIS mystique. The MIS or Information Services departments now have five or so subgroups all fighting each other for recognition, budgets and control of their respective domains. They are the keepers of the host, applications, the desktop (dumb tubes and/or PCs) and telecom. Now more so than ever each group has dozens of technical issues to deal with in their particular discipline so "fighting off an aggressive user with a compelling strategic business plan" is a great deal more difficult.

The economic buyer (purchasing) is looking for equipment to do the job, at the right price and under enforceable terms and conditions. He looks to the advice of the technical buyer as to the adequacy of the system. If the manufacturer describes the system as an ACD, it must be! However this is again a definition subject to the background of the designer, amplified by the marketing organization and broadcast by the sales organization. There are many manufacturers that want to force your customer call center applications and expectations into their "solution."

The end user, who will live with this choice on a day-to day basis, is almost always assumed to want more than is necessary to do the job. Often the end user is treated as having less weight in the final technical selection and decision. Here is the challenge for the end user buyer.

Making Your Application King And Being Heard!

The customer call center manager must take on the role of the educator. First understanding the subject of your customer call center economics and the tools necessary to achieving the corporate goals of building sales and/or delivering customer satisfaction. The next step is educating those critical to the decision, in the strategic and operating issues that must be dealt with on a daily basis. Once this knowledge shared with the other influential buyers, the customer call center manager should wield more influence in final equipment and service selection decisions. Hopefully the paradox of capital versus operating expense will be resolved in the customer call center managers favor.

Do not neglect potential allies in the sales, marketing and service delivery parts of your company. They need the center to work so they are not burdened with additional work "falling-out" of a less than effective customer call center.

The Small User Options

As a user with twenty or fewer positions to staff with telephone representatives, the first question to ask is, "what are my current options?"

☐ Is the center to occupy existing space?
☐ If so, what telephone equipment (if any) is the space served by now?
☐ With new space, will there be other company occupants?
☐ What are their telephone system plans?

As part of a larger organization occupying the space, the customer call center can generally use a portion of the PBX that will serve the space. Most modern PBX systems offer in conjunction with the administrative PBX system, an ACD of some sort. How sophisticated this system may be dependent on the manufacturers understanding and commitment to the application.

Unfortunately few PBX manufactures have embraced ACD operation in their PBX with much sophistication, although they have improved. But just as they have added more sophistication, the standalone ACD vendors have raised the hurdle again. They tend to take short cuts based on the architectural and feature decisions necessary in building a PBX. This is an area that deserves more explanation which we will do in Chapter Thirteen when we compare operational compromises of PBX and CO based offerings against stand alone ACD systems.

Customer Call Centers Need More Of Everything

Beyond twenty positions, the customer call center starts to consume space and telephone resources, far out of proportion of the number of staff and telephones this group represents. Typically the customer call center management also begins to request services and information beyond the capabilities of the generic PBX. At this stage there are many more options to consider.

Starting a customer call center from scratch, with no previous switch decisions to live with, the customer call center manager can choose what appears to be most appropriate. It may be a key system, PBX/ACD, or a standalone ACD. At twenty positions the cost dynamics of the center clearly justify specifically designed call distribution equipment.

Below twenty, with knowledge growth will occur, the options are richer today than even a year ago.

1. A call sequencer can be added to a PBX or Key system, provided both have the capacity to support the customer call center.
2. A PBX system with a UCD system and effective reporting.
3. An ACD package can be added to your PBX or key system, provided the manufacturer provides this for your given PBX system.
4. A small standalone PC based ACD may be the option.
5. Central Office ACD services offered by your local phone company.
6. Network based ACD systems with intelligent customer based servers (mini-network control points) that drive remote network switches (network action points and even other ACD systems.)

Automatic Call Sequencers

An automatic call sequencer (ACS) may be the solution as an add-on to an existing PBX or key system. This is typically an add-on product to which are attached a group of trunks or station lines. When all agents are busy, the ACS answers, plays an announcement and places callers on hold. After the delay message music may be played. The ACS alerts the agents to call presence by some lamp illumination technique (flash rate) or add-on station display. This also indicates which call has be holding longer than another so an agent can pick up and serve the longest holding call. They provide some reporting capability and provide increased status monitoring capability.

The big difference between an ACS and an ACD is the ACS is "passive." The agent must initiate the answer. There is no compulsion to answer the call. The hold status is broadcast to all agents and it is up to them to pick up the call. Most ACD systems deliver a call to an agent and they are obliged to answer. Removing the decision and discretion from the agent is considered desirable in a production customer call center.

Both ACS and ACD systems, report via a combination of call count and call length information, whether or not the callers were served and agents were answering as planned.

At five to ten positions an ACS may make sense. Selecting an ACS is a short term solution as the missing features incur a number of operational and cost handicaps.

Key and PBX systems, although cheaper than a true ACD also have some important operational shortcomings as ACDs. Above thirty positions, the economics clearly advantage a true ACDs.

Today, with the availability of inexpensive standalone PC based ACD and voice response technology and the availability of sophisticated used systems, smaller centers have access to better systems at lower prices and need not compromise operational efficiency.

Secondary Market Alternatives

Do not ignore the option of used equipment. A customer call center may be very handily satisfied with a machine of relatively recent manufacture, that is no longer large enough for its original purchaser. Customer call center equipment is often removed from service for reasons other than obsolescence and age. Some of the earliest installations of true ACD systems are still providing reliable daily service to their owners after 20 years. Among the secrets to their longevity has been superior reporting and customer programmability. These systems have paid for themselves many times over.

Whole systems and parts for existing installations are readily available on the secondary market. The thought of a customer call center acquiring used equipment is not overly attractive to a manufacturer. This is like buying parts for a car that is already owned. There are not the options for alternative parts sources after you have committed to one or other manufacturer by buying their system. Knowing this manufacturer's price upgrades accordingly. The gross profit margin that may have eroded in the "competitive heat" of original sale, is not threatened nearly as much when it is time to upgrade. Today most of the popular systems are available in the secondary market. Some of these systems have seen as little as twelve months worth of use.

The thought of acquiring a machine of recent vintage at thirty to fifty percent off the list price is very attractive to a customer call center manager on a limited budget.

The question that immediately arises though is how old is old and what is the upgradability of these systems? Will the buyer of equipment give up important modern features?

Because most of these systems are predominantly software driven, they can be upgraded to the most recent versions of software, for the cost of the software. Successful manufacturers are in the enviable position of having a large customer base. The new systems these manufacturers introduce must maintain a degree of "backward compatibility" with systems they have already sold to existing customers. Backward compatibility is a fancy way of saying that they cannot ignore history and arbitrarily obsolete systems sold to earlier customers. End users do not like to buy systems at the tail end of their market cycle, so are generally assured that their purchases will not be arbitrarily obsoleted. Hence the backward compatibility strategies and assurances that most manufacturers provide their customers.

A manufacturer's history of protecting customers from obsolescence is normally a matter of pride, that is relatively easily determined. The vendors with smaller businesses are more concerned about this issue than the larger vendors, as they have more to lose by ignoring or abandoning a product and user base.

In this age where software development and maintenance of a system is an immensely expensive proposition, PBX and ACD system manufacturers can not afford to introduce completely new software packages very frequently. The two most well respected ACD systems have control software that has evolved over nearly two decades. The systems subsequently introduced are typically hardware upgrades with the previous software version enhanced to reflect the new hardware and introduce some additional features. This is called "value engineering." Getting the most value out of the product supposedly to the benefit of the existing base and the manufacturer. A joke goes, "do you know how God created the world in seven days? Because he did not have an installed base!"

These new features may be minor, or may introduce a new strategy and direction. The latter approach is usually accompanied by a high degree of marketing effort. Take your time to understand your way through the vendors marketing position.

There may be little new being introduced. The positioning may be defensive as another competitor may be effecting the success of this manufacturer. All of this is important to the customer call center considering the secondary market.

If a company is introducing a totally new machine which does obsolete an existing ACD model or product line, financial arrangements may be made in the way of discounts to prod existing customers into the newer machine. The replaced machines typically find their way into the secondary market.

There is also an opportunity for the customer call center on a limited budget during a manufacturer's product transition. Offer to buy a newly superseded machine at a reduced price. Generally the manufacturer has been making presentations under nondisclosure agreements to key prospects and customers. The timeframes for installation precede the production delivery of the "new" machine, so interim arrangements are made to provide "old" versions, then a later replacement. The "old" equipment needs a home. These traded systems are often available directly from the original manufacturer at substantially reduced prices.

Buying from another user who no longer wants the machine is one alternative, as is buying from an equipment broker who specializes in this brand of system. Most of these machines have been used up to the day of deinstallation. They therefore have been maintained by the manufacturer or his authorized maintenance representative. Obtain assurances from the seller and ensure you are provided some limited warranty. Refurbishing may occasionally be necessary. Most manufacturers will refurbish the equipment for you at their factory and at an arbitrarily high price. Field refurbishing is often adequate at greatly reduced cost.

Negotiate payment terms and do not make final payment to the seller until the machine is installed and working to your satisfaction.

Software Title Ownership And Support

What about title to the system software? In most cases, the original manufacturer does not grant title to the software that drives the system. A license to use the software is sold with the title to the hardware. The vendor of the used equipment may have title to the hardware but legally cannot transfer the software. Inquire of the seller as to the status of the software or call the manufacturer and ask what their policy is regarding software title.

Also determine that if you acquire used hardware, what position they take, if any, to support you.

Most vendors have an unpublished rule; we would sooner see a customer call center buy our equipment, even though its used, than lose the system to a competitor. The reason for this is, successful customer call centers will grow in size and sophistication, and the user will eventually need to do business directly with the manufacturer. Then there are certain manufacturers who have never understood this and levy punitive software licensing fees on those individuals who buy on the secondary market. There is the added disadvantage in that most of the newer features such as CTI and VRU links require the latest software version, typically not available with a system available on the used equipment market. Though by the time you read this CTI "plumbing" is generally being stripped of its "marketing panache," and being relegated to utility software. Secondary market sellers are quick to point out that software licenses are not needed if the secondary market purchase is only parts to upgrade an existing system. Not obtaining a software license for a new site is also an alternative, but do not expect any support from the manufacturer until you establish a relationship.

Make sure you obtain all the user documentation. Training may be available from the manufacturer. If you are a licensed user, a manufacturer will not deny you training. Negotiate terms carefully and ensure to obtain possession of all of the equipment in good working order before the final payment is made.

Chapter Seven

Introducing The Automatic Call Distributor

Introduction

Throughout the text we have frequently talked about customer call centers and the equipment they use. Let's focus on the automatic call distributor (ACD). This is the hub of any customer call center reengineering process as this device provides the services "rationing," balancing and reporting that allows a customer call center to best deliver on the promise of service. What is an ACD and why is it different from other call handling devices such as key telephone systems (KTS) and private branch exchange (PBX) equipment?

An ACD -- automatic call distributor -- is a misnomer. The name suggests the primary function is to distribute a large volume of incoming calls in a predetermined and equitable fashion, to customer call center personnel. That is its day-to-day advantage. But its primary function -- and justification for why they should be discrete from administrative switching, -- is that it collects and stores information. Lots of information in a way that a generalized administrative switch (PBX) does not. And you can, as the ACD manager, manipulate that information in a myriad of ways to better understand the character of your business and so manage the business opportunities offered by the callers, the service your customer call center delivers, the cost of delivering this service and the image it projects for your company. Never take your eyes off the information gathering and presentation aspects of the system. Never accept less than you believe you need and never accept fitting your business goals into a vendor's often limited vision. This is particularly true as you move into the applications value offered by the new customer call center technology platforms of CTI, intelligent desktops and client/server technology.

"This Ain't No Party, This Ain't No Disco, This Ain't No Fooling Around!"

Apologies to someone! There has been an interesting shift since CTI became a marketing buzzword. Someone sold one, then had to deliver on the expectations.

The writer was privy to a recent presentation by a major computer manufacturer, where they "pushed" CTI and the related mainframe host and gateway software. They have similar products for midframe environments and what appears to be a "telephony server." They had the gall to say that the average price to build a full CTI application using their technology was between $100,000 and $400,000 with a payback of less than a year!

In talking with this product manager after the presentation I challenged him on this as I have not seen a significant CTI project ever deliver a payback of less than a year and, in most cases, require an average investment of up to $3,500 per workstation, NOT including the existing telephone switch or a desktop PC of recent vintage and significant power. He countered by saying that they recognized that CTI was really just plumbing and the truth of the matter was that this was really process reengineering and workflow management. His excuse for not presenting the opportunity in this way is that "it scares most call customer call center managers who do not have the vision or authority to embrace or initiate projects of this breadth!"

From his perspective building a market demand is totally justified, while the goal of this book is to equip the reader with the tools and expectations to embark on realistic customer call center process improvement that may involve CTI.

Call Flow

Of late there is a new focus at how this whole call management process works. This shift is as a direct result of employing workflow analysis and reengineering disciplines. It begins way "upstream" of the actual call, beginning in the promotion or information broadcast that stimulates the customer to pick up the phone and call. It is most important that the customer call center know why. The next issue is the number of calls or customer opportunities offered. This may be an order, a request for help or information. From a business and applications point of view, clearly each of these have a desirable and measurable outcome; that is an order or a satisfied customer.

Each call follows a "state profile" that can be simply compared in microcosm to a sales cycle. Taking the customer state from "suspect," to "prospect," to closed order or satisfied customer. Over the course of transaction (but not ignoring the bigger relationship concept,) the numbers of opportunities diminish. If 100 prospects call the customer center, yet only 10 result in sales, what caused the attrition and how can it be corrected or conversely, what can we do to "disqualify" unqualified buyers before they pick up the phone, call and waste your customer call center resources. The new thrust in ACD reporting is to get to the reasons for and the information to allow remedies to this lopsided "conversion ratio;" that is offered opportunities to results. This is being done in numerous ways we will discuss throughout this book.

The leading edge standalone ACD systems are no longer simply "a better telephone system," but a better way of doing business. This is because of the process reengineering thrust offered by these standalone systems and the adjunct services delivered by these vendors really attack business transaction management. The PBX based ACD vendors are still stuck pitching "phones." These transaction and process management tools are what gives your ACD system power.

Let's go back to basics and begin by focusing on what an ACD is best known for -- distributing calls to agents.

The Concept Of Call Demand Concentration

The basic notion of a customer call center is the processing volumes of telephone homogeneous telephone calls. Serving inbound calls is typically the primary function of the center. Trunks carrying calls into the center, or a telephone position in a customer call center, are busy more often and over longer periods, than a typical trunk or telephone serving other parts of the business.

A major difference between customer call center applications and regular administrative telephone use is that call centers carry disproportionately large amount of call traffic when compared with typical administrative (that is, normal office) telephones, circuits and switches. The exception to this statement however is CO (central office or the telephone company exchange) switches and network circuits. In both the ACD and CO example, some phenomenon has occurred to concentrate and focus the unusually high volumes of telephone traffic on the customer call center or the network service.

In the case of the long distance telephone network components, physical concentration of administrative traffic has occurred at subscriber PBX systems, local and other devices. When it is clear that the calls are for the long distance network, then resources allocated. Concentration of the traffic has occurred. The network is engineered for the anticipated demand. Typically this is done for average demand

In the case of a customer call center, this concentration has occurred through the establishing and advertising the customer call center as a focal point for customer and prospect inquiries. Instead of these inquiries being vaguely directed to the main company switchboard number or PBX, these are now concentrated on a specific service group. Hence the concentrated telephone traffic, occurring in disproportionately large volumes for the number of trunks and staff present in the customer center. All calls to a customer call center can be considered as having the potential to generate or protect revenue.

Being a focal point for a volume of customer or prospect calls, there is also the necessity to ensure the callers are answered and served correctly. This introduces two additional concepts that are extremely critical in the world of customer call centers and the reason that ACD systems came into existence; massive data gathering and user progammability. We will discuss these later.

Call Distribution

The people that staff a customer call center, typically called agents (from airline sales "agents") or telephone sales or service representatives (TSRs), are organized into groups or teams, who are trained to serve the requests from a particular type(s) of inbound customer. These customers are routed to the agent group based on their request for service.

Less and less a UCD (Uniform Call Distribution) system may sometimes be used. A UCD tends to be less expensive and more rudimentary than an ACD. It may be perfectly acceptable in certain applications, though these are typically restricted to overflow or backup, not primary service groups. Since the price of basic ACD software bundled in a PBX or key system has fallen so low or in some cases is provided "free," there is little or no reason to accept the operational inequities and information limitations posed by a UCD.

A UCD uses a top-down or round robin call routing. A **"TOP-DOWN"** routing or search (sometimes call "hunting,") means the system begins to look for an idle station at a physical hardware or station address from the top of a list of stations. To illustrate, we will name this station #1. Once the first incoming call of the day is received and is in process (at station #1) any subsequent calls follow the same search pattern. Beginning at the top of the heap and searching down the list until an idle station is encountered. However calls end at the low number stations and new calls are passed to them while stations later in the numbering plan remain idle. A number of "hot seats" are created where the agent works more than their peers. This is considered inequitable.

In an attempt to remedy this work distribution inequity, a **"ROUND ROBIN"** distribution technique was introduced. It worked just like top-down but was distinguished from the top-down search because it began the search for an idle station at the next station after the last station that was delivered a call. This produced more equitable inequality yet still did not distribute calls truly equally.

A UCD using either top-down or round robin distribution cannot deviate from these predetermined routing plans. That is these systems are not easily reprogrammable, particularly by the user.

The issue of user reprogrammability is a significant user feature we will discuss at a later point. Suffice to say, that if the customer center management does not have control of their systems and its ability to respond to customer demands, they are already behind the service curve.

An ACD differs from a UCD as it typically routes a call to the agent who has been idle longest, unsurprisingly called the **"LONGEST IDLE"** technique. The ACD maintains an "availability" or "free" list of agents in a particular group. As an agent finishes the last call, they become "available" and are added to the bottom of this free list. As time passes and they remain on this list, they progressively rise to the top of the list until they become the target destination of the next call. They receive the next call. To do this an ACD has to have substantial processing and memory power.

A well designed ACD system will also allow the user to employ rudimentary UCD routing. There are times when there is a distinct need for a top down distribution technique in conjunction with the more equitable call distribution provided by the "longest idle" technique. An example of this occurs in a low traffic period, when there is a minor amount of call overflow to a second group. Rather than randomly interrupting everybody in the overflow group from alternative work assignments, the system biases the interruptions to a few agents assigned to the stations at the "top" or beginning of the agent group. The rest remain focused at some other job -- updating the mailing list, entering previous orders, outbound calling or whatever -- unless the call volume really picks up. To repeat the basic concept which distinguishes ACD systems from other systems. An ACD system will tend to equalize the workload across telephone agents or telephone representatives. This allows for higher productivity based on the knowledge that all agents are being treated equally as far as work distribution is concerned.

The most recent generation of ACD systems introduce a number of newer routing "wrinkles" such as conditional call routing, skill based call routing, knowledge based call routing, the inverted queue, and most recently intelligent call routing.

Conditional Call Routing: This uses the concept of the free list but also allows "interrupt" routing based on encountering a service, time, caller identity, call type or traffic load condition. This causes the machine to look to a table of conditional instructions which reflect call treatment based on the desired business objective. As an example, the queued million dollar stock trade, identified by a special called number (directory number, 800 etc.,) inbound caller identification or voice response prompted account number, is recognized and served ahead of the penny trader even though the larger trader called seconds later. It may be that once a predetermined queue length is reached calls are overflowed earlier to backup groups than under the normal queue scenario.

Skills Based Routing: This is a wonderful concept but as executed simply allows agents to sign on in more than one group, identifying the second classification as having certain properties or skills, that match specific customer demands. For example a customer call center may have a requirement to serve both Anglo and Spanish speaking customers. However the offered Spanish speaking customer load is not sufficient to dedicate Spanish speaking agents to that service. If that happened, the Spanish speaking agents would carrier a lighter load than the general Anglo agent group. So the strategy is to build a primary general group of all agents (Group 1) and build a second shadow group (Group 2) of bilingual agents. The system has the ability to differentiate Spanish speaking customers from the general caller population. This again is done by a publishing a distinctive telephone number for Spanish speaking callers wishing to be served by Spanish speaking reps. This can be done via Dialed Number Identification Service or DNIS, or a DID number. Or by a specific caller id being gathered from the network (ANI) or voice response unit (VRU) and being compared against an existing customer database record that identifies this agent as desiring Spanish speaking service. The ACD system then looks at the shadow group and the shadow queue that only Spanish speaking reps are part.

What happens here is that the system, because of this skill "interrupt," reduces its search for an eligible agent, based on the unique skill required to serve this caller.

Skill based routing is a significant feature that can be overused and dilute the effectiveness of the call center. Some of the worst examples can be found in software support where a caller identifies the software type, platform and version, only to be routed to such a small universe of skilled agents that the queue becomes extended, the service is diluted because the economy of scale is diluted to the point of defeating using and ACD.

Knowledge based routing is another version of Skill Based Routing that purports to consider more than just a particular agent's skill set and eligibility to serve a particular customer.

Intelligent Routing: This is the latest iteration of trying to connect a particular caller to a particular agent and offers all the potential to turn an ACD into a inefficient PBX call processing system.

The real difference with intelligent routing is the fact that the routing process considers more than a single call center, but caller data such as when they last called, the subject, to whom they last spoke and the feasibility of connecting that customer to the same agent. Of course all the issues of service level and prompt response to a customers request are factored into the routing decision so that callers don't go into impractical and an infinite queue, however the whole economy of scale concept is diluted.

The Inverted Queue: Another inbound routing feature that has gained popularity in the leading standalone ACD systems is the ability to invert the call type. That is when an inbound customer call encounters a delay, the caller is given three options, to wait on the line for service, hang up and call back or leave their number via a VRU prompt, hang up and expect a call back. This latter call back feature may be driven off the ANI capture. Here the system captures the inbound caller number and because the customer hung up before service was received, inserts a callback event into the inbound queue.

The ACD system then can automatically interleave the outbound call back with inbound calls. What happens here is that the nature of an outbound call is changed to "look like" an inbound call. Most inbound agents claim to not be good at proactive calling, but fine at reactive calling. That is if a customer or prospect asks for something, that's fine. But if they have to initiate a sales contact, they have a real objection to the process. This comes up as an issue when we discuss 'call blending," as offered by some of the newer outbound predictive dialing systems.

A recent tool being introduced in leading customer call center is a tool called call or case tracking. The goal of this is to gather topical case data so the state of the customer inquiry can be tracked so should a called call back and speak to a second agent, that second agent is answering that call and customer in the context of the customer relationship. Inquiry state management is also descriptive of this process. It has a myriad of uses in many different customer call centers, the most obvious of which is to equip as many possible agents with the knowledge to answer this customer call better. This begins to build the ACD back to its original goal of rationing the supply (your call center resources and agents) across as larger demand (customer calls) as possible. Back to economy of scale as described below.

What Makes Up An ACD System?

This section will deal with hardware, the architecture and the relationship of the parts of a switching system and in particular, an ACD system.

There are seven groups of components or subsystems that make up any switch;

1.   **The common control or intelligence of the system,**
2.   **The internal switching network of the system,**
3.   **The ports into and resources attached to the switching system,**
4.   **The backplane or signal distribution subsystem,**
5.   **The internal power supply,**
6.   **The power distribution subsystem, and**
7.   **The mechanical packaging of the system.**

All these elements are packaged together in a physical housing that allows integration of these subsystems with the software that is stored in the memory of the common control or "brains" of the system.

FIG. 7-1

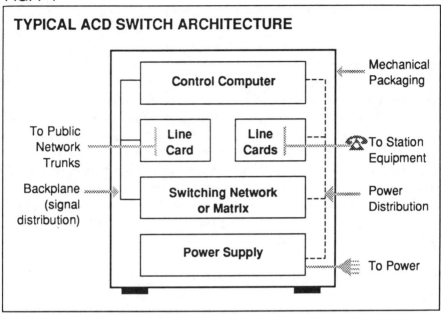

TYPICAL ACD SWITCH ARCHITECTURE

Control Computer

Mechanical Packaging

To Public Network Trunks

Line Card

Line Cards

To Station Equipment

Backplane (signal distribution)

Switching Network or Matrix

Power Distribution

Power Supply

To Power

An ACD has key features setting it apart from other call switching devices, the most significant of which is the traffic carrying capacity.

1.   The Common Control Or Intelligence That Drives The Switching System

All switches that are available today are computer controlled. At the core of the system is a specialized computer running specialized code, to allow connections to be set up between two (or more) ports in the switch. Each port represents the party to the conversation. An inbound caller occupies a trunk and the agent staffs a station. Unsurprisingly this path between the parties is called a "talk path." The two parties to this connection may not be both people. For example a queued customer listening to music, is attached to a port attached to a music source, announcement or whatever.

This computer technology has evolved from earlier processors and architectures to the more powerful 32 bit processors available today. Despite increased raw processing power, often tightly written machine level code runs well on older smaller processors. This is often why a manufacturer is reluctant to upgrade core processor technology for the sake of technology. Often the many hundreds of man years invested in software would be unsalvageable. Old, therefore, is not necessarily bad. There are ACD systems that have been in service for over 20

years that are still providing reliable service. However the cost of supporting some of these systems is becoming prohibitive. While the newer technologies offer greater potential for ongoing development and evolution. Code development is easier and faster in these newer environments. The common control or intelligence of the system manages the system resources and allows call origination, completion and feature use. The system brain may be one single computer or a number of distributed computer processors that talk to each other in a parallel (shared responsibility) or on a hierarchical (master/slave) basis. How this is achieved becomes important when a system fault occurs. How the system recovers from this, so as to cause little or no disruption to service and your business, is important. Remember these callers represent revenue now or eroded goodwill and lost revenue later.

The common control system manages a number of processes. These may include;

The switch resource status management process,
The switching process,
The data gathering, and,
The utility and diagnostic programs.

These programs run on an operating system, that uses various program tools to execute these various functions.

Resource status management; This process merely keeps track of what is going on in the switch. Resources are all the ports occupied by a device. A device may be a trunk, an agent or station, an interactive voice response connection or utility device of some kind. These devices are typically in one of two states, idle or busy. To change from one condition to the other, these devices "request service" from the common control device. The computer then looks to a table that tells the computer what to do with the request for service. The computer may expect to receive further data from the device in the form of the dialed digits that make the request more specific.

The switching process now allows the setup of a connection between the two resources requested by the device (for example, a caller station), or by following the treatment instructions residing in a table in common control memory. This then enables the common control computer to set up a connection between trunk

A and agent Y. The status resource management aspect of the system will monitor the connection for the duration of the transaction and "breakdown" the connection and return the devices and communications path to idle, upon completion of the call transaction.

Throughout this process, **data is being gathered about the transaction**. This may be minimal and be used for internal system management and diagnostic purposes or may be more extensive. With more extensive data many more applications can be addressed.

These may be call accounting, network optimization and/or trunk and station productivity analysis. Remember the more information you have the more insight and control over the application. But also so the management burden. When you have more information you have to do something with it. Otherwise the having or not having this information is irrelevant.

State vs. Record Machines

It is important to recognize an important philosophical difference in switching system design which particularly affects ACD operation and management. Some systems are defined as "state" machines, others record machines. This is defined by the way they gather, report and record call processing data.

A state machine collects and reports every change a device or call goes through. This data is delivered in real-time and can be used in a number of ways. This data allows real-time screen updates on a field by field basis. If it is written to disk it allows the collection of a complete audit trail of transactions, device, resource and personnel productivity.

A record machine must complete a transaction, typically a call, or wait for a system "snap shot" to be "taken" before the total machine (by device) status is reported. The machine never catches up with itself and is incapable of producing real-time displays for the supervisors. Most PBX based ACD systems are record machines. Watch a supervisor system screen and if the whole screen goes blank and repaints at regular (10 seconds?) intervals it is a record machine. One leading PBX based ACD system, starts shutting down reporting functions as the switching process demands more processing power!

There are always many other program modules running in today's switching computers. These are programs that allow the system to do more utilitarian things. These are described as utility programs.

2. The Internal Switching Network Of The Switching System

The system switching network or "matrix" is a series of components that allow the connection of any trunk, any station or utility device, to any other device. A utility circuit or device is a service device that is switched into the call transaction to allow use of this device in the call setup. For example, a tone generator delivers dial tone during call setup, a tone receiver "hears" and interprets the digits. In the case of an ACD, utility devices are also music-on-hold and announcement devices. These consume ports when present, and switching capacity when in use.

The network or matrix has addresses. One where the communication enters the switching system network and an address where the communication leaves the system. These are called ports. In turn these are occupied by a component such as a trunk, station, or utility device.

The majority of these systems are now digital. Analog systems use a less flexible, but extremely reliable scheme, that views the network as a matrix of X and Y coordinates. The common control sets up a connection by referencing the physical X/Y switch coordinates and "crosspoint" switch that accomplishes the connection between the particular X port and Y port devices. These switching matrixes were originally a network of physical switches. Subsequent solid state networks did away with physical switch networks by accomplishing the same function in silicon chips.

To find the number of simultaneous conversations the system will support is governed by the number of talkpaths or crosspoint connections which can be set up.

There are still many analog ACD systems in service today. This technology will continue to provide reliable and cost effective service for many telephone callers well into the next century. All of the popular ACD systems offered by standalone and PBX vendors in the US are digital systems.

There are many great good ACD deals to be had in the used equipment market. Many of these systems have analog networks. These are renown for their simplicity and reliability. If you have an important application and a small budget don't overlook this alternative.

All digital systems use an addressing scheme that allows a device to access a communications buss or pathway. This pathway resembles a freeway with entrances and exits. Each entrance and exit represents a port. Each port offers traffic in the form of "slices" of a message. These are like cars entering a freeway. Each message has an intended address, just as the driver of the car has an intend destination or exit. Unlike the car which represents a complete unit, a conversation is made up of potentially millions of message parts. By assigning each message with an identity "flag" and an address, the "digital parts" of a conversation can be connected between port A and B. These are the respective parts of a conversation albeit in tiny increments. By assigning the message with (entrance and exit) addresses, the buss connects port A to port B. This must occur thousands of times a second for this one connection.

Messages are sent backwards and forwards between ports. Our freeway example assumes a one way or asynchronous transmission not a two way or bisynchronous conversation. There is a second timeslot assigned for the second port.

These systems transmit conversation samples 8,000 times a second. They divide time vertically like a sliced loaf of bread. Each slice represents one 8,000th of a second conversation sample. This sample is sent from port A to B on a time slot. B responds and sends a message (also sampled 8,000 times a second) back to A. This occupies a second time slot. Each conversation requires two time slots. To find the total number of simultaneous conversations the machine will support, take the total time slot in a machine and divide by two.

When considered in the context of hundreds or thousands of ports, and hundred or thousands of calls in a busy hour, the load on the common control computer managing all this activity, is high. This leads to a second question of system capacity, because all computers have a finite load capacity.

3.   The Ports Into And Resources Attached To The Switching System

The common control and the switching devices make up the core of the switching engine in any switching application. Attached to and controlled by this switch are the devices that accomplish connection and communication to an from this engine.

The switch package is made up of a rack(s), and the shelves within the rack(s). These contain the various components or resources that make up the remaining elements of the system. These elements are the reason the switch exists. They represent the trunks, stations and service or utility circuits that need to be connected to accomplish the particular call transaction application this switch serves. The customer call center or business communication system.

Each trunk or station port is considered a "user available" port. That is a port the user can assign a resource or component to, such as trunk, station or with growing frequency, voice processing devices. Other ports in the system are occupied by utility devices, shared or "pooled" across the system, thus shared by the entire universe of user ports. These are the utility circuits. Ports may be dedicated to a single function. They may be preassigned to be occupied by a trunk, station or utility device. A system with "universal" ports allow almost any switched device to occupy almost any slot within the switched device slots.

4.   "User Available" Ports

The reason the term "user available" is used is to identify the net size of a system. Vendors talk grandly about the "capacity" of a system yet when put into use by a user, the system does not support the devices talked about by the vendor. Gross and net capacities differ because there is more to a switch operation than hooking up stations and trunks. Utility devices and also real life limits discovered in the computer processing power prevent a machine from reaching its maximum advertised capacity. Utility devices occupy ports whereas computer limits mean ports cannot be occupied even though they are vacant.

A vendor may give the user some say in the amount of utility devices in the system. Typically that are engineered into the system to meet anticipated traffic load. These are the tone generators, receivers, conference links etc. Today more of these devices are single integrated circuits (chips) and no longer need to occupy a unique slot.

When these are discrete devices which occupy a port, the vendors tend to be conservative in making sure the system is configured with enough of these devices. They often provide more than are necessary. The ports these devices occupy may be freed up to support an extra couple of analog trunks, agents whatever. Check with your vendor. You may be able to "squeak" through some tight capacity situations by displacing utility devices. This is a secondary or transient strategy only. Most vendors discourage this as it unduly complicates system administration for vendor and user alike.

User Devices

a). Public Network Components

- Trunks, Analog and/or digital circuits consisting of;
    - Local loops,
    - Foreign exchange circuits,
    - Intra and Interstate WATS lines,
    - Other bulk service long distance lines, and
    - Tie lines.

When telephone service is delivered in an analog format it can be bought a trunk at a time. Digital service generally arrives 24 lines at a time in a T.1 span.

b). Customer Side Resources

- Telephone Terminal Equipment or Instruments,
    - Plain old telephones (2500) sets,
    - Proprietary telephone set,
- ACD devices
    - ACD Agent instruments,
    - Integrated desktop workstations
    - Supervisor instruments,
    - Monitoring and Training instruments or access ports
    - Announcement devices, for delay announcements,
    - Music or promotion-on-hold devices for delay purposes,
    - Training or emergency recording devices,

- Automated attendant devices for call screening and call prompting, and
- Ports for accessing voice messaging and voice response devices.

Utility Devices

These are the tone receivers, tone generators, modems and other devices that are necessary to process a call. These may be either physical or logical devices.

The underlying rule in detailing each of these devices in a system is that each discrete device needs an address to enable it to participate in the call transaction process. Each discrete address therefore consumes communications capacity and displaces an alternative device. This principle will become increasingly clear as we move into capacity issues, number, throughput and control limitations. First the public network devices,

Telephone Circuits Or Trunks

Attached to the matrix or internal network are the public network devices. These are the circuits which allow calls to be placed to or from this switch to other point on the public network. These circuits exist for specific applications. Some cost based such as WATS. Others allow call or caller type discrimination. Dial 800-555-1234 for Sales, 800-555-1235 for Service. In the case of an ACD, although cost is a consideration, specific circuits may exist for reasons of geographic coverage. They serve specific regions that you wish to receive customer calls from.

Combinations of cost, call type and regional coverage add to the apparent complexity. These circuits may be digital or analog. Today, analog service is still predominant but this is changing quickly based on the fact that it is more economic for to deliver service in digital format. The signals on analog circuits arrive in analog form that are converted to from waves of electrical energy to sound waves by the telephone instrument headset or handset.

This is contrasted with digital circuits that transmit acoustic representations in digital form. Digital services are regularly available as T.1 service. A T.1 channel offers both the telephone company and the user substantial gain in circuit capacity and reductions in circuit cost. A two pair circuit (4 wires) can now carry 24 channels or separate voice conversations. Formerly a circuit pair (2 wires) was limited at one conversation or voice path. With telephone calls

arriving in digital form, your switching system or an interface device, called a channel bank, must unscramble or decode these signals, first to individual conversations then natural speech. To break up this data stream into 24 separate incoming conversations, the switch or channel bank must demultiplex (or "demux") the data stream on the T.1 span into 24 conversations. The outgoing conversations are multiplexed ("muxed") into one 24 channel T.1 span.

As a rule when planning for trunk types, trunk group organization and sizes, look to the business objectives first. Then, and only then, look to achieve these objectives in the most economical manner. By all means seek technical advice but don't start there. Strange results occur when technical judgment is first applied to select the types, groups and quantities of trunks to serve a customer call center.

Telephone Terminal Equipment

On the user side of the switch, there are the user resources. These range from a simple 2500 series telephone instrument, (a black phone!) a modern electronic telephone set, a high call volume ACD agent instrument, or an integrated voice and data workstation. These devices may address voice applications only or more frequently, may be they hybrid voice and data devices.

There are two schools of thought in delivering instrument features to the marketplace. They originate in either hardware or software philosophies. Many instruments have features hard coded into them. That is there is a specific button for every feature. A feature change may require an additional button. Then there is the software based feature philosophy. Here the manufacturer adds features vis software, thus can add them more easily and without hardware changes.

Some of these features may be controlled by a user feature control table known as a class of service table. That is each instrument (user) has features extended to them based on a table granting levels of permission. Much like a system security access. The higher the class of user, the more features are available to the user. There is a renewed importance attached to the integrated voice and data workstations. They will be discussed in Chapter 14.

Supervisor, Monitoring And Training Terminals

Unique to ACD systems, these devices resemble the category above, but are designed to supplement the supervisory, monitoring or quality assurance and training functions in a customer call center. These devices often differ from the normal telephone service representative or agent instrument because of unique hardware and/or software based features that extend the instrument beyond general ACD agent functionality.

A position that is equipped for monitoring must allow a supervisor or call auditor to patch in to a call as a third party without affecting the quality of the call. Typically this can mean a reduction in the volume of the call. The monitor position ideally also should not introduce extra sound on the line when the supervisor plugs into a particular call, hence the term "silent monitoring."

Software vs. Hardware Class Of Service

Take care when you are evaluating an ACD that these devices all the same for agent, supervisor, or monitor. Any feature differential should be controlled by software based class of service definitions. In this way you avoid stocking more than one type of instrument.

Announcement Devices

These devices provide prerecorded announcements to an incoming caller. They were simple message playing devices such as tape or solid state memory devices. They should not be confused with the newer voice processing technologies of automated attendants or interactive voice response (IVR) with call prompting, triage, screening and direction devices.

They are informational in content and they were originally designed to deliver a "delay" message. These have been expanded beyond the inevitable "...please hold, one of our agents will be with you eventually. This is the only boring message you will hear...." to provide information, specially provided user specific promotions. With the newer voice processing tools such as automated attendant and IVR, call screening and prompting for service selection and other functions expand the possibilities of call greeting.

The simple announcement devices occur in two forms. A mechanical continuous loop recording (a tape recorder and player) or solid state digital devices. They may be a integral part of the ACD system or a port allowing attachment to a discrete external device.

Digital announcement devices are preferable due to sound fidelity, instant reset and replay (the caller always hear the beginning of the tape) and reliability issues. A mechanical playback device runs at a constant tape speed and continuously playing the delay message. Calls that are to receive the message a queued up in a micro queue ready to receive this message. This is so they don't barge into the middle of a nearly completed announcement. All new call arrivals must all wait till the beginning. Calls do not arrive simultaneously, therefore they are all queued different lengths, until the announcement is completed. This adds to individual call length, anywhere up to the entire length of the message. This increases line occupancy and circuit hold time. A powerful and expensive nuance!

FIG. 7-2

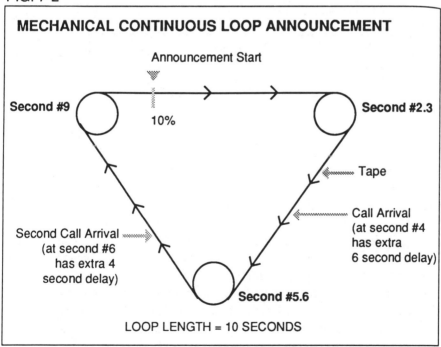

In many cases these devices use multi-track tape with multiple channels per individual tape. That is two or more announcements can be recorded simultaneously on the same tape and be played back to two or more separate callers. These announcements must be of identical length. This leads to decreased inflexibility because of the constant length announcements over all applications. Even though the words may not take up the same space on the tape the first, second and night announcement occupy the same tape space. A short announcement will still take up the same physical tape length, and therefore time, as it occupies a channel with the time predetermined by the longest announcement on the tape loop.

FIG. 7-3

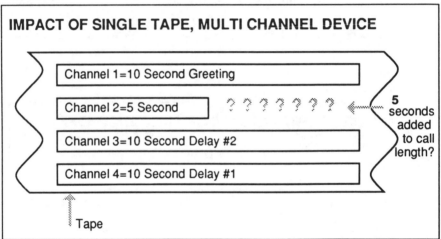

Most systems now use solid state announcers that eliminate this and recording degradation problems induced by wear on the moving tape and playback heads. Because digital announcers have no moving parts they are more reliable also.

Most significant is the circuit time saved. When a caller "barges out" of an announcement as an agent becomes available, the digital announcement is instantly reset to the restart point and is immediately available for the next inbound caller. No additional delay is imposed on the caller while the mechanical tape loop winds on to the beginning of the next play cycle. Though this may be seconds, seconds add up quickly when hundreds or thousands of calls are being processed.

Recorded Announcement Flexibility

Adding business applications in a customer call center demands more announcements and many of the major popular PBX based ACD systems have significant limitations in this area. Take care to understand how many unique recorded announcements can be played simultaneously to incoming customers of the same and/or different types.

Disk Based Announcements

A number of the major ACD vendors have elected to do away with separate recorded announcement devices and load these onto a disk based voice response system. One example has even driven their delay music through this vehicle.

The advantage is almost unlimited flexibility. The disadvantages occur in the cost of acquiring and bulletproofing a disk based announcement system, then the additional time added as each call requires disk access, versus the time it takes to access the "flash" memory of a solid state announcement system. It takes longer, even though this is just microseconds, to access disk based announcement data.

Substituting disk based announcement technology to additionally deliver on board automated attendant functions, ACD voice mail and rudimentary IVR capability, on the surface, a great idea. In the case of simple greetings and announcements this is total overkill and expensive to acquire and to operate. Disk access, as any PC user will attest is quite measurable. It takes time to determine where the file is, access and play it back. This potentially adds unnecessary overhead to call processing time to each call.

A number of larger production based customer call centers are not considering this technology, particularly if it is the only way an ACD can handle routine announcements. The reason for this is the additional costs that are added due to this overhead. In large customer call center, an additional second per call average can amount to as much as $1,000,000 a year in expense impact.

There are three other "gotchas" that these vendors don't emphasise either. **First,** if the system is configured as a redundant system to allow non-stop operation, the "B side" of the system must duplicate the "A side" disk based voice technology and database. If it does not, operation in an outage of the A side cannot be duplicated by the B side, as there is no disk based voice services redundancy. This is a vendor trick to keep the price down in a competitive bid situation. They often leave it out. Truthfully they can say it is a redundant machine, but it will not operate as a mirror image of regular operation.

Second; if the voice databases are not maintained as absolute replicas of each other, mirror operation is also impossible.

Third; often these vendors heavily pitch their ability to offer integrated announcements, auto attendant, voice mail, and integrated voice response. However as of this writing, the IVR function is so rudimentary, that should the customer call center require sophisticated IVR scripts and data communications with a host, these ACD vendors introduce yet another IVR from a third vendor. This means a redundant ACD system with fully redundant voice services and sophisticated IVR requirements needs three separate disk based voice services devices. This is costly and a announcement and script database management nightmare.

Music And Promotions Devices For Broadcast To Delayed Callers

The customer call center industry knows a caller is less inclined to disconnect during a queued delay, if the caller is provided some feedback that confirms they are still in queue. This is feedback is provided by the announcements and the playing of music during the delay. The implication is the caller has not been forgotten. This has been expanded to include promotional messages and even "all news" broadcasts.

As an alternative there are many providers of professional announcement and music on hold programs which can be extensively customized to your business applications. These suppliers provided the license to unlimited use by the customer call center.

Voice Messaging And Voice Response Interfaces

These interactive announcement and tone recognition technologies, allowing a caller to "converse" directly with a computer system using a touch tone pad. This can be used as a "call prompting" device allowing the caller to select the service they wish to receive, (push 1 for service, push 2 for sales) ask for information and participate in other transactions, without the involvement of an agent. With the right programming, many callers can actually have their requests satisfied without ever speaking to a live agent.

These are sophisticated devices increasingly making their way into customer call center applications. They offer great service enhancing and labor saving potential when correctly applied. This market has become extremely confusing for the average buyer as there are so many offerings which may or may not be appropriate for use in your customer call center.

The problems is there were five distinct applications that were typically supplied by four different types of machines. Each vendor type extended their devices reach to capture more market and reached into vaguely related applications. The result was over reach and a number of dissatisfied customers who reached machine limitations well before the machine was obsolete in its original purpose.

There are basically five different types of voice technology applications beginning with the humble home answering machine. This serves as a model and a basis for explaining each of the different types.

☐　**The answering machine:**

An answering machine serves one line, has local memory and is non interactive. A call comes in, delivers a message and then will record a message. These systems are typically narrow devices with no other applications, though a number of PC board systems are available for use in your PC. The answering machine in its purest form requires no other interface other than connection to the telephone line. The user interface is based on recording the original outgoing greeting message, then recovering and clearing each of the incoming messages.

☐　**Automated Attendant:**

This serves more than one trunk, delivers a message to an incoming caller, asking the caller to select their destination. This may be a function (Press 1 for Sales) or an extension. The system expects entry of touch tone (DTMF) digits to select the address. It interrogates a local table that dials the appropriate extension identified as sales or the desired extension. In the early automated attendant systems, local memory and storage were limited as they had but one role, call triage.

The automated attendant is connected to a key system or PBX. In its original application of call triage, it did not generally interface with any other devices such as computers.

❑ Voice mail:

This is as application designed to allow interactive non-simultaneous messaging. Voice mail is an ideal description. The system is served by a number of trunks or connections, serves a large universe of callers, is highly interactive with extensive local memory, computing power and message storage.

The automated attendant is connected to a key system or PBX. In its original application of exchanging voice messages between users, it did not generally interface with any other devices such as computers.

❑ Audiotext:

This a machine that manages a huge library of information for playback to a caller at the callers demand. Each piece of information represents a volume in a library, directed at answering one specific request. The audiotext machine stores these volumes and allows the caller to access the appropriate information message via a directory of services that are available. The caller must find and select the information they want via touch tone selections. These systems are served by many trunks, have significant local processing power and vast local storage. Based on the limited interactivity of the recorded data, this may be disk or tape based. There is typically no communications with an external computer or database.

❑ Integrated Voice Response (IVR) or Voice Response Units (VRU):

These systems connect to multiple trunks (or extension lines,) have significant local memory and processing power. They differ in two significant ways from voice mail devices. They are expected to follow sophisticated user programmable scripts and interface and use external data from another computer.

These are among the most sophisticated applications of voice technologies. This is because they go beyond simple messaging into actual data gathering, interface to external databases that require a separate computer look up, then articulating the data delivered by the external computer.

As you can see from the original mission of voice technology, each device had a specific function and architecture which did not make an automated attendant a good voice mail machine, a good IVR and vice versa. These were typically function to cost trade-offs. Therefore selecting the correct platform for use in your customer call center application is critical.

Voice Technology Connection

There are a number of ways these devices can be connected to the system, and a number of ways they can be implemented. Connectivity can be accomplished in two ways, via analog (2500 set emulation) or digital links. In the case of analog links, these are less efficient and occupy more switch real estate than compared to digital service.

Recording Devices

Frequently the occasion arises to record a particular call. This can be for reasons of;
- security, tracing the "crank call,"
- maintaining an audit trail, in a high value transaction, such funds transfer or high
- chances of exposure to liability such as a 911 call,
- training purposes,
- monitoring or quality assurance and counseling purposes,
- or sales verification.

These devices may be a simple tape recorder or a commercial grade multitrack tape recorder, and even in VCR formats. They may attach to a single recording port or attach at the agent station termination blocks and not require dedicated ports. The application determines the termination.

Where all calls are being recorded for audit, training or sales verification, a voice activated multichannel tape works better when terminated concurrently with the agent stations. A system-wide recorder for crank calls needs only one recorder port assuming your center does not receive more than one crank call at a time? There are a number of device considerations.

Emergency Recording, Logging (Or Audit) Systems, Training Tapes And Interactive Monitoring

There are a number of recording devices in the market that have application in the customer call center. However just like the early days of voice response, each application and the technology solution is very specific and typically cannot be forced to perform a function it was never intended to. It is necessary to understand the applications segments and the devices used in each. There are four segments in the recording device market. These are:

1.) Record a call on demand

There are two different flavors of applications for record on demand; these are agent initiated and more recently, call type based on a computer telephony link that identifies a specific call type that the customer call center wishes to record.

These systems are used to record agent's conversation based on an agent or supervisor request. Applications are "Sales Verification" and "Over the Phone Transactions." where active customer consent can be used to execute a contract. In these applications, the agent needs to record the customer saying, 'Yes I want to buy your product'. There are also the emergency recorder applications to catch crank calls, bomb threats, etc.

These systems usually connect via a physical link to the switch. They receive a request to start recording an agent, then receive a request to stop. Access is usually done from an analog link to the tape recording or maybe disk based.

2.) Record "all" calls

These systems as known as voice loggers. This type of device has received recent coverage for its role in the Bankers Trust scandal of October 1995. They record all calls that an agent takes or makes on their phone.

The system connects to either the incoming lines or to each agent's phone. This connectivity option means that each monitored line or phone has a dedicated port on the recorder. For large customers, this can run into hundreds of thousands of dollars. Play back is usually done from a dedicated PC that has access to the recorded voice. Recorded voice can be digitized or recorded on VHS tape technology which allow up to 32 parallel channels on the tape.

The problem with playback is actually finding the call you need to playback. Since it records ALL Calls, the only two items you have to "find" the call is agent number, (this corresponds to channel number, if the channel is connected to the agent's phone) and time. For non-digitized systems, voice access is sequential, meaning that you have to start from some point and fast forward or rewind to the requested part on the tape that you think has your target recording. On VHS tape systems that means going through the parallel channels up to 32 times or until you find the target call. Companies that distribute and or build this product are Dictaphone (about 70% of market), Racal Milgo and others.

The big flaw with logging and demand call recording systems is there are seldom a digital data tag that makes recovering a specific record easily. Again it is necessary to know the physical location of the recording on a tape to find it, or if disk based, time or port information. The recording is not accessible as a digital computer file and therefore cannot be tied back to any call transaction data generated by the ACD system.

3.)   Scheduled Recording of agent voice calls for quality assurance

This is a new entry in customer call center management systems and offers significant break through in monitoring. This is what interactive monitoring system does. The supervisor "schedules" recording and the system records the agent(s) based on that schedule. These systems typically connect to the switch like a "Supervisor Phone". This connectivity option allows the customer to utilize a small number of channels to monitor a large number of agents. Play back is done from any standard touch tone phone, much like voice mail. This type is primarily software based and generally more flexible than a hardware based systems that require the supervisor to play back from a dedicated PC or from one equipped with additional monitoring hardware.

From the interactive monitoring system, the supervisors can access voice files by group, subgroup, or by agent ID and since they are digitized, the system can go directly to the requested voice files. These files can be tied back to any digital data generated by the ACD for reporting purposes. This is an important and critical difference between this and the two previously discussed systems.

We will discuss the uses and benefits of these systems when we get to discussing customer call center management style in Chapter Twelve.

4.)   Data Recording

With the advent of monitoring came the need to concurrently view the data screen being used by the agent so the reviewer could see the rep was correctly articulating the information displayed to the customer. There are two ways of doing this, the older and hardware intense screen duplication represented by

Witness Systems, Marietta, GA. The better and more flexible way to do this is via software that allows a mirror of the screen, (via software driven port replication,) to be displayed by the review equipped with a similar display device. This is the solution sold by IBS Systems of San Diego, CA

These systems can record what's happening on the desktop device, terminal or PC. They record either host based sessions or the entire desktop's activities. This becomes important when a company moves from real-time monitoring (expensive and inconvenient) to monitoring past recordings. This is desirable as the reviewer does not need to be on the phone concurrently with the agent waiting for an appropriate customer call. These systems usually have a logical link through the network or reside on the host computer itself. Access is usually done from a dedicated PC or from any PC connected to the host.

Recent work has been done to connect the voice and data recording monitor systems to provide an even more complete view of the customer/agent transaction to be reviewed.

The applications for recording systems, particularly monitoring quality, is discussed more fully in Chapter Twelve.

Ports

All these devices are attached to physical ports in the switching system. When they are in use they occupy a path through the switching network consuming network resources.

4. Backplane Or Signal Distribution Subsystem

A backplane or signal distribution system may be made up of a single printed circuit board in a single shelf system, or a complex of backplanes interconnected by ribbon cable or other mechanical path. The single shelf backplane is called a "mother board." These devices have both finite physical capacity on a shelf, rack and system basis. They may be simplex or duplex to ensure redundancy.

5. The Internal Power Supply

As expected, electric power is the lifeblood of a computer controlled switch. Along with receiving and providing a degree of power conditioning, your system's internal power supply reduces the voltage of the incoming power to the voltage required by the individual components in the system. The internal power supply may be just one device (simplex) or multiple devices in serial or multiple devices arranged in parallel (duplex). These power systems may be redundant. Check: just because there are multiple power supplies they may not be redundant. Also check for that single point of failure such as a single fuse buss or fuse.

Power supplies generate heat. This heat needs to be dissipated. Always leave room around a power supply. The bigger the power supply the greater the heat. How is it cooled? Convection or mechanical fans? Where is the power supply? At the bottom of the device (heat rises!) or at the top. In a system where cooling is mechanically assisted, what happens if a fan, (or fans,) fail?

6. The Power Distribution Subsystem

The power distribution subsystem is the power distribution network in the machine that allows electric power to be distributed at the right voltage to each of the components around the system.

This can be the weakest part of the system -- especially when it is overloaded. It can be overloaded by supply (the front end) or demand (the back end). That is the power being fed to it or drawn from it. Power variations are a common source of problems for all computer controlled devices.

Also what options do you have regarding electric power? AC (alternating current, or the power coming of the electric company's grid and through the standard wall socket,) or DC (direct current provided by filtering commercially available power through an inverter and batteries which "steps down" the power to the switch.) By using a DC power source you have a higher degree of power regulation and reliability.

The more the computer companies got into the switch business, the less attention was given to delivering conditioned (DC) power which was considered a telephony standard. However providing AC power and the batteries and inverters necessary to power a switch add additional installation and maintenance cost, and in a competitive sales environment, considered undesirable. The cheaper alternative is standard AC, but with any move to increased reliability, the cost of acquisition and ownership is higher, but consider this against the mission critical nature of your customer call center.

The more critical your customer call center is, the more critical it is you pay attention to power regulation and backup. Our humble opinion: a full-blown DC battery backup system powering a DC machine makes most sense. An AC system with an external power regulator is typically fine and less expensive in small applications.

Case Study -- Power "Ups and Downs"

An ACD was installed in Las Vegas in a medium sized 24 hour a day hotel reservation center. Needless to say in this 1000+ room hotel, the guest reservation center was critical to their revenue and competitive position in the market. Every morning between 8:30 and 9:30 and every afternoon between about 4:00 and 6:00 the system would "crash" in a big way. The service organization did not find the pattern or frequency of the failures until they put power monitoring equipment on the power outlets. Not before they had changed out the computer control and power supplies, did they discover the ACD shared a circuit with a large three storey hydraulic elevator to the executive offices! This elevator drew massive power requirements as the pump fed the elevator ram. The sag in power was more than this AC powered ACD could stand.

Now with complex applications becoming available from CTI and customer call center process reengineering, the need for redundant servers, LAN connectivity and robust desktop machines, becomes even more critical, yet most systems integrators and available hardware are short on answers that have been de riguer in the telephone industry.

7.   The Mechanical Housing Of The System

All of this technology must now be packaged up in a effective unit that meets regulatory, manufacturing, marketing and cost objectives. The package consists of rack or cabinet mounting for shelves, which contain slots for printed circuit boards and subassemblies. These represent the various components. These are connected to the backplane at right angles from where they receive power and communicate with the system at large.

The Switching Engine

In calling out the various components and subsystems of a switch, it becomes clear that a device, a component or a system, has finite capacity. These finite capacities occur at all system levels and exist in three dimensions;

    a.   **The number of devices that can be physically accommodated in the mechanical housing,**

    b.   **The number of simultaneous communications paths supported by a single stage switching network, and**

    c.   **The raw call transaction processing power of the common control computer(s).**

The questions that should be asked in any switch purchase are;

A.   Physical Capacity

    1.   **How many devices can it physically support?**
    2.   **Are there any tradeoffs if analog versus digital circuits are used?**

This is a switch "real estate" question. That is how much room is in the switch to accommodate all of the required devices? Digital devices (such as a T.1 span of 24 channels) may be one card, whereas analog trunk ports may be four, eight,

twelve or even 16 to a card. The impact is more cards are required for the same number of physical connections.

    3.   **What are the maximum number of devices per shelf?**
    4.   **What are the maximum number of shelves per rack?**
    5.   **What are the maximum number of racks per system?**
    6.   **What is the maximum port capacity of a single stage switch?**
    7.   **If it is possible to connect single stage switches into a large switching complex;**
            ■   **how is this done?**
            ■   **what are the trade offs, and,**

- **are existing ports displaced?**

At this stage we are only looking for physical system blockage and not considering the impact of software being unable to logically support a physically nonblocking configuration.

B. Switching Capacity

1. How many devices can be supported by the switch?
2. How many simultaneous conversations can be carried by the switch?
3. What is the actual traffic capacity of a single stage switch?

C. Common Control Computer Capacity

1. What is the largest referencable installed customer?

What we are looking for is the ability of the switch to handle calls. You must watch the language the various vendors use. Some refer to "BHA" or busy hour (call) attempts, which means what it says, but attempts only, NOT completions. Whereas other more honest vendors talk about BHC or busy hour call completions. A switch can deal with more attempts, if it does not have to route, connect, monitor (call status) and "housekeeping" the data following a completed call. You are looking for the largest single stage switch installed.

Vendors may try and show you a multi-module site, that is more than one switch tied together. This is not a single stage switch and there are significant inefficiencies and higher costs for following this strategy.

Why An ACD System?

Processing an ACD call is from FIVE to SEVEN TIMES more complex than a an average administrative call processed by a PBX, and therein lies a key issue as to why a generalized switch such as a PBX or CO does not make the most desirable ACD platform.

It consumes more resources, it is switched more times, is more intensely managed by the switch, ideally more data is gathered and reported about the call status, status changes and outcome. And this is only getting more complex as we add IVR, and CTI applications such as call tracking or customer inquiry state management in an attempt to reduce customer call center staffing. Because of the revenue and /or goodwill implications, the call carries a great deal more importance and emotion than the average administrative PBX call. Simply put,

the customer call center is considered a "mission critical" application in most businesses. Manufacturers have recognized this to different degrees and offer differing levels of system features and robustness to fit every type of customer call center.

The features and values of an automatic call distributor system can be categorized into five broad areas;

1. **The architecture and capacity of the switch,**
2. **The ability to provide service to callers in a system outage,**
3. **To provide a high degree of information about all facets of the system, its operation and customer call center resources,**
4. **To be easy to use at every level so effort in using the system does not impair the primary caller transaction,**
5. **To provide open control system architecture so that the ACD system can interface with other customer call center resources.**

1. ACD Architecture And Capacity

The first question to ask of a switch provider, offering to sell you an ACD, is the history of the switch.

☐ **What did this system start out as?**
- **A key system,**
- **a PBX, or**
- **a purpose built ACD?**

A CO, PBX or key system based ACD, did not begin life as an ACD, and is consequently encumbered with certain design decisions made for the originally intended application (administrative phone support) and market (size.) When a system is designed certain engineering compromises are made to meet marketing and manufacturing cost objectives. This expedience often caused the last generation of switches to become generalized PBX solutions.

With generalization, comes a lack of clear engineering focus. "We are designing it to be a multi-purpose switching engine capable of serving any voice application." Yet competition, market reality and engineering design considerations dilute this. An ACD system is a very particular application with the need to accommodate the many human factors and management issues of a real-time cultural and business environment. Many of the needs of customer call center management and ACD design, contradict good PBX design.

These generalized switches, with their intended market application, often become the manufacturer's basic platform for the application or market next identified. The system may provide modifiable call routing, can be programmed by the user, can produce call statistics, and maybe can be sold as an automatic call distributor. But is it an automatic call distributor?

Manufacturers generally do not lie, but if they do not understand the application well, they do not understand why specific features exist and "shoehorn" the application into a less than ideal machine with a constrained computer power, compromises are made. The user of this crippled system subtlety loses opportunities to save money and take control of their business destiny. Nobody lied, but neither party to the transaction may realize what they are giving up from a business perspective. And the lower initial acquisition price may appear to favor the PBX or hybrid platform.

A generalized approach compromises three aspects of customer call center management:

❑ **direct control of operating costs,**
❑ **ease and convenience of real data for analysis, and**
❑ **the business insight and business advantage that comes from this data.**

The various opportunities to control operating costs, (trunk and staff,) over the life of the system, far outweigh the increased acquisition cost of a standalone ACD over a PBX based ACD. In spite of this many buyers balk at the increased system cost compared to a PBX based system. It is important to understand the critical mission of the customer call center and the operating costs to be saved. If you can live with the compromises offered by a PBX based ACD system and your business loses little or no advantage, then an PBX based ACD may be just fine. Once a business understands the compromises brought by a PBX based solution, this is seldom the case. Figure 7.4 explains the architectural differences between a production ACD and an administrative PBX based ACD.

FIG. 7-4

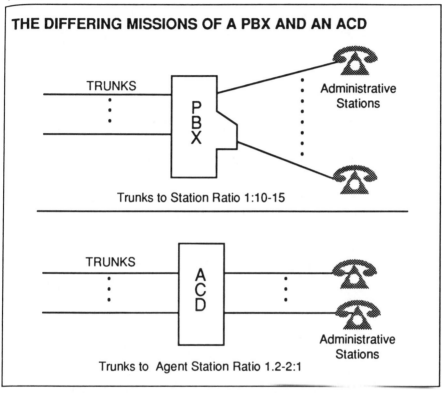

A true ACD system has very specific user focused properties;

a.   **The system must be both physically and logically non-blocking so the system can connect any two ports (resources) attached to it, at any time.**

b.   **The system must allow a high degree of flexibility to the user, to allow trunk, agent, routing and reporting arrangements to reflect user requirements.**

The user should be able to easily manipulate the call routing tables at any time, so as not to abdicate customer call center flexibility to vendor service availability or cost. Ease of user "programmability" is a significant issue. "User programmability" does not mean writing system code, rather it means the changing of system tables to reflect your business objectives. On demand, easily and quickly.

c. The system must offer a high degree of reliability.

Because of the critical nature of a customer call center as there is a great need for its uninterrupted operation. Typically some degree of resilience is built the machine to retard failure.

This is a world of subtlety, but expensive nuances, that are reminiscent of certain military "don't ask, don't tell," stance. If you don't understand the issue, you don't ask the question, you are never aware of the implications.

A.   Physically And Logically Non-Blocking

It is important that all calls be answered and served promptly, because of the revenue and image maintenance issues associated with the call.   There are few exceptions to this rule.

Physical blockage is the inability to connect a caller, desiring to reach another person or device, to that person or device, due to a lack of talk path capacity in a switching machine.

In the case of an ACD, a talk path is the communication pathway that is established between any component and another.   For example, a trunk and an agent position, so the conversation can occur between a caller and an agent. This conversation may result in an order or request for help.   This is a physical path in an analog switch, or adequate timeslot capacity in a digital switch.   Most switch manufacturers claim to provide non-blocking switches to their advertised capacities.   A little known, and unadvertised fact is that many of physically non-blocking switches can introduce blockage.

This occurs when the software that queues and routes the calls, is written in way that does not take advantage of the non-blocking switch capacity.   For example, when an inbound call has waited for an available agent in the primary answering group, beyond a certain predetermined threshold, the call is intraflowed (overflowed) to a second group of agents.   If an agent in the second group is not immediately available, the call continues to wait in queue. In some systems, if an agent becomes available in the first group, the group primarily responsible for the serving call, the call cannot be answered by that agent, as the software does not allow for "look-back" capability. This is an example of "logical blockage" occurring, even though the physical talk path exists to serve the connection.

This has the effect of increasing the number of agents in the second group to meet the increased or "stimulated" traffic load and service level they now must meet. In outbound call routing, "look back" capability in queuing tables is known to contribute approximately a 15% increase in trunk group efficiency when the trunks involved exceed thirty.

Although no research or writing is known to have been done on customer call center efficiency, the lack of multiple level simultaneous queuing is believed to incur a similar efficiency penalty. The sizing of the secondary and subsequent agent groups must now allow for the extra load that is now offered to them due to the lack of the look-back feature. The logically blocking routing scheme stimulates the traffic load they now must serve, and more staff is required to continue to meet the desired service level.

This type of problem is typically encountered in PBX based ACD systems. The effect on increased operating costs becomes significant.

Since the addition of conditional and skills based routing, there has been an increase in the ability of these systems to focus the call on a increasingly definitive agent resource based on a specific skill set. This however has two effects: I greatly increases the complexity of setting up optimal and efficient routing tables and queues. If done badly or employed too frequently can significantly reduce the efficiency of the ACD. That is whole reason for the customer call center (many served by few) now has the potential to become fragmented to the point of denying the reason for this center which was to take advantage of economy of scale.

New strategies are being developed to deliver the agent significantly more tools to allow almost any agent to serve the caller again. Although the notion of a truly "universal agent" is probably illusory, there are many things that can be done to expand the skill set of your agents so as to expand the pool of agents available to serve your callers. That is back to being a true ACD. We will deal more with this in Chapter Fourteen on Advanced Customer Call Center Strategies.

B. ACD System Flexibility

An ACD system must allow a high degree of flexibility. Though most ACD vendors allow a great deal of user access to the system for reprogramming of the routing tables and parameters, a little examination of the philosophy governing this feature is necessary.

First it is absolutely unnecessary in this day of microcomputers to deny a user control of his or her own destiny. We now have the power of a 1970s mainframe in a chip, and the on-line storage capacity in a battery driven lap top PC. As an aside, almost this entire book, with the diagrams, was written in ZEDIT, on a battery driven lap-top at 35,000 feet, and can be stored on a single 3 1/2 inch disk. It is absolutely unacceptable for a customer call center customer to have to build their business and call handling processes around the limitations of a vendor's shortsighted decisions or machine. Yet in the world of ACD systems a number of vendors expect call center managers to do just that.

The background that has led to this is understandable when you examine the software philosophies that were popular at the time the system was designed. ACD systems that are available today reflect four attitudes to user programmability. The effect of these philosophies are typically experienced by a user when making call processing changes to the system via an administrative computer console or CRT screen.

1. **The "system build:"** This era allowed extensive user flexibility when originally specifying the system, but did not allow for extensive subsequent changes on site, by the user. Changes are possible, but are normally conducted with the assistance of the manufacturer. There are costs, inconvenience and time delays associated with any change. A very technical user can make changes to the system, but not without extensive training and skill. More recently personal computer have been introduced to "front end" the change process and make it less difficult for a user to make a change.

2. **The "table driven" system:** Programming of the system provided for the control software to look to user accessible tables. These tables could be changed by the user, at will, to reflect routing steps, agent groups, agent properties and other system aspects. These system use plain language in their command structure, and a simple command syntax; noun, verb, and optional modifier. An example of this is "Revise Route (number) 01." The objective of

this strategy was to reduce the skill and labor content necessary to manage the system. System operation still required considerable training. However, the resultant independence from the manufacturer and customer flexibility is a substantial value.

FIG. 7-5

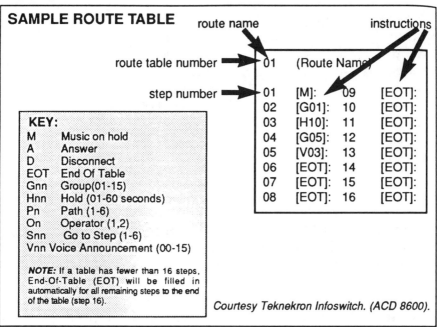

SAMPLE ROUTE TABLE

Courtesy Teknekron Infoswitch. (ACD 8600).

3. **"Menu driven" systems:** This is the most recent advance in ACD user interface techniques. In this case all of the options are arrayed on the administrative CRT screen as the system manager steps through the system revision. The manager merely selects an alternative by moving a cursor and pushing enter. The change is made. A variation of this is the introduction of LOTUS 123 like header screens, with cursor/enter selection sequences.

EXPLANATION:

Although the phrase "user programmability" is used, no literal programming skills are necessary to manage a modern ACD. However, there is an advantage in giving the system management responsibility to people not in awe of technology.

FIG. 7-6

```
┌─────────────────────────────────────────────────────────────────────┐
│ SAMPLE MENU SELECTION TABLE                                           │
│                                                                       │
│ ┌───────────────┐ ┌─────────────┐ ┌──────────────┐ ┌───────────────┐ │
│ │ Status        │ │ Resources   │ │ Users        │ │ Update Records│ │
│ │ Trends        │ │ Groups      │ │ Trunks       │ │ View Table    │ │
│ │ Database      │ │ Call Control│ │ Voice Trunks │ │ Print         │ │
│ │ Reports       │ │ Outdial Plan│ │ Instruments  │ │ Delete        │ │
│ │ Procedures    │ │ System      │ │ Workstations │ │ Status        │ │
│ │ Forecasting   │ └─────────────┘ │ Stations     │ └───────────────┘ │
│ │ Administration│                 │ auX. Devices │                   │
│ │ Options       │                 │ Data InterLink│                  │
│ │ Maintenance   │                 └──────────────┘                   │
│ │ Log-off       │                                                    │
│ └───────────────┘                                                    │
│                                Courtesy Aspect Telecommunications     │
└─────────────────────────────────────────────────────────────────────┘
```

4. **Object Oriented User Programming:** Here icons or symbols are used to represent actions, objectives or sequences. The user merely takes the object and places it in the order they require same to be executed.

Today, most systems have updated their interface standards to make the ACDs easier to use. The penalty a manufacturer incurred for not being easy to use, was confinement to markets that could afford to invest in the staff necessary to use the system. This is changing.

Take time to understand how hard or easy it is for you to make changes to the system. What staff commitment and training levels will be needed to support this. Also understand the scope of these changes, both system and component level. Understand to what level in the machine rule changes operate.

Command Granularity?
Systemwide, Trunk Group, Trunk Or Call!

What is the extent of your ability to change the system? Down to what level of detail? A good example of control over your ACD (command granularity) is answer control. Here a call answering rule is applied by the system.

If a call arrives on a trunk and there are no agents immediately available to answer the call, it may make sense to allow it to ring. The logic behind this is the fact that not all telephone calls are answered immediately, so it is quite reasonable to expect the caller to accept two or more rings, until an agent becomes available. Here is the key. If the call is not answered, billing does not begin. This is a major advantage to an inbound WATS subscriber, because the alternative is; to answer the call, and while the caller waits to speak to an agent, play them your expensive "elevator" music. It's not the music that's expensive but the phone line to play it on.

The question of command granularity is this: when the delay parameter (or any other like parameter) is set up, does it effect the entire system? Just the trunk group, an individual trunk, or is it dynamically assigned on a call by call basis?

Ideally you should be able to control the smallest logical unit your ACD effects. This is a call. If you are restricted to constant treatment at a trunk level or worse, trunk group wide, or worse still, system wide, you become increasingly unable to adapt to the instant business conditions.

When Is A Call A Call?

Next issue is the optimum delay dynamically adjusted to reflect agent availability. If there are agents available, does the system provide the minimum one ring then

immediate "cut through" to the agent, or does it introduce a flexible caller delay period that can be longer or shorter based on agent availability.

A little telephony explanation is required here. This is just like setting up a computer to computer communication. There is the hardware connection, the wire! Then there is the signal requesting a response; essentially "is anybody out there?" Then there is the answer and handshake between systems. A CO once it has a call destined for your pilot ACD number, selects your physical trunk (access) and sends a supervision in (ringing voltage (analog) or digital equivalent

(digital or ISDN trunks.) Your ACD recognizes the inbound call service request and responds with answer or "answer supervision." The call is connected and billing begins. The following comments are directed at network expense. There is a commensurate or alternative labor expense also.

The ultimate question of the vendor is this; do you offer dynamic call-by-call answer supervision delay? Unfortunately they will all answer yes! Typically because they do not understand the nuances of the answer.

The next question is this; at what point does your system return answer supervision? Again this is the signal to the telephone company to connect the call and begin billing. The answer is when the ACD answers the call.

The next question is this; can you delay answer if you have no agents (IVR ports, whatever) to serve the caller? Again they will answer yes. Here is where the answer becomes critical in two areas:

First, what governs the return of supervision, the trunk card settings or an interrogation of the routing tables and agent availability.

Here is what all the PBX based systems do. On a trunk card by trunk card basis they will allow a fixed ring delay to be set. That is X seconds. The trunk card or trunk group can be set to deliver a 10 or so second delay. **No matter what!** What these systems don't do is detect the inbound call and ask the central computer to check the agent database to determine if an appropriate agent is available before they return answer supervision. The reason they do not do this is the basic architecture of a PBX/ACD versus a true ACD.

When any computer based system is designed, the system designer is tasked with building the system as inexpensively as possible. This is a relative statement.

One of the easy ways to reduce cost in switching design is to provide less computing power and storage. (It is as though these folks have never visited a PC store to see how cheap computer horsepower, memory and disk storage have become!) One of the ways to reduce computer processor demand, is reduce the number of repetitive tasks the system processor needs to be involved. One such task in a phone system is answering a call. It the logical next step if a process is always the same, to relegate that task to a lower process than the central processor. In a PBX system, one such task is answering an inbound request for service. This means that any call to a trunk card is answered with no further question asked of the central processor. When a system originally designed as a PBX is pressed into service as an ACD, there are certain things it can never do without dramatic redesign. Coupling an inbound request for service, with the dynamic interrogation of a routing table by the main processor, when there was no physical and logical design linkage, is next to impossible.

The absence of this feature may mean thousands of dollars a year in higher INWATS expenses to your customer call center.

Subsets of this feature are;

"When is a inbound customer call recognized as a call?"

Supervision in or supervision out?" (System answer?) As we have just explained, the reason this is important is first, for the issue of dynamic answer and recognizing the presence of a call so that the routing database can be questioned. If the database cannot be interrogated as a linked question, the system will answer all calls blindly and add unnecessary call length and billing to your customer call operating expenses. The second issue is;

"A fox watching the henhouse"

A manufacturer may have you believe this is an insignificant a feature, but it costs American business millions of needless dollars a year to long distance carriers because their systems cannot search for an available agent before answer supervision is returned on a call by call basis. One major PBX/ACD makes light of the lack of this feature in their ACD systems as they make their money on the long distance services they sell to attach to the ACD!

"When is the call counted as data for reporting purposes?"

Supervision in or supervision out?" (System answer?) If a call is not measured before answer a   significant amount of trunk performance and potential network problem identification data such as "ghost calls" is lost to management.

Is the presence of a call measured before answer supervision is returned?

Again for the same reason as mentioned immediately above. In the case of an ACD that allows CO ringing to be factored in as part of the queue cycle (much to the chagrin of the long distance carriers,) it is important to determine how long a caller is in this state, so tolerance can be measured.

A ring cycle is six seconds in duration; two of ringing and four of silence. If no one (or nothing) is available to answer the call, two rings saves 12 seconds of billable WATS time per call and so on. It is important to understand the length in the ring pre-queue for true service level and queue management purposes. In the case of one call center the writer works with, a second added to the length of the average call, adds $1,000,000 a year in expense to the teleservices budget.

Move this off your "books," and back to the carrier, and although you still will require available trunk capacity, it is cheaper that billable trunk capacity, carrying expensive music.

This little shortcoming will cost a customer call center owner bunches.

Here's how to measure the impact on your customer call center:

- First, how many calls does your center queue a year?
- Of all the calls, how many exceed 6 seconds in queue, before being connected to an agent?
- How many exceed 12 seconds, 18 seconds etc.

A system that can retard answer supervision on a call by call can save you at least six seconds of billed INWATS time per queued call, or 12, 18 or more respectively.

One recent customer call center visited by the author received 75,000 calls a day of which 74% were queued per day to add WATS costs of $29,000 a month. This WATS vendor also sold this customer their PBX based ACD.

The ability to drive this command and management detail is first an issue of the manufacturer understanding the issues in a customer call center, providing the features by providing adequate computer power and software. When an ACD began life as a generalized switching device, this type of detail is next to impossible to deliver to the user.

Is dynamic barge out of the CO ring cycle available?

Now if the system provides a fixed delay, such as 10 seconds or so, what happens if an agent becomes available during that time? The desired answer is that the system will detect the available agent, answer the call and deliver the caller to the available agent. This is called "barge out." Because the delay

decision is limited to the realm of the trunk card or trunk group, no other issues, such as an agent becoming available in the target group, there is no barge out! Available agents, queued callers = logically blocking! Available agents twiddling

their thumbs while callers wait for service. Again these are the subtle limitations of a PBX based ACD system. As subtle as they may be these shortcomings conspire to cost a call center owner thousands of dollars in inefficient operating practices.

2. System Reliability And Failure Resistance

A true ACD system is also built with the knowledge the system will fail at some time in its service life. An outage may also be occur as a planned event. This knowledge of the system not being available is a critical design consideration. There are ways to minimize the impact of an outage. These range from totally redundant components to nothing at all.

Understanding the levels of progressive system degradation available from your chosen vendor, can equip you to minimize the impact of a failure. Then be intelligent in how you spend money to reduce the impact of a failure. You may not need the diesel generator on the roof. If the MIS department already owns one, hook it up to your battery recharge system. You are a mission critical application.

ACD systems can be taken down intentionally for a number of quite logical reasons. A hardware or software upgrade or physical move of the equipment. If the center operates 24 hours a day there is no ideal time for this to occur, so an ability to continue to serve the incoming callers is desirable. Understanding how system reliability and failure resistance is engineered into the system is important.

Power

A system can fail due to the unavailability of power. To minimize the impact of power failure, three strategies can be pursued. These may be used individually or concurrently.

1.   Conditioned power

An ACD can be driven with AC or DC power. AC or alternating current is normal commercial power, coming out of the nearest power socket, delivered by the power company, off the local grid. It is subject to all the vagaries of surges, spikes and drops in voltage, that disturb computers.   When the office lights flicker, its a power disturbance. If these are not considered of significant

consequence, wall power can be quite satisfactory. To mitigate transient power problems, a voltage regulator may be used. This is a device which is plugged into the socket power source. It contains voltage buffering or regulation electronics designed to catch and isolate momentary power transients. This isolates the

system from very short term power problems, but does not supply power in an outage.

2.   Uninterruptible power

The other extreme of power protection is a completely isolated system with its own or alternative power source. In this case the ACD is completely isolated from commercial power. The ACD is typically DC powered. The power is provided by a DC or direct current system. This DC system "floats" the ACD away from the commercial power. There is a battery which is constantly charged by the commercial power supply grid. The ACD is supplied by the battery source which has a life of an hour or more. ACD power is supplied by the battery. An inverter maintains the battery charge. When power fails, the batteries supply the system until they are used up, or the power returns. Statistically most power failures are less than 60 minutes in duration and within the planned battery capacity.

3.   Backup Generator

The building housing the customer call center may have an AC power generator, that "kicks in" in the instant of a power failure. The question becomes how fast will the power be available and will it be transparent to the ACD. If it takes a minute or two to come on line the ACD will die, unless the power system (typically a bank of DC batteries) is engineered to accommodate this. The MIS department cannot tolerate this either, so the building management should understand the problem.

If you have access to such back-up power, make sure your company includes your customer call center as a candidate for back-up power support. Having the order entry terminals running on the telephone reps desk and no phone calls is a little ludicrous. Get the ACD on the same system. Once again, selling your management on the mission critical nature of the application is necessary. If you have an external generator, make sure you have gas or diesel in the generator's fuel tank! Don't laugh, we know of a huge credit card company which got caught running on empty! These strategies only ensure power is available to the system. Now it is necessary to consider building a redundant system.

A Redundant ACD System

Here we make the assumption that the failure is caused by a failure within the actual system. A processor fails, a disk crashes, a controller or switching network hiccups. Any number of system glitches can cause the system to stop processing calls. The major element is the brain or control processor. In the area of common control technology, the system can have redundant computer systems. That is a second computer system that backs up the first in the event of it's failure. It is important to understand what redundancy really means in the case of your chosen vendor. Is it the entire system or just large parts of the system deemed to be critical? The control computer, the internal system power supplies, power distribution, switching technology and the individual line, station and utility components are all indispensable elements. Are these redundant? Typically this is not the case. A new generation of technology is promising to introduce more redundancy than simply duplexing the common control. Check which components your vendor means when they say "redundant!"

Common Control

Common control can have two types of redundancy:

a.   **Mirror image or "nonstop" computing** - as Tandem Computer calls uninterrupted operation. This first method uses mirror image processing. Two computers "mirror" each other until the point of final execution and one completes the last step or process after comparing the consistency of the separate results to this stage. The last step is completed by one of the processors and everything begins again. This type of redundancy in the control system should insure constant uninterrupted operation. To implement a system of this nature is more expensive in the short run. Cheap insurance in the long run, because the business you protect us short term revenue and long term goodwill.

b.   The second and more popular method is **"hot standby,"** where a   second processor kicks into operation when the first fails. A duplicate or B side system stands ready to kick into operation should the A side system "die." The problem with this technique is that calls in process can be "dropped" during the system swap over. Newer systems do not drop calls and look more like the mirror or nonstop application mentioned first. Again initially expensive but cheap business insurance.

This redundancy only effects the system intelligence. If other major parts fail, the system still dies.   Typically a vendor will identify the maximum number of elements that can be effected by any one outage. A system outage will effect no more than xx lines or agents...a shelf...a cabinet.   Consider this as a percentage of the customer call center and it can take on a whole new meaning.   If "only 48 ports (trunks, agents, etc.) are effected by any outage" and your customer call center only has 96 ports, you just lost 50% of your customer service capacity.   If they are just your trunks or just your agents, you may be dead in the water.

In the case of some systems, especially those using onboard voice processing subsystems, they require a   complete duplication of the voice processing subsystem on the B side to perform identically to the A side in an A side failure. As we mentioned earlier this may not be configured the same to lower costs in a competitive deal. It is absolutely critical that not only must the B side mirror the A side, but the database must be synchronized so that everything works identically.

Another issue is the **software redundancy.** This is important if the reliability "bug" resides in the software. Is the mirror software an exact replica of the first, bugs and all. Well designed redundancy typically runs a second and unique copy of the software that does not inherit the errors occurring in system A over a lifetime of use.

c.   A third strategy is **power fail transfer or onboard bypass.** This is really a **fallback strategy**, is to build onboard bypass into the system so that with any failure, (power or system), telephone calls on analog trunks, can still be received, as they continued to be supported by CO provided power.   The system must be equipped with sufficient power fail transfer trunks to allow the system to operate.

A typical PBX ratio of 5 to 10% of the trunks being equipped with power fail bypass trunks, is totally inadequate in a customer call center. Power fail transfer

(PFT) trunks are telephone lines from the central office are hardwired to a specific phone instrument during a switch outage.   The PFT feature must be present in the line card for it to work.   These individual phones become single line instruments much like a single residence line.   They are not switched by the PBX or ACD during the outage as it is dead, yet they remain directly connected to the phone company exchange and can receive and originate one call at a time.

PFT trunk cards are also more expensive than regular telephone line cards. They also take up more space in the switch.   As an example 8   regular lines may occupy a single slot but when PFT line cards are specified they only allow 4 or even 2 per slot. One vendor trick used to keep the proposal price of a PBX/ACD low in a competitive battle against a standalone ACD is to omit PFT trunks or keep them to a   minimum.   When bypass features are incorporated in a PBX/ACD quote, the price gets a lot closer to the more fully featured system.

FIG. 7-7

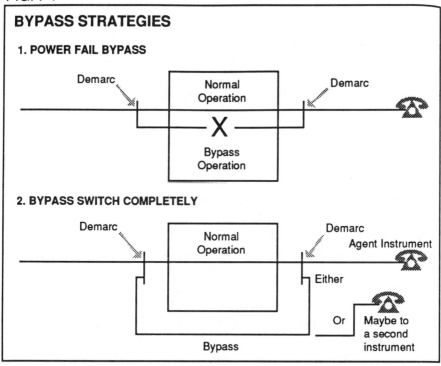

Key questions:
> **Do you provide power fail bypass?**
> **Response: Yes.**
> **How many trunk to agent power fail connections are included in this price proposal?**
> **Response: Some, 5, 10 all!**

What you need and the answer to this question can dramatically change the PBX/ACD system price and bring it closer to a standalone system. Upon system failure and fall-back to power fail transfer or bypass, two methods are used.

First, where the first trunk now is directly connected to the first agent position, and always is. The second method is to preassign each bypass trunk to a specific station. The latter technique is more flexible as you do not have to staff quite as rigidly. The only rule to be aware of is, that you cannot simultaneously process more calls on bypassed lines than there are manned positions.

As the system fails, before the power fail trunks start carrying the calls, all calls in process are interrupted. The actual switch to the bypass mode may be manual or automatic. Restoral of the switch to full automated operation may also occur in either method. The vendor should take great pains to explain how this occurs. Take time to understand how it works. There are some expensive and inelegant solutions.

New features and technology will increase the complexity and cost of redundancy. Since a number of the standalone ACD and now PBX based ACD systems think that basic announcements and music can be better delivered by a disk based system, they must also configure a duplicate disk based voice response system in cabinet B (the back up system.) This adds significant costs. In a competitive bid, if a buyer is not watching carefully, they will sell redundancy, and leave out this feature. This means in a switchover, the routing tables of system A are going to go and look for announcements, music and the like, that are not present in system B. This means that the process and subsequent databases are out of synchronization and the caller will encounter unintended processes. The vendor acts surprised, as if they didn't understand what you meant when you asked for redundancy. It also takes a significant time to resynchronize the database and restore operation. The solution is a $50,000 to $100,000 mirror voice response system in system B. And the user has little choice.

Be aware that any T.1 service coming into the system will not operate as the system needs power to maintain and decode any calls carried on a digital circuit. The reverse is also true of analog trunks on a digital switch. Calls arriving on analog trunks, attached to a digital switch, will not work in a system or power fail condition unless there are separate arrangements to wire these around the switch. A simple and inexpensive way around this is to wire the customer call center with separate analog telephones, and install manual bypass directly to the analog trunks. This technique and bypass block has the quaint name of "calamity switch". They work fine and constitute a simple and elegant solution.

3. High Visibility Into The System

The ACD system must provide a high degree of visibility into the system, its operation and the resources attached to or working with the ACD system.

There are "choke points" in a customer call center which can negatively affect call processing.

1) **Inadequate network capacity**
2) **too few trunks (or local loops) to carry the offered inbound call load,**
3) **Inadequate switching capacity,**
4) **Misunderstanding the demand to staffing ratio, so extended queue delays inflate caller abandonment,**
5) **Poor training and motivation of the agent staff,**

Added to these choke points are now;

6) **Inadequate VRU capacity, and**
7) **Poorly designed and ambiguous voice response scripts.**

A well-thought through ACD system will provide an extensive array of tools to allow a great deal of insight into the flow of your business, with both real-time and after-the-fact reports. Because of the intensity of the customer call center application, the staff with the responsibility of managing this center on a day to day basis are best qualified to judge what is necessary in the management reporting tools.

The customer call center business has a great preference for the capture of the lowest level of call detail at all times, that is every keystroke generated by an agent, and trunk, delay and process detail by call.

4. Ease Of Use

"If it is hard to use, it won't be!" The ACD system must be easy to use at every level. A customer call center is a demanding environment to begin with, without adding a whole new level of discipline on the agents, the supervision, the administration and management.

The effort involved in using the system must be almost transparent to the user. The agent instrument or workstation should reduce keystrokes and confusion so

the agent can focus on the caller and the business at hand.   Use of the ACD should not impair the reason for the primary caller transaction.

The staff, supervision and management should have accurate and unambiguous reports. Plain language is essential.   No jargon. Check the report column headings. Do you need a Ph.D. in abbreviations to understand them? Administration of the system should be simple and not require layers of specialized staff.

Large centers do need skilled people to manage these systems and the telephone network interfaces. Small to medium centers do not need dedicated staff, although two or more people trained in the use of the system, trained to deal with the system vendors and telephone network are essential. This however need not be their primary function. A complex ACD system increases management insight. It should not unduly increase management effort.

Today, your corporate telecommunications department is probably completely overworked trying to buy the most reliable and least expensive network, maintain the PBX systems, move the phones and do other administrative tasks. The last thing they need or want is a bunch of demanding managers in the customer call center constantly asking for changes, then changes to the changes. What they do not understand is that a customer call center is involved in sales or service as opposed to a relatively predictable task like accounting.   Both of these tasks demand taking advantage of change and opportunities.   If the ACD system administration is difficult and requires outside help from your telecommunications department, or worse still, the vendor, business opportunities are often ignored because of the degree of difficulty introduced by a hard to use system.   The command language and ease of user administration is a key differentiator for true ACD systems.

5. Interface With Other Customer Call Center Resources

Increasingly sophisticated systems and business methods have arrived in the customer call center. These are voice response, database and list management, interfaces, workflow management, work force planning, and autodialing systems attached using Computer Telephony Integration or Client/Server Computer Telephony connections.

Connection with host and customer database applications for delivering screen "pop" information concurrently with the call, is becoming increasingly popular.

Computer telephony integration is a technology whose time has arrived. The use of these techniques speeds up the call process, has the potential to repersonalise a homogeneous transaction, reduce the workload and allow the customer call center to do more with fewer resources.

If the ACD system does not easily interface with these typically external systems and processes, considerable inefficiencies can arise. Complexities increase and response times suffer to the point the business goal of the call is impeded.

These complexities have severely hampered the deployment of third party computer to telephone links due to the complexity, time and cost of making these connections and applications run as advertised.

One very expensive lesson that few ACD vendors have yet to learn is this; the switch has to become subservient to the customer application and database. The switch must become yet another input/output device. This is particularly true when an ACD is used in conjunction with outbound applications.

Today there is still a battle for ideological supremacy between the switch and the computer vendors. The ideal solution is to let both win, give them the crumbs of victory and install a client/server based first party solution using a desk top PC based workstation. Most of the time, cost and complexity of early CTI implementations are reduced, while the success of these customer pleasing and labor reducing hybrid solutions enure to the benefit of the customer call center. More in Chapter Fourteen.

CHAPTER EIGHT

Automatic Call Distributor Basics

System Categories

From the beginning of this text there have been references to system sizes and varying levels of system sophistication. There is no easy way to categorize systems and the way that they fit specific applications and sizes without offending the vendors and those users who have chosen to apply them to call centers beyond their typical capacity and sophistication.

Annually, the system vendors report to various market research bodies that their average system sale is of a given size. Using this data and the system size categories discussed earlier, it is possible to assign certain general market domains for each vendor and product model. Unfortunately, this approach ignores exceptions to these rules and dignifies generalizations. The underlying assumption is that the market finds the correct application level for a given product. Fortunately this remains a relatively consistent measure of a products suitability to a given market.

Sizes Revisited

In the under 20 agent position size there are a number of key telephone systems (KTS) or hybrid key/PBX system providing rudimentary ACD functionality. The majority of PBX based ACD systems also provide ACD features of varying

sophistication. A new generation of PC based small ACD systems, promises the features of their larger low-end standalone systems.

Standalone ACD systems also are found in this segment, though these vendors primarily pursue markets above this size. The reason that a customer call center manager in this market, would consider a more powerful system (such as a standalone ACD system) is primarily because of planned growth. In other cases, users have experienced the advantages of using powerful ACD systems in their domestic operations, and have exported this advantage to smaller domestic applications or overseas operations.

One Fortune 100 company regularly installs $150,000 ACD systems in customer call centers with as few as fifteen inbound/outbound telephone marketing representatives. They found the improved productivity, the increased sales and lower cost of sales for a center equipped with a true standalone far outweighed the capital cost of the system. When the domestic systems were made redundant for any reason, they were moved to their overseas markets with the same sales growth and cost containment effect. It is no surprise that this company is the leader in their market and has now pioneered the deployment of desktop productivity tools and customer call center workflow management.

20 To 50 Positions

At 20 to 50 position the annual cost of ownership of an ACD system of any type is less than 10% of your total operating expense but can allow significant control of you line and staff costs.

PBX based ACD systems are most frequently encountered in this segment and again the most popular PBX systems provide ACD features of varying sophistication. Central office based ACD systems are beginning to make headway in this market segment also.

Due to the financial dynamics of customer call centers above 30 positions, standalone ACD systems start showing up frequently in this segment. The reasons for this are;

1. the recognition a customer call center of 30 agents is costing owner a million and a half dollars or more a year and there is a serious need to manage this. Today the feature and reporting state of most ACD systems

with their origins in a PBX architecture materially compromise the ability to manage this center precisely.

2. A customer call center of 30 or more agents take a disproportionate amount of switching and system resources. From the switch capacity point of view these thirty agents are the functional equivalent of between 150 and 300 administrative (regular telephone) users. Therefore a standalone

ACD outside the company PBX keeps a potentially disruptive application off the main company switch and maintains the status quo.

When you combine an ACD and a PBX together you bet neither system will grow unchecked. We have already discussed the growth dynamics of a customer call center reflect business success, new campaigns and new market offerings which require phone support. When the business is successful often the customer call center sees growth first, immediately followed by an increase in administrative staff to support the new business. As both the ACD and the administrative PBX requirements begin to grow they "step-on" each other.

The disadvantage which is cited by PBX proponents is system disintegration. Advantages cited for including the ACD on the PBX are ease of dialing (from a common station numbering plan) and ease of transfer between the ACD and the administrative portions of the company. The standalone ACD proponents counter with the arguments that a good standalone ACD installation reflects as close as possible the PBX dialing plan and transfer protocols.

Neither are totally correct. There is little comfort in seamless integration between the PBX and ACD functions as other disadvantages occur. Typically each agent position is now served by a minimum of two PBX hardware ports. One for the ACD group number (this is how the ACD portion of the PBX allocates calls) and one for the agent station number (so the supervisor and others can call the agent directly). A standalone ACD does not typically do this as an agent can be dialed by station (software defined) or by agent identification number. Calls from a PBX station to an agent on a standalone ACD can also use the ACD dialing logic. Because of the functionally separate hardware ports, management reporting of agent ACD and administrative activity on a PBX based ACD is also disintegrated. The ACD data is reported in the ACD MIS system. The administrative activity such as outbound calling or intra switch calls are reported on the administrative (SMDR) reports. These fragmented reports defeat objectivity in reporting employee performance.

These are the main disadvantages of trying to "stuff" both applications into one machine. The car/truck analogy. Though the combined vehicle can do both tasks, it is not great at either. The potential compromise in a PBX based ACD may be your business.

Why not distribute the ACD function to an application specific switching system external to the PBX. We already have the example of distributed applications in the computing business.

Generally everybody gets more business done more quickly and at a lower price. The technical staff gets upset because the user population has not adhered to corporate standards. We chose an effective departmental system (witness the minicomputer boom of the 70's and early 80's) and the continuing PC boom.

50 To 150 Positions

At this size center, the price of ownership of an ACD system amounts to less than 4% of the operating cost the customer call center.

Features become more and more important, particularly when they address operating expenses. The less sophisticated systems have less of market share due to the increased appreciation by this market of the issues and the solutions offered by the standalone ACD system vendors. Vendors in this market segment are duplicated again, although the less sophisticated offerings depend solely on price to compete.

150 Positions To 500 Positions

At this size the ranks of the PBX vendors thin, despite what their specification sheets claim. There are three standalone vendors effectively competing for this business. A number of PBX based ACD systems and CO-ACD systems compete but the feature shortfall and engineering compromises make these less attractive. Central office based ACD systems have immense capacity but are short on control and MIS features. In the last edition of this book, published in 1990, this was forecast to change. Well, the more things change, the more they stay the same!

One really interesting wrinkle that has occurred is the advent of VRU based announcements. This has real merit when complex routing is required prompting and expecting customer touch tone feedback.

Above 500 Positions

The logistical issues and options for an owner of a customer call center in excess of 500 positions have little to do with ACD system selection. For those who consider this an attractive customer call center size, the choices remain limited. Only a few true ACD vendors provide nonblocking switching systems over the 1000 agent position range. Other vendors can only begin to portray this capacity by linking switching modules together. As they do this the database management, physical and logical blockage all conspire to complicate an already complex project. There are other reasons -- facilities, potential staffing shortages, disaster recovery, etc., that seriously challenge the wisdom of such huge incoming customer call centers.

Features And Definitions
System Features

An ACD system has key features setting it apart from other call switching applications;

1) **The physical and traffic capacities of the switch,**
2) **The trunks and agents capacities and tradeoffs, and**
3) **The call processing capabilities.**

1)   CAPACITY; PHYSICAL SIZE - This is measured by the number of devices that can be attached to the switch.   Typically an ACD system size is expressed on a trunks to agents ratio, for example, 256 trunks x 200 agents.

Although many vendors talk about the "trunk side" and the "agent side," ideally a switch should have universal porting. That is every slot in the system can carry any device, whether it be a trunk, agent or utility component.

Analog trunks generally take up more "real estate" than digital trunks. Talk with the vendor and determine what the compromise is and this may push you to T1 spans earlier in your planning. This is now increasingly cost effective to do this as even the local telephone company is pushing digital service to extend their plant capacity by promoting lower tariffs.

The physical capacity may be limited by the internal network of the switch. This is the number of talk paths or simultaneous conversations that can be connected

by the switch. This may brought about by the internal communication path capacity of the switch and then there is the capacity of the common control.

Traffic Capacity

This can be illustrated by comparing the switch and common control to an intersection with a number of converging streets, managed by a single police traffic control officer. There may be sufficient lanes to carry the traffic (physical size), yet not enough time or space for all the traffic fed from the lanes, to cross the intersection safely (communications pathways), all under the control of a single traffic control officer (insufficient common control capacity).

In an analog switching system the physical switch capacity is limited to the number of talk paths. A talk path includes two ports, one for each participant in the conversation (the caller and the agent, music or voice processing port) and the actual communication link through the switch. The maximum number of calls which can be connected simultaneously is the same as the talk path total.

In a digital switching system similar resources are consumed. Two ports and a path through the switch linking these ports. As this path is an electronic buss, typically using time division multiplex switching technique, the conversation capacity is measured in timeslots. One for each conversation/transaction participant. A call, at minimum, needs two simultaneous timeslots.

The maximum number of conversations which can be connected simultaneously is exactly half the number of timeslots the system supports.

CCSs or Erlangs is another measurement used in measuring the traffic capacity of a switch. A CCS is one hundred called seconds. There are 36 CCSs per hour. An erlang is an engineering term for an "hour of traffic." A manufacturer will rate the each switch port at 30 CCS per hour. This means although the talk path capacity may exist, the switching computer is incapable of matching the capacity with processing power, if all the ports were attempting to make and receive calls simultaneously. This type of rationing is common in PBX engineering but causes real trouble when a busy ACD function is added to the same switch.

The traditional measurement of the common control or the computer controlling the switch has been "busy hour call attempts" (BHCAs). This means the theoretical capacity of the switching computer was is rated by the number of call attempts it could recognize and attempt to process.

A more reliable measurement is the number of "busy hour call completions" (BHCCs.) Here the measurement is the number of calls the switch control can recognize, process under the call processing rules, connect to the correct resource(s,) maintain the connection for the duration of the call, end it and break-down the connection returning all the resources to idle status, track and report the call progress and write a final transaction record to disk. Again this is theoretical, however there is a significant difference between attempts and completions.

The real measurement is the "sustained call processing rate." this is the number of calls the system continue to process over a sustained period of time such as a shift or a day, without degradation in the call processing switching or report preparation and presentation (display or print). One major PBX vendor strategy is to momentarily suspend report gathering, supervisor screen up dates and printouts during high traffic periods.

Growing out of one's incoming phone system remains the single biggest problem facing today's incoming customer call center manager. It is difficult -- if not impossible -to explain to top management the likely growth of an inbound center.
   The consequences of buying too small are too high in terms of annoyed and disenfranchised customers -- especially if they have become used to a good level of service from previously god customer service.

There are three steps to avoid being trapped into an inadequate system;

> **1.   Have as clear an understanding of your plans and size potential as humanly possible. As difficult as this may seem, take the time and assume growth and success will occur. (It will!).**

> **2.   Scrutinize the official manufacturer documentation carefully, watching for small manufacturers warnings to distributors and users to avoid this configuration and that application. Insist on getting everything you can lay your hands on. And in writing. Availability, amount and quality of this material will tell you a lot about the manufacturer and vendor. If they aren't helpful during the sales process, what about after they have you money?**

> **3.   Have the vendor/manufacturer sign up to spend time understanding the underlying growth trends driving**

your business. **Ensure the vendor stands by the recommended configuration from both a traffic capacity and a "no surprises" agreement.** **There will be no additional cost, effort or abnormal inconvenience placed upon the user working around some undisclosed system limitation.**

Remember, a vendor is more likely to grant price, support or contractual concessions upon the initial order, than on subsequent upgrades. This is less likely true after all payments have passed to the vendor.

4. **If the vendor offers price concessions to win your initial business, attempt to have these apply over a reasonable period from the date of installation.** **Reasonable means as long as possible, though not so it is punitive to the vendor.**

2) Growth Strategies

A vendor uses two strategies to grow a system; First, fill the system cabinets to their maximum designed capacity.

Second, when growth occurs beyond the single initial system, tie two or more together as transparently as possible. This is done with intermachine links or tie lines and can be accomplished relatively effectively. The key to the effectiveness of this strategy is the transparency of the implementation. Does it add to the effort of managing the resulting system, and does it work as one system.

The answer to this can only come from a user who has really implemented this solution. The "no problems" response from the vendor, although well meaning and self serving, does not mean that much to the new user who has more systems than he bargained for. Make sure the explanations provided prior to contract are adequate, in writing and understood. Additional protection from over representation by a vendors, is to make all correspondence and proposal material part of the contract. Tell the vendor this in the any proposal solicitation.

The switching modules may interconnect quite elegantly and the call control software may balance the load equitably, but what are the database management and administrative issues, if any? If you update call processing on one module, does it apply to all. How is this database synchronization accomplished? Is the all report data consolidated on one report system.

Alternatively, the implementation may be a crude intermachine tie lines with no intelligence associated with the routing of an interflowed call. While the system produces elegantly integrated report formats and data.

The concern is that two machines with adequate cumulative port count may be placed in service in the same application, and act independently of one another, merely passing calls off system A to system B, with no heed for equitably balancing the call load between machines, agent groups or agents. The large standalone ACD vendors understand the implications of this and have built big, single stage switching machines or implemented the interswitch load balancing, to all but do away with any objections to this strategy. Take the time to understand the process and the tradeoffs that accompany such an engineering solution. The problems that can arise in poorly implemented solutions manifest themselves in one or all of the following ways;

> **i.   Inability to manage as one system, thus additional effort at the supervisor level, i.e. managing two systems**
> **ii.   Increased staff to accommodate for the inability to look back from switch A to switch B when an agent becomes available at the entry point/switch, and**
> **iii.   The managing and synchronization of two or more system databases.**

A clever solution to this inequitable call distribution over one or more systems is to provide a second stage switch that acts as a systemwide traffic hub. This works to broadcast a request for service across the second and subsequent switch modules, without the entry switch system or module (the system at which the call enters the system), relinquishing call control. This allows for more equitable call distribution to occur.

Physical allocation of the traffic loads and the call processing task, associated with trunk and agent splits, must be observed. This is generally satisfied by paying attention to the communities of interest in the call center. The only issue that remains is the consolidation of the databases and the realtime and printed reporting processes. Vendors pursue varying strategies to do satisfy this.

FIG. 8-1

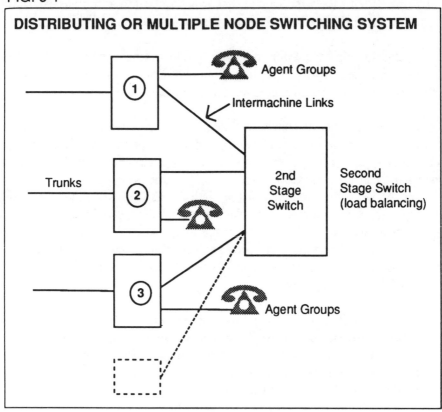

DISTRIBUTING OR MULTIPLE NODE SWITCHING SYSTEM

3)   Call Processing

i)   Trunks

All trunks arrive at the switch in one of two forms; analog and/or digital.   In the old days, most trunks were analog and arrived on your doorstep on one pair of wires.   Trunks are increasingly digital as digital technology has dropped in price and brings increased capacity on existing facilities.

Despite this most local trunks or local loops that are commonly available to a customer call center are delivered in analog format.   A digital switching system must provide "reverse" channel bank technology, albeit single circuit and a great deal more integrated, and efficient than traditional channel banks.   This technology is necessary to digitize the analog circuit for transmission through the digital system.

Today in North America, a T-1 span represents 24 multiplexed voice channels arriving on two pairs of copper wires.   Now due to telco plant preservation strategies and lower tariffs, these are now as commonplace as analog circuits.   In Europe, the standard is 32 channels. A circuit is either one pair or one analog channel or two pair and potentially 24 or more channels.

When an analog phone pair arrives at your doorstep, you can attach a $20 black phone directly to it (in telephony nomenclature, a 2500 set,) dial numbers and speak and be heard. Nothing could be simpler.   When a T-1 link arrives on your doorstep, life is more complex. The only thing that can be attached is a digital switch with line cards that can "untangle and decode" digital messages into 24 separate conversations.   Until recently this was called a "channel bank." A "channel bank" is an electronic device that the splits up the T-1 stream of 1.54 million bits per second into 24 discrete analog circuits that can be terminated on a standard analog telephone switch -- PBX or ACD.   More recently most PBX or ACD systems allow for direct termination of T-1 trunk as they have this technology directly built on to the trunk cards.

FIG. 8-2

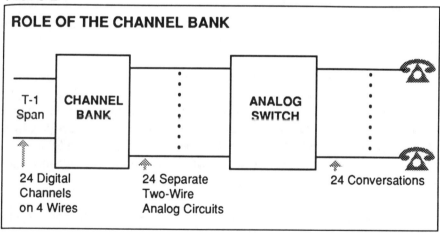

- 161-

Analog And Digital Trunk Terminations

One of the big advantages of digital technologies is the downsizing in componentry, space (switch real estate) and power consumption. Because of this the circuit cards required to terminate digital and analog circuits are typically of different technical and physical properties. The size issue is most significant at this stage. Digital circuits can be supported on considerably denser cards, typically 4, 8 or 16 discrete devices per card, whereas an analog card may only support 4 or as few as one discrete analog circuit. This means the system is physically larger and the shelf that may support 64 digital circuits, can support a lesser number of analog circuits. Watch for the analog to digital tradeoff issue and the physical capacity impact on your intended system configuration.

ii) ACD Trunk Termination

Trunks are physically attached or terminated on an ACD either singly or in trunk groups. In the case of a T1 circuit, 24 or more based on the span capacity are terminated on a card that "demuxes" the 24 channels and into discrete circuits which are in turn considered individual trunks or ports. This port is considered a physical address. It is important to understand this as this is one of the ways an ACD figures out how to handle an incoming call. These methods are described as either physical or logical.

     a. **Physical.** Where the trunk is attached, either as part of a trunk group. This physical trunk is assigned to a split or gate in the database. This split or gate indicates the type of call or caller, and therefore the type of treatment the caller will receive. When a call shows up on this port, the switch points to the database, decides which route applies and routes the call following a predetermined software table. The call will be routed to the intended agent (answering) group based on the rules applying at the time of arrival.

     b. **Logical.** Alternatively, despite the physical trunk group, split or gate the call may arrive on, the call will be preceded by 4 or more significant digits sent by the network (DID, ANI or DNIS). The switch expects to route the call by looking at the database table that applies to this physical port. This is the default route. That is unless digits are received. Once these digits are recognized, the physical routing is ignored, and the logical table addressed.

These are interpreted by the ACD system and the call is routed to the intended agent, or group of agents based on the caller or nature of the call based on the digits received. These digits may be "direct inward dialed," "automatic number identification" or "dialed number identification service" digits. This is logical call by call identification. Physical trunk groups generally refer to the telephone trunk type, whereas a gate or a split refers to the call or business type that arrives at that gate or split.

iii) Incoming Calls

A caller, by virtue of dialing a particular number, (published as the number to call for satisfying this particular request) presorts this particular call type into the intended ACD gate. As a call arrives on a given trunk, in a predetermined split, a number of things happen. The inbound call supervision request from the carrier central office is detected on the trunk and the system reacts.

An important and crucial difference in how calls are handled begins at this point. The true standalone ACD and the PBX/ACD begin to separate into application specific and generic groupings. The resulting differences, although in many cases potentially written off as mere subtleties, make major differences in the manner in which the customer call center is managed and at what cost.

An ACD system can react in one of two ways: Answer the call, or upon detection of "supervision in," look to a call processing control table for step by step instructions. PBX design and architecture dictates the system answers the call now, (unless there is a preprogrammed delay,) whether there is an available agent or not. A true standalone ACD asks the routing control instructions what to do before anything else happens, then proceeds through a list of steps and conditions that apply to this call.

When Is A Call A Call?

A telephone call is considered to be completed when the caller is connected through to the intended party or caller. Under standard telephony signaling this is accomplished when the last central office sends ringing voltage (analog circuit) or a "supervision in" (digital circuit) message to the intended party telephone or system. The called party or system responds by answering the call, and sending reverse voltage ("reverse" or "answer supervision") back to the CO and then back up the circuit to the calling party CO, to establish the connection and begin the billing cycle. In a digital world all these voltage changes and supervisory signaling is achieved with digital "start," "stop," "set-up" and timing messages. In an ISDN world these travel on the out-of-band "D" channel, or in an in-band as unique digital messages signaling the switches to begin, set-up or end a call.

Completed calls are not the only events occurring on an analog telephone line. There are often spurious voltages that look like "supervision in" requests. An ACD will react by answering and treating these events as calls, if they are of sufficient strength and duration. A true ACD system will begin measuring these "calls" from the time they appear on the line, before or after answer. These events show up as lost calls if the ACD is sensitive to reporting these events. There is a clear reason to measure all events and their duration so circuit transients, such as these do not distort reporting or displace valid calls.

Traditionally most inbound call telephone systems IMMEDIATELY answer the call upon receiving the request for service. Next, the system looks at the call treatment table that indicates the call should be served by a particular station number or group designated by this station or directory number. The call is routed to that directory number (extension number.) In the case of a PBX this may be the operator station or pilot number in a hunt group. If this station or group is configured as part of a PBX based ACD group and the number or phone stations represented by this directory number is busy, the caller should then be routed to an announcement, a subsequent group, and so on. Answering a call and sending it to busy phone(s) intended to serve the call is not smart.

This indicates the designer tended not to understand the nature of the ACD application particularly well, because automatically answering a call when the agents intended to serve the caller are busy, is not optimal. When this happens, the owner of the ACD typically gets to play callers expensive "elevator music."

Answer Delay

A smart ACD might let the call ring (no answer) for up to 24 seconds or even longer. While this happens the carrier is not billing the inbound WATS user. Also callers do not perceive ringing to be a traditional delay or "queue," provided this is not extended unreasonably. Three to four rings "buys" 24 seconds when there is no one to serve the caller. Ideally this happens dynamically on a call-by-call basis. This more desirable process is used by most standalone ACD systems and integrates the answer process as an optional step into the call processing rules. By doing this the ringing cycle can become part of the queuing process. This feature is known as "ring delay".   This is a misnomer. It really means "answer delay."

By adding a fixed or a flexible number of ring cycles to the answering process actual answer or "supervision out" can be delayed. Supervision out is the phone system "return handshake" to the CO saying it is ready to accept the call. A standard ring cycle in North America is two seconds of ringing, four seconds of silence, for a total of six seconds.   When a call comes into (a central office or switch) the caller may not enter the ring cycle at the beginning.   The reason for this is that it is a continuous cycle being generated and switched to incoming calls as needed.

There are key human factors issues, associated with intelligent use of the ring cycle, that work for the customer call center manager. First, a caller, calling a business will typically accept ringing from 2 to 7 times or 12 to 42 seconds. An intelligent ACD system can use this time to the customer call center advantage by actively including this as part of the delay. Good reporting of delay and abandoned call statistics will allow a customer call center manager to really determine the actual "threshold of pain" callers are willing to accept. The logic being that it's cheaper to let the phone ring than to answer it and put the caller on hold on your expensive 800 line.

Second, there is a apparent temptation to reduce call length by immediately cutting-through an inbound call when there is an agent immediately available.

This would bypass the ring cycle completely, and eliminate part of the six seconds associated with a normal ring cycle.

Experience indicates this does not save the time per call as would appear at first glance. Our phone use conditioning causes us to expect some amount of ringing when making a telephone call. By eliminating all ringing, the inbound caller becomes disoriented and uses up more than the six seconds to figure out what happened by discussing this with the receiving party. Any saving is thus offset.

A standard trunk delay means there could be agents available but the caller must go through the fixed system, trunk group or trunk delay cycle. Both the caller and the agents are "twiddling their thumbs" while the system blindly follows the inflexible delay rules. More staff and more trunk time is needed to accommodate this.

4) Call Routing Tables

Although the process of handling inbound call routing appear similar, they are filled with nuances and subtleties that are critical to a customer call center. This process is the core of customer call center management and is a process that must be understood clearly before selection of an ACD is made. Operational costs are directly and dramatically impacted by how these tables operate.

Manufacturers call this process by different names. For example; Call Control Table (CCT), ACD call routing, Call Vectoring or routing table. A call processing table is a set of preprogrammed steps that reside in system memory.

These may a standard set of steps, preprogrammed into the machine prior to installation. Or, more often today, these are tables that may be changed, by the user, to address the particular call processing demands as they occur. The simpler these changes are, the more flexible and therefore more functional the ACD becomes. If these changes are only possible with effort or factory support, the less likely and the more expensive adapting the ACD to meet the customer call center needs becomes.

Simple rule: flexibility means you can control your destiny more, though with this control comes a greater need to understand your objectives and the ACD tools available to help you meet these objectives.

The Anatomy Of An Incoming Call

An incoming call, arriving on an ACD, can be segmented into four elements;

- ☐ Call setup and ringing,
- ☐ any call queuing necessary,
- ☐ Talk time, (agent or VRU,) and
- ☐ Disconnect.

FIG. 8-3

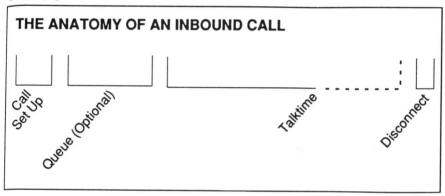

Early UCD and ACD designers assumed the only portion of call length actively manageable by a user occurred once the call was answered, namely the queue and the talk time of the individual agent. This was challenged by the modern ACD systems designers. Understanding a basic rule of telephony, shorter calls cost less, they set about extending greater control of the call, and call length, to the user.

If a switch knows when a call arrives, and if it has no agents available to serve the call, then why can it not delay returning the supervision signal to the central office? Don't answer the call unless there is an agent available to serve the caller

FIG. 8-4

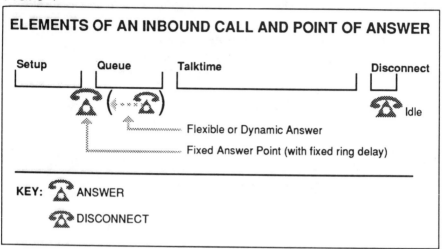

ELEMENTS OF AN INBOUND CALL AND POINT OF ANSWER

Setup   Queue   Talktime   Disconnect

Idle

Flexible or Dynamic Answer

Fixed Answer Point (with fixed ring delay)

KEY: ANSWER

DISCONNECT

A true ACD switch can "watch" a ringing line and agent availability simultaneously. If an agent comes available and there is a ringing line or a queued caller, answer and immediately send the caller to an agent. If an agent is not available, intelligently use the ring cycle as a delay until this is no longer courteous, answer and play a greeting and delay message. Should an agent become available at any time in this process provide a "barge out" step should be activated so the delay can be interrupted and the caller served.

These steps have been implemented by the major standalone ACD manufacturers. After 15 years of competing with them the major PBX based ACD vendors still build pale replicas that cost a call center owner additional operational costs. The biggest area remains "command granularity." Earlier mention was made of the how deep a command definition could be forced and the effect of doing this. Ideally it should be down to the smallest common denominator in a system; a call. Data gathering should be granular down to the agent keystroke, trunk number and clocked second for every call and call state change, internal or external (in and out,) complete or incomplete. This is particularly critical now a new generation of call tracking applications are beginning to emerge.

Called Party Disconnect

In Chapter 4 and Figure 4.5, we discussed the nature of call setup and break-down control residing with the caller. This does not change with an 800 call, even though the responsibility for paying for the call shifts to the call center owner.

Control still resides with the caller. If the caller is slow to hang up after completing the call, or is served by an older slower CO, there may be an appreciable time before the CO (local to the customer call center) senses the circuit has been returned to idle and breaks down the local loop, making it available for the next incoming caller. Two things occur, the call length may be extended by a few seconds. Second, the trunk is effectively busy so a second inbound call will be unable to access this trunk. The overall load is increased and more trunks are required to carry the same load to compensate for this few seconds of disconnect overhead.

Modern ACD systems recognize the instant an agent releases or hangs-up on a call, relays this to the local CO and requests immediate disconnect. This frees the circuit for the next call. Meanwhile the agent has gone on to serve another caller arriving and possibly queued on another trunk. The breakdown signal can now arrive from the calling party end of the call, immediately, late or never at all, and this has minimal effect on trunk occupancy and required trunk capacity. The impact of any delay is eliminated by this feature. How does you proposed vendor handle this? Most PBX based ACD systems are passive and wait for distant end disconnect on an inbound call or a trunk "time out," whichever comes first.

NOTE: One aspect of the ACD call from a staffing and event duration, may include a state known as wrap up or after call work. If this is required on a call by call basis, this adds time per call and effect the number of calls an agent can handle and thus the overall capacity of the system.

Measuring The Duration Of A Call

Before leaving the call answering process, there is one other issue of importance from a data gathering point of view. When does a call begin to be measured?

a. **when it is answered by an agent,**
b. **when the ACD system answers, or**

c. **when the request for service occurs as "supervision in" is raised by the CO?**

From a reporting point of view, this is important for three reasons:

i) **Measuring actual trunk occupancy,**
ii) **Measuring the actual point of abandonment by a caller, and**
iii) **Discriminating between real calls and spurious events or "phantom" calls that could be mistaken for real calls, thus distorting reports.**

Optimally, the ACD system should recognize and measure a call from the instant "supervision in" occurs, record the time of system answer, time duration in queue before system answer and after, follow the route steps taken by this call and record time of any IVR participation, any requeue and time of agent answer.

5) Position Organization

On the user side of the ACD system there are agents organized in teams, groups and splits. The reason for the segmentation can be for any number of user reasons;

a) **Span of control** -- a supervisor or lead agent is assigned a team of agents or TSRs, up to the maximum the supervisor or lead can effectively manage. Typically the more complex the transaction or business type, the higher the lead/supervisor to agent ratio. The more complex the business, the fewer agents a supervisor can manage.

b) **Competitive Teaming** -- often the customer call center is broken up into groups matching a responsibility. The individual groups are then pitted against each other to encourage better performance.

One of the most innovative uses of this strategy, maximizing network and ACD technology has been using DNIS and more recently ANI to obtain regional origin of inbound calls made to one published 800 number. The calls are then routed to the responsible group who competes with their peers to satisfy the caller with prompt service, and request satisfaction.

c) **Application separation** -- where a call is routed to a group of agents trained to serve the callers request. This is sometimes called "skill based routing." The system adds a database that categorizes agents in two ways; the physical group they are assigned to and a logical or skill based category. This means the agents are determined or trained to serve a particular type of caller or caller problem. An example would be English and Spanish speaking agents, assigned to serve 90% of the English speaking callers and that 10% wish preferred to speak Spanish. A skill based routing system will override the physical group organization (that is the majority of English speaking target agents) and search for an agent with a specific skill, (that is an agent who is bilingual.) This confuses a call center organization to a degree as it applies a responsibility matrix versus a hierarchical structure to serving callers. By becoming too sophisticated in assigning skill based logic, or primary and secondary responsibility assignment, a call center begins to dilute economy of scale. The customer service, market and business issues in your customer call center may make this a trivial consideration, but then again may add unnecessary cost.

All vendors and users interchange the terms team, split, subgroup and group to suit their needs. Be aware of the number of hierarchical levels or cross group responsibility in your organization and whether the ACD you choose will allow you to reflect and report on this structure. The more hierarchical levels the ACD vendor provides the better, as this allows greater flexibility and a higher probability of reflecting the way you do business and wish to manage your customer call center. Three is acceptable, more is better.

Make very sure that the ACD system you choose, tracks all calls as they are queued AND overflowed (interflowed) to each progressive group step in your customer call center. This allows you to understand work load by group and any artificial increase in Group 2, based on understaffing or other deficiency in Group 1 and so on. Once the call is in the system, load management and understand the destination and service dynamics are no less important to providing responsive service while still maintaining costs. This becomes even more important if an interactive voice response device is part of the call answering process.

Primary, Secondary And Tertiary Gate Assignment

How your customer call center is structured is critical to your ACD system selection. For example if you have small groups of specialized agents attending to specific tasks as their primary responsibility, that do not have adequate workloads, you may wish to assign them to secondary groups.

6)   Special Call Processing Treatments

Along with user programmable routing tables found in modern ACD systems, there are other control tables that allow greater flexibility and freedom from the drudgery of reprogramming as time of day, day of week and day of year changes occur. One vendor offers a system which allows up to 256 different command sequences to be built. Some are preprogrammed system housekeeping sequences such as report generation and database indexing and backup. Others are user start-up, reconfiguration or shutdown procedures. These are written and may triggered by a time clock in the system. For example, at midnight, the system will close the daily accounting files, clear all the daily statistics files, accumulate totals, allow reports to be generated and files sent to other applications servers, etc. All automatically. Other system functions can be executed in batch files. At other times of the day the user may setup a set of procedures to be executed, files to down or uploaded on schedule.

These sequences are rather like AUTOEXEC.BAT start-up procedure files found in an MS-DOS based PC. In this case these sequences are triggered on a time schedule. These time schedules are setup to follow a daily pattern. However, these clock-driven sequences may differ on different days of the week, and again, differently on statutory holidays that fall out of sequence throughout the year. To accommodate this your ACD system should ideally have a day-of-week and day-of-year table to allow exception schedules to be followed. This means a system can be left knowing it won't print reports devoid of data over a weekend, or won't turn off the "night closed" announcement and open the unmanned customer call center over Thanksgiving. This increases flexibility and leaves management to focus on running the business, not a machine.

People vs. Technology

Be careful. Care needs to be used to effectively implement these devices. Every channel between the switch and the voice response device equals another occupied port. So the device can be a drain on the ACD capacity.

Be aware with interactive voice response and automated attendants, technology is not the issue.   Caller acceptance is the issue. Great attention must be paid to the design of the human interface.   Callers can still be "turned off" by being greeted by a recording. Acceptance can be accelerated by the application and the script. Where recordings are used and what is said. There are many tricks to ensure your use of voice technologies is successful with your callers and fulfills the promise of service improvement and cost savings.

WARNING

ASCAP (American Society of Composers and Publishers) have been attempting to levy royalty fees against users of music on hold, as this is considered the unauthorized rebroadcast of copyrighted material. This has encouraged the use of promotional material and the "all News" alternatives. ASCAP even alleges this is not a way out as even commercials contain copyrighted musical material. There is no clear solution to this royalty issue. ASCAP is calling small businesses and trying to intimidate them into paying. Sadly many succumb without questioning this. There is no absolute answer to this but ASCAP can be caused to back down by disconnecting the allegedly copyrighted programs.

Solutions

Make the recording short, the choices simple with a brisk script with a thrust toward solving the caller's problem. Choose your audience carefully, educate them extensively. Take as much time with coworkers (internal customers) as external customers. Do not surprise your audience otherwise confusion can turn to anger and a feeling of no longer being important to your business.

Chapter Nine

The Automatic Call Distributor

How They Work

The whole notion of an automatic call distributor is to ration as few as possible agent and other resources, such as interactive voice response ports, across as large a caller demand as possible.

This must be achieved as expediently as possible, balancing good customer service, good employee working conditions, against the lowest expense to revenue ratio as possible. An ACD goes a long way to achieve this. Use of a good forecasting and planning package can ensure this.

An ACD achieves this by imposing some delay in the service received by the inbound callers. This delay or queue is perceived to be tolerable and customary in the call center marketplace. To achieve this, maintain a happy customer base and make a profit, is nothing short of an endless real-time juggling act. The core tool in this act is an ACD. The core features of an ACD is the ability to expediently and intelligently assign service resources automatically and as transparently as possible.

The one feature that accomplishes this is the automatic customer call routing methodology. Coincidentally, this is the one feature that is given little analysis and attention by most ACD designers, vendors and buyers alike, is the routing and queuing structure.

Call Routing Tables

Although the processes appear similar, are filled with nuances and subtleties critical to a customer call center. This process is the core of customer call center management and is a process that must be understood clearly before selection of an ACD is made. Operating costs are directly and dramatically impacted by how these routing tables operate.

A call routing or call processing table is a set of preprogrammed steps that reside in system memory. These may a standard set of steps, preprogrammed into the machine prior to installation. Today, more often than not, these are tables that may be changed, by the user, to address the particular customer call center call processing demands.

The simpler it is to make these changes, the more flexible and more functional the ACD becomes. If these changes are only possible with effort or factory support, the less likely and the more expensive adapting the ACD to meet the customer call center needs becomes.

Routing Control Elements

We broached the subject of call processing or routing tables in Chapter 8, as far as the call answering process is concerned. We did not however approach the steps beyond the point of answer. These steps include;

- **The management of the status of all trunk and agent resources,**
- **The answer step,**
- **The connect step,**
- **to available primary agents/group,**
- **announcements,**
- **other service devices such as voice response units,**
- **The delay steps,**
- **The overflow trigger points or steps,**
- **the selection of secondary or subsequent groups,**
- **the use of voice messaging and other load shedding strategies, and**
- **the overflow off this system to second and subsequent systems.**

There is increasing appreciation on the part of the systems designers of integrating all these decision points into one decision process. Today few systems do this Trunk level components detect a service request and answer the call, independently of knowing the status of the target agent group. This is typical of PBX based ACD systems. Even retarding answer does nothing to alleviate occupancy, call or billing duration, if the "hardware answer" decision is not coupled with agent availability status and call aging.

The key in all of this customer call processing, is to view the system and resources at any point in time, as a whole. This increases both call processing speed and economy by addressing the largest possible universe of resources.

The more agents or applicable voice response ports available to serve an offered call, the better the service received by the caller. Basic economy of scale rules.

With a functional ACD system and active and involved management, not only will the callers receive good service, but at the best cost to service ratio possible in this customer call center environment. Why is this possible?

Shorter calls still cost less, so it is critical that the routing process shave a second here, seconds there. These add up quickly to large amounts of time. A large California based bank estimates that every second increase in the average customer call, costs them an additional $1,000,000 a year in overhead expense.

It is simple to make this calculation. Take the total cost of your customer call center operations and divide it by the number of calls received. Now determine the average call duration in seconds. Divide the total call center operational cost by the number of seconds in a typical call. You'll be surprised and will have a powerful tool in your "financial justification kit." An incoming call uses a number of costly resources during the process.

- **A trunk,**
- **The switch, at least two ports and a talk path,**
- **An agent and a portion of their day,**
- **Optionally a voice response device and the computer system it is attached to, and**
- **any supporting computer system.**

All these elements are used sequentially and in some cases concurrently as the incoming call process proceeds. Thus shorter calls can save more than just talk time on expensive long distance trunks.

Call Processing -- The Basic Steps

a.   **Answer**

A telephone call is considered to be an ACD call when it is connected to the ACD system. This is occurs when the receiving central office sends a "supervision in" message. At this point one of three scenarios can be followed;

1.   Immediate answer and the triggering of a request to the call processing control table in the switch common control for inbound call routing

instructions.   This tends to be a "reflex" reaction that is built into a trunk component as this is the desired reaction when a trunk requests service in a PBX application.

This is considered a "hardware" level answer decision. This is termed "hardware answer." The logic for this technique is sound in a PBX application, though not necessarily in a customer call center ACD.   In a PBX, there is no need to continually ask the common control computer what to do when a new call arrives.   The same answer always applies; answer the call and send it to the operator or a specific extension.   Responsibility for the answer decision is delegated to the trunk card, using a "distributed processing" philosophy.   This keeps the processing load off the PBX common control and frees it for more important PBX feature control.

FIG. 9-1

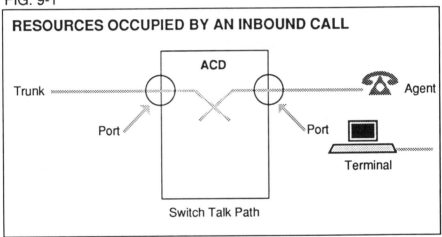

RESOURCES OCCUPIED BY AN INBOUND CALL

2. Retarding answer for a fixed duration, then answer and interrogate the common control tables. The delay time duration can be established at one of three levels. It can be a system-wide, trunk group or individual trunk level parameter. Upon exhausting this delay, the system behaves in the same manner as the first scenario. This is also termed "hardware answer," as even the fixed delay is built into the component (in this case, a trunk card).

The question here is whether or not the system is built to "barge out" of the fixed delay period, should an agent become available. Don't take it for granted all systems do this. The big standalone systems do but it is not an absolute rule on systems that began lives as PBXs. The implication is this; agents may be available but the ACD system insists on delaying the inbound caller. The ACD

blindly follows the fixed delay parameter, oblivious to the state of the available agents.

3. The final method is termed "dynamic answer." Here the CO sends the "supervision in" signal requesting return answer supervision. The switch reacts by recognizing the presence of an inbound call, and looking to a routing table that instructs the machine to determine if anyone in the target group(s?) of agents is available to serve the call. If no one is available, do nothing other than maintain data recording the first indication of the call appearance. Meantime, the system scans the intended agent group looking for an agent to become available. The system lets the call continue to ring. This ringing (voltage) is provided by the CO.

Concurrently the call is now being timed and aged against the route parameters.

Two things will end the delay:

i.   **if an agent (or optionally and IVR system) becomes available, or**

ii.   **the preprogrammed delay period is exhausted and the routing table commands the system to answer the call an optionally provide an announcement.**

Extending the answer up to the preprogrammed delay point, coupled with immediate answer and barge out to a now available agent, are the components of dynamic answer. Assigned by the route table, this feature can save six or more seconds of billable time, per delayed call. Given the fact every second counts, this can be a very large number. As software controls this answer decision it is termed "software answer."

b.   Connection to the first intended resource.

This resource may be an agent position, a delay announcement or with increasing frequency, a voice response or voice mail machine. Again there are basically two methods this connection can occur,

1.   Upon "hardware answer" the call is connected to an available agent, an announcement device and/or music on hold. The agent begins the transaction or the delay announcement is played. This assumes a desired target

resource is available.   If not, all queued calls go to music or a delay announcement, thus queuing the call at the call center owner's expense.

2.   The second method, is the route table driven or "software answer" Here, no agent has become available so the system, realizing the call has aged beyond a reasonable ring delay, answers the call.   Depending on the manufacturer, this may be a discrete step in the inbound call routing table, or be inherent subset of the announcement step.

In both cases, two issues need to be carefully understood on the part of the buyer; the flexibility of the announcement technology, and the ability to "barge out" of the delay or announcement to an agent who may become available during the software managed delay or announcement.   At this stage, if the call   is answered by an agent, under any of the described scenarios, no further discussion need be had. The call is connected and is subsequently processed by the primary or intended group.

c.   Selection of second or subsequent agent groups.

After the routing process has looked to the first agent group for service and found no agent immediately available, the system can react according to one of two parameters:

i.   If the number of calls (call count) in queue, exceed a predetermined number, immediately look to the next group, abandoning the primary group as a potential resource to serve this call, or

ii,   Look to the time parameter in the routing table. Once this has run, the system then looks to the second or subsequent step.

Upon encountering either decision parameter, the system looks to the secondary agent group. The immediate question, does this overflow step prevent the call from being served by an agent in the first and most ideal group, should one become available while the call is queue for the secondary group.

When we started this chapter, the warning was given we were going to examine nuances and here we are. Subtle? Yes. Worthy of ignoring? No. The issue is maintaining the largest pool of resources to serve a service request. Scale produces economy only if it is intelligently used.

Simultaneous Queuing To Multiple Groups

Vendors of ACD systems are not quick to provide clear definitions of how things really happen in their systems. This is generally due to the fact there are no

accepted frames of reference or standards to judge which is a better way of doing things. Consider the following scenario; Three different ACD systems manned with three agent groups, the primary, secondary and tertiary groups.

1. Trunk Vectoring.

This popular technique instructs the system to receive a call and look at the first group for a predetermined time. Once this time is exhausted and no agent has become available, look to the second agent group and so on.

The important issue here is the number of agents (or resources) being simultaneously scanned for an available agent to provide service. Typically the pattern is group one, then two, then three, so that the largest number of agents being simultaneously scanned is only equal to the largest agent group.

In most PBX based ACD systems, the original designers pressed the "call forwarding" feature into service to implement overflow, hence the inability to do simultaneous look back when call forwarding features are used.

2. Overflow call count.

Like trunk vectoring, once a time or call waiting count parameter is exceeded and the call is passed to the secondary or tertiary group for service. In this case, typically this overflow decision is triggered by the number of calls already queued for the particular target group. If the queue call count limit is exceeded a queued inbound call will completely ignore that group and immediately "jump" or overflow to the second or third step.

A subtle, but important, intellectual shift occurs here. A process becomes the target for a call, not a physical device or person. This is a small demonstration of the evolution away from classical telephony thinking where a hardware address (station) or device is the primary call target. This is one of the primary reasons designers of true ACDs spend more time with logical targets (agents who sign on) rather than physical telephone instruments or port numbers, DNs, vectors or whatever. This means data is credited to the logical unit (agent or group) rather than an extension, then need to be interpreted to provide "people statistics."

3.   Multistage queuing.

In this case all inbound calls target a call processing control table and are handled as targets of this logical resource or table. The system then looks to match the caller with the most desirable agent/group and only when time parameters are exceeded does it "add" the secondary and tertiary agent groups as additional answering resources to the call queuing process. The word "add" needs further explanation.

In all three of our scenarios we have almost identical systems with small variations in the call processing schemes. The system with multistage queuing will have a smaller and more productive staff complement because the queuing table takes advantage of the economy scale.   Also it employs simultaneous "look-back" queuing.

Look-Back Queuing

Look-back queuing is a much used, yet little understood phrase. Being able to "look back" at a previously questioned resource is technically look-back queuing, but does it take advantage of the total available agent complement at that point in time?

It may be just a "snap shot" process. The system looks at group 1, then group 2, then group 3, then back to group 1 and cycles accordingly until the call is answered.

The look back difference occurs when coupled with multistage queuing. Two processes occur simultaneously. First, the ACD with a call in queue, following the call routing table, looks at the first group waiting for an agent to become available. When a certain amount of time expires, the system adds a second group and so on. The second process which comes into play is the scanning of the primary agent group, then secondary group as the additional agents are added

to the logical prospective pool of answering agents. Typically the system has a preference for the first and most desirable group. In this way the largest pool of agents is built up to serve the caller.

Economy of scale becomes meaningful at about twenty five to thirty agents and begins to improve from that point. Statistically, the greater the calls to trunks to agents, the more efficient the system becomes. Trunk vectoring and overflow, without simultaneous look-back capability, deny this building of scale. See Fig 9.2.

Overflow, Intraflow And Interflow

These terms essentially mean the same thing. A decision point is reached in a call processing sequence and the caller "overflows" to the next intended agent group. Overflow is the general description of this step. Intraflow is overflow internally to another group in a single ACD. Interflow is overflow to another group in a second or subsequent ACD or other system.

FIG. 9-2

RELATIVE AGENT UNIVERSE WITH MULTISTAGE QUEUING		
	Number of Agents in Each Group	MULTISTAGE QUEUING Without vs. With
Group 1	40 Agents	40 40
Group 2	60 Agents	60 100
Group 3	20 Agents	20 120
	TOTAL	20 120

* Maximum # of Agents = Current Group Size
vs.
Cumulative Total of Agent Groups Call Queued GAP

Selecting An Agent Within A Group

Once an agent group has been selected to serve the call, and assuming for the moment there are a number of available agents to answer the call, how is an individual agent selected. There are three common ways, "top-down", "round-robin" or "longest available".

1.   Top-down selection method

In this case the system uses a technique common to uniform call distributors (UCD) and early ACD systems. Here the call is directed to a target directory number in the system that amounts to a group pilot number. The call begins hunting for an available agent at the top of the list of extension numbers these agents occupy. The call hunts through the list from the top until an available agent is encountered. The call is then connected to this agent. When a new call arrives it begins at the top again and rotates through the same hunt sequence. If all extensions in the group are busy, the call "returns" to the top of the extension list and cycles through the list again, looking for an available agent. The effect of this hunting scheme is to always place an inequitable workload on the agents early in the hunting sequence. Agents refer to the seats (extensions) as the "hot seat(s.)"

In some limited applications this may be a desirable. Take the example of a back-up agent group primarily assigned to do non-phone work unless service levels deteriorate. With this top down hunting method, all the agents are not randomly interrupted with overflowed calls unless the incoming call load is high, then they are all pressed into service as intended.

2.   Round Robin selection method

Less frequently encountered, like the top-down method, begins with an agent extension and hunts in a rotary fashion, looking for an available agent. The difference here is the hunt sequence begins at the last agent extension which answered the call, plus one. Although, less of a "hot seat" effect occurs, the workload is still not equitably or logically distributed.

3.   Longest Available Agent method

Here the ACD maintains a table known as an "available" or "free list", where each agent is assigned upon going into the available (for a call) state. As each agent joins this list, they are assigned an arrival priority. That is when they became "free" to join the list. The "oldest member" of this list is the next agent to receive a call.

Again there is a subtlety in the shift to logical assignments of values, in this case the time the agent has been in the available state, that allows a substantially greater degree of flexibility, and the ability to more appropriately reflect a

customer call center structure. Traditional telephony uses hardware addresses and does not allow this interaction between hardware and software tables.

Secondary and Tertiary Group Assignments

Most modern standalone ACD systems also allow more specificity in targeting certain individual agents in the customer call center, based on the skills or specific services these agents can provide. The typical example cited is the use of foreign language agents in a predominantly English speaking center.

The problem that arises is this. the call volume to this particular skill split is low enough not to keep them constantly busy. As a result the total call load is not balanced across the agent group. Some agents will work harder than others. This results in inequity of work distribution. This has many implications beginning with perception and going as far as compensation.

To solve this problem, the standalone vendors provide for agents signing on to multiple groups, based on their skill, then having the system manage the equitable distribution of calls, preferring those agents with a given skill, when such a caller calls. Yet still ensuring everyone shares an equal a work load as possible. This ensures equal work and plays the economy of scale game as closely as possible. Reports are delivered based on the primary, secondary and tertiary splits, assignment and ultimate routes.

Other Call Processing Steps

Other Agent Groups

Modern ACD systems allow connection to as many agent groups as desired, under a single call processing control table. The limits here are the number of allowable steps in the table, or the total number of agent groups in a single system. This does include interflow to a second or subsequent remote site.

Delay or Hold

This a delay step, allowing for a delay of a predetermined time. Some ACD systems allow this to be inserted prior to the trunk answer point. Ensure if this is the case, "barge out" is inherent in this pre-answer step. All delay or hold steps after the trunk answer also should allow barge out to a newly available agent. Do not take barge out of a pre-answer delay for granted. Check with the

vendor. Watch for the fixed "forced delay" step (in lieu of dynamic answer) many PBX based ACD vendors sell. Some do not have barge out. This means you can have available agents, queued callers and no ability to connect the two for five or ten seconds, depending on the fixed delay. Five seconds a call, for all calls that are answered immediately, quickly adds up to significant additional trunk and labor costs.

Announcements

These are optional resources that allow informational messages to be played to the incoming caller. How the system is instructed to whom and when to play these is generally a function of the inbound routing table. Some older ACD and UCD systems assign these in hardware. Ensure barge out to a newly available agent is standard.

Interflow

This is an overflow step, most developed in the larger more sophisticated ACD systems. The intent of this techniques is to allow multiple, geographically dispersed ACDs, to be networked together. This allows even larger "pools" of agents and resources to serve an inbound calling population. Large airlines and catalogers make extensive use of this technique to great effect, to shift workload, optimize staff and cut overtime expense.

Other resources -- interactive voice response, voice mail, etc.

The discussion of whether to use them or not, is over. They are proven. Customers have accepted them in appropriate applications, while they can dramatically improve a company's service delivery at relatively minor incremental cost.

Companies use interactive voice announcement and response technologies to supplement their agent forces. Introducing of voice response technologies into your service options present many intriguing possibilities to be discussed later. The most critical issue at this stage is the perceived delay they additionally introduce to the caller service level. Typically these voice or audio response systems are inserted as a call prompting or overflow step in the call processing sequence. They can be used to ask the caller to enter critical identification information for coupling with your account databases and so on.

Call Prompting

This was a term and a technique first used by AT&T in Enhanced 800 Service. It inserted a step into the call process as the caller arrived at their intended destination. This step used interactive voice technology to ask the caller to identify with more specificity, the department or function they were trying to reach. The greeting script may go like this... "Thank you for calling Acme Corporation. To better serve you please enter the number of the department you wish to speak to, 1 for Sales, 2 for Service etc...." The caller enters the number on their touch tone phone and is queued directly to the functional group they desire. The advantage occurs in the fact functionally dedicated trunk groups are no longer required, i.e. publishing one number for Sales, another for Service etc.... Now with the call prompting greater flexibility occurs but now secondary queuing also becomes a concern.

The AT&T service was embedded in the 800 service, but now this feature can be obtained as a part of any voice processing scenario from the cheapest auto attendant to the most expensive IVR available.

Your marketing department can use this feature to reduce the number of 800 numbers they use to advertise your sales and service numbers. "One number service" becomes viable as an alternative to multiple circuits for different customer services.

Call Overflow

Here the same technology is used, but at a different stage in the call. Here the voice response device is used to backup the live agents during a busy period when service to a minimum of callers may be unreasonable. Instead of "eternity queue" the voice response device takes a call back message or provides a service alternative. In this case though, successful implementation depends on how quickly and conscientiously the call back occurs.

Voice Messaging as Overflow

Adding voice messaging as an overflow feature is a two edged sword. Unless there is a compelling reason for an agent to pick up the phone and return calls, this is not going to work.

First; most ACD systems are marginally staffed. The ACD was bought to aid in carefully match supply (agents) to demand (callers). If this is the case the agents have little or no time left to return calls left in the messaging system. **Second;** it is a well known belief that inbound agents (reactive) are not good at making outbound (proactive) calls. That is the perception and many agents act this out. The last thing they wish to do after a heavy inbound call session is to begin making outbound calls. **Third;** the calls have to be retrieved from the voice mail system. This can occur three ways. First have the agents call the voice mail and physically "transcribe" the message, caller name and caller phone number and then make the call. Second, assign an agent to this task and distribute the call back calls to agents. Neither of these are particularly seamless or transparent. The third method is to integrate the voice messaging system with the ACD common control.

One ACD vendor has done this to great effect. This system offers callers in an extended queue the option of leaving a request for a call back and hanging up. Part of the message requests the caller dial their call-back number into the system. The system records the voice message and the touch tone digits. The system then monitors the customer call center service level. As the service level improves it "inserts" these call back requests into the inbound call flow. The system "plays" the voice message to the agent and automatically outdials the phone number.

A newer strategy is now available when callers enter their account identification using a social security, account, phone or some other number via IVR, the computer system builds a call back list and presents these call backs to available agents while allowing passive or active preview dialing.

This is particularly elegant in that it removes the call back decision from the agent, occurs almost seamlessly and makes the outbound call "look like" and inbound call. After all, "the caller wanted to talk to the customer call center." Using automatic number identification or ANI is another way of capturing the inbound caller's number. The ACD system must be equipped to gather this data and do something with it. This offers a secondary challenge in that you do not capture the individual identity of the caller. This can be done in real-time or at month end when the 800 billing is rendered. The lead atrophies quickly, so "after the fact" direct mailings from the abandoned caller list to a caller denied service, will have little effect unless they are particularly innovative and compelling.

Chapter Ten

Bulletproofing The Center

There's Nothing As Dead As A Dead Customer Call Center and that includes your Business!

Strategies

One simple question: How much revenue and profit will your company lose if your customer call center crashes for one hour? For a day? For a week? For a month? And if you don't think it can happen to you think of the hapless companies who sat at the end of 35,000 Illinois Bell phone lines after the infamous 1988 Hinsdale central office fire. Many lost their phone service for as long as a whole month. Four weeks without calls, without revenues, with no profits from the customer call center driven portion of your business. Lost business opportunities and erosion of business credibility. Forget the money, think of the company anguish and the possibility of furloughing or laying off employees. Think of your career. How it could have been enhanced if your preventive plans had saved the day. Think how far it would be put back if you do not buy an ACD and build a customer call center which can resist almost the worst possible disaster, including earthquakes. It takes money though surprisingly little more in terms of the capital investment you planned to invest in the center. When measured against the revenues and profits at risk should an interruption occur.

Disaster Recovery And Business Resumption Plans

The notion of disaster recovery is a flawed notion to begin with. Unless you are a very small business with only one business location, putting all your "customer call center eggs" in one basket is a risky strategy as a minor disaster as simple as a telephone pole being hit by a car, can take you out of business. The fall back is then to develop a business resumption plan, but again this language assumes the business experienced a hard interruption.

This recalls a business win some years back when a major mutual fund manager lost power to their ACD as an contractor inadvertently severed an electric cable to the building. That day the company had launched a major new fund and placed full page ads in major financial and city news papers to the tune of many hundreds of thousands of dollars. They could not answer one call! Because the installed PBX/ACD, a competitor for the next generation switch, could not work in a full power fail bypass mode, they lost millions. A true ACD should normally be configured to allow for this.

A Business Continuity Strategy

A far preferable and realistic strategy, once your business grows to a size that justifies this, is to balance business across to geographically separate sites. Equipped and staffed to handle business operations on a day to day basis. For a small business, putting together a back up strategy with a telephone service bureau is a partial and effective intermediate strategy.

Here is why this makes sense. Looking at it from a business resumption perspective means having staff and equipment available at a second site and that becomes problematic if you treat this as a switch from site A (that has experienced the disaster) to site B (the back up site in times of emergency.) In a disaster recovery mode, you will find that staff and operations processes don't transport as easily as hardware and software. Having a continuously operating second site with staff as the alternative site for overflow means something other companies characterize as disasters are really lesser events for you.

Hardware strategy: Maybe you will wish to over-configure the system shells and populate them with extra components (gleaned from site A if accessible or rented for the duration of the event from your vendor,) in the event of a major call traffic redirection. This avoids your company carrying expensive inventory just for a once in a decade event.

During the January 1994 Northridge (Los Angeles) Earthquake, staff could not enter condemned buildings, even though some equipment continued operating, freeways were jammed, streets closed and no one wanted to leave their homes and families out of fear of subsequent aftershock damage etc. Many local COs were effected and calls in and out of Southern California almost impossible. Emergency agencies were telling people to stay home so the thought of moving staff to a contractors retail back up center was illusory. Flying them out of state, impossible. Callers from unaffected regions kept calling, and if there was no business continuity plan, those calls went unanswered.

Details

"Bulletproofing" the customer call center is not limited to the reliability and failure resistance of the ACD.

The more you protect, the inbound circuits, the power source, the automatic call distributor, the computer support system, building lighting and air conditioning, the better off you will be. Then planning an "off site" business resumption strategy is also the ideal. The author has observed a number of business and natural disasters and customer call center recovery strategies. The basic rule is, the longer you take to recover full customer call center operation; minutes, hours, days, the longer the residual effect.

The other uncanny corollary is how quickly a company can forget the effect of a catastrophe, when they discover the cost of a backup plan! There are a number of major businesses in the Los Angeles Basin with single call centers, who were mercifully out of business for brief periods of time during the 1994 quake. In the cases the author directly experienced, it was not the systems that died, but building closures until inspection and granting of structural safety clearance and the availability of staff, that kept customer call centers off-line.

Circuits

Circuits have five elements involved that need to be examined from a reliability point of view. Without adequate circuits or no access to the public network, the customer call center is effectively out of service.

Tracing a circuit from the public network to the customer call center switch identifies three separate elements;

- **the long distance network provider "point of presence (POP),"**
- **the link between the network provider POP and local CO,**
- **the local serving company Central Office,**
- **the outside plant or cable route between the CO and the customer call center, and**
- **the building entry and termination point.**

a.   The POP office and Central Office

Myth has it Central Offices never die. Although generally unbelievably reliable, they are occasionally known to break. Sometimes they burn. There is little a customer call center manager can do to guard against this. Having a disaster contingency plan is mandatory for the customer call center manager. The more valuable your incoming calls (in terms of revenues) the more compelling the argument is for a disaster protection and contingency plan. It is not very comforting blaming the local telephone company for your lost business, despite reality. Tariffs protect the local telco and the long distance carrier for direct and indirect damages due to nonperformance of their service. The most generally recoverable from the telco and/or carrier is the abatement of the telephone bill for the duration of the outage, provided it exceeds 24 continuous hours.

A strategy rarely followed, because of the cost, is the termination of circuits at two separate central offices. Now, on notice, the long distance carrier can alternatively route inbound calls through the second central office and back-up cable path to the customer call center. Obviously, a physically separate route for the outside cable is recommended.

A major long distance carrier offers an arrangement with 800 service where they will guarantee no calls will be lost after you have notified them to redirect your inbound 800 telephone calls to a second site or sites. Take a look at this it sounds like a great solution. Understand EXACTLY how it works and WHAT IS REQUIRED of your company to ensure a "switch" to a second site would work. If it works as advertised, test it with real traffic before you "take it live." There is more to making this work than just the redirection of your 800 service.

As discussed earlier, setting up a relationship with a company that provides disaster recovery or back up services is a great idea. There is only one flaw in that they have limited resources also. There is an assumption that only a limited number of customers will demand their services at any one time In the case of the 1994 LA Quake, these companies quickly ran out of capacity to support their subscribers. This argues for an exclusive company based business resumption plan. Remember your advertising campaigns are not typically effected by disasters and they take more time to turn down than you customer call center. The volume of service requests are effected in a positive way in that call volumes increase.

b.   Outside Plant (From POP to your CO and the CO to your premise.)

Every customer call center is linked to the public network via a local CO. Between the CO and the customer call center is a connection called the local loop. A similar high volume connection exists between your CO and your long distance providers POP. This may be analog or digital. It may be cable or microwave radio link. All are subject to interruption by way of physical cutting of cable or loss of power. In the case of microwave, loss of line of sight connection is an issue also. Somebody builds a building or one of your antennae blows down. To guard against this a second alternate local loop is often used. Again, on the face of it, not an inexpensive measure.

When considered in the context of the business and the revenue at risk, back up circuit routes can be cheap insurance. One major domestic airline books $16,000 per minute. Loss of any portion of the customer call center or reservation system is tremendously costly. If this option is pursued, the routing of these local loops should be absolutely separate even down to the building entry point.

c.   Building Termination point

The local loops or trunk elements may arrive in either a digital (T1) or analog format. At the point of termination, prior to literal attachment to the ACD system, there will be connecting blocks allowing the individual trunks to be broken out into their individual wire elements. In a either an analog or a digital environment, total power loss ends all call processing unless uninterruptible power is supplied to the switch and in the case of T1 spans terminated on channel banks and then an analog switch, the channel banks.

There are four different scenarios.

- **a fully digital environment, Digital trunks and digital ACD,**
- **mixed analog/digital trunks on a digital ACD,**
- **mixed analog/digital trunks on an analog ACD, or**
- **a fully analog environment with both analog loops and ACD.**

We have discussed the issue of digital trunks and switches requiring uninterrupted power for operation. Channel banks are necessary for terminating digital trunks (T1) on an analog ACD. They must be supported with uninterruptible power if they are to receive and decode 24 channel T1 spans into a single analog conversation during a power outage.

Power

In the case of the most digital ACD systems, DC is the required power source due to its predictability and stability. AC systems are likely to require more power conditioning and be subject to potentially higher maintenance requirements due to the less precise power source.

With an analog ACD system, a fall back position is often taken to avoid back-up battery or DC power systems. Power fail cut-through or bypass capability is included in the system. This allows the ACD to receive calls on those particular trunks, connected to predetermined instruments. Power from the CO is used and the instruments act like a single line home phone. All other system features are lost during the outage. Check that the number of cut-through trunks configured are satisfactory to meet a substantial portion of the total trunking. Ten percent is inadequate, while one hundred percent is unrealistic unless this is a standard feature. Remember, each power fail position must be manned to take a call.

With a digital ACD system, there are two strategies. Complete DC power support, either from a battery source or UPS (uninterruptible power supply). The latter is more expensive while batteries need to be recharged or they too run out of power. All systems bet that the power outage will not be for an extended period of time, so battery is typically provided in minute or hourly increments. The longer the battery support time, the higher the cost. Years ago Bell Labs did a study and found that over 90% of all power outages lasted fewer than five minutes.

One innovative approach is taken by a recent entry into the ACD arena. They provide full time DC power and full battery support for the system. Should power be lost to the inverter which charges the batteries, the batteries will support the entire system, disk drives included, until the batteries become substantially depleted. At this stage the system bypasses the switch to digital instruments still supported by the remaining battery to allow simple call receipt and origination. In this way the system can still operate over an extended outage. Overlooked in this discussion is the fact anytime power is lost, other customer call center facilities are also lost. Air conditioning, lighting and any supporting computer system. People are unable to work in the dark, so often natural lighting is designed into the center. Not all regions are dependent on air conditioning year round so there may be provision for natural circulation.

Simple call transactions may be able to be completed with pencil and paper or messages taken for call backs.

Don't forget to include your long distance carrier(s), suppliers of your 800 trunks in your disaster planning. With some prior planning, they can move all or part of your incoming 800 calls from one customer call center where a disaster has occurred to another operational center in a another part of the country. Just make sure the target center has the physical and staffing capacity to accept the redirected call load.

Telephone Systems - Redundancy

This was discussed in Chapter 7.

Computer Systems - Redundancy

Over the last decade there has been an upsurge in the use of completely redundant computer systems for "mission critical" applications. These systems were more expensive than there non fault resistant counterparts and like all other systems needed clean power, 100% of the time to operate. The prices of these "fault resistant" or "nonstop" systems have come down, while the options have increased dramatically. These systems are increasingly finding their way into mission critical customer call center applications such as credit authorization, customer service and order entry. Rule: When the MIS department insists their application needs uninterruptible power, do not allow the call switching process to be overlooked as a candidate for the same treatment

Computer Telephony Applications - Redundancy

There are two architectures that are promoted for CTI applications. These are;

1. **the typical host/terminal "star" configuration. Terminal data is provided by the host, using a local "wall power" source.**
2. **Desktop PC, LAN and server configurations.**

If the host, PC, LAN, server or CTI link is lost, so are the applications they support. As you integrate CTI applications in either environment it is critical that a fall back strategy or redundancy be built into the system. This is more simple with a centralized computer ("host") system, as you only   have to "bulletproof" that system. You can still lose terminals and connectivity to the ACD switch.

Client/server CTI environments are proving to be increasingly popular in CTI applications due to lower cost, faster deployment and increased flexibility. However they offer more failure points than tradition terminal systems.

To build a integrated nonstop customer call center with linked computers and switches you need to consider bulletproofing the following components:

1. **The ACD switch.** The switch needs to have redundant common control and MIS processors. This is typical of most standalone ACD systems and some PBX based ACD systems.

2. **Any IVR systems.** This can be mitigated by having more than one system and balancing trunks across these. Redundant IVR systems are available but are still costly for the utility they provide.

3. **MIS links between the switch and the host.** The voice signal   coordination typically comes from the ACD MIS. If there is a redundant MIS system there must be two parallel links to the computer system holding the application and the database. Watch how the vendors position this. In some cases they deliver more than one link (for load distribution purposes only,) but the message traffic is distributed across both links. They do not exist for redundancy purposes! Two redundant CTI links are ideal.

4. **The database system.** Building nonstop computer systems is an established art. However the cost of buying a hot standby computer system is still expensive In a recent experience, the cost to equip a call center with a hot standby system added 83% to the price of the CTI project, versus 18% to deliver a warm standby or failover database server. The difference was about 50 seconds to accomplish the application switchover, with no loss of calls, just the "screen pop" and related functions during that 50 seconds.

5.   In the case of client/server, **the local area network.** This
is a relatively stable technology that can be bought in redundant
configurations, but again, is the additional cost worth this to your
call center. LAN problems are readily diagnosed and remedied
with competent people.

6.   **The Desktop PC.** This is important when "soft phones," that is
where the desk top telephone is a "window" on the PC screen.
If the PC is lost, so typically is the telephone functions, unless the
manufacturer provides an external (to the PC and its power source)
device that allows continued operation via manual bypass.

Chapter Eleven

The Desktop And Telephone Devices

Introduction

Since this book began life as The Incoming Call Center in 1987, much has changed in the use of personal computers and applications. Back then we made the observation that the arrival of the PC in any business remade the economic landscape like a swarm of locusts remake a lush landscape. The PC first began to remake the customer call center with its use as a replacement for the computer terminal or dumb tube.

Now that robust PC multi-session systems like recent versions of Windows and OS/2 Warp, they are becoming combined voice and data terminals almost 15 years after they were first mooted as Integrated Voice and Data Terminals (IVDTs) of the early 1980s. Both Microsoft (TAPI) and Novell (TSAPI) have promulgated PC telephone interface standards in an effort to get into this market. In both cases however the suggested standards are not "industrial strength" enough to meet the requirements of a production oriented customer call center.

The keys to the successful adoption of integrated desktop work environments are twofold:

☐ **demonstrable economic justification for adding PCs and dumping telephone instruments, and**
☐ **real applications that deliver measurable economic benefit.**

Customer Call Center Performance

Agents are employed to handle incoming calls. There are other agent and staff performance goals also. These are;

▪ **to process as many calls as possible,**
▪ **in as short a time as possible, and**

- provide as high a level of satisfaction to the caller as feasible,

From an agent point of view these goals can be reached more readily if ;

- the terminal, instrument and system are simple to use
- unambiguous in its use,
- key strokes are kept to a minimum,
- does not introduce any undue fatigue factor into the task, and,
- does not "step on" the primary business transaction.

Many customer call center or telemarketing applications require the agent to follow complex scripts and enter data while conducting an intelligent conversation with the customer or prospect. It is important the terminal (ACD, PC or CRT used) does not get in the way of the business at hand. Try it yourself -- try to talk intelligently and type accurately at the same time. Now add a dumb phone and listening and responding persuasively!

The PC based Agent Instrument or Integrated Desktop

Of late a number of the leading ACD and computer vendors have been discussing providing ACD instrument functionality in a window on a PC.

Unfortunately most of the vendors discussing this approach to integrating the telephony function in some sort of PC or smart terminal have an objective which reflects their position in the marketplace. If they are a computer vendor, their position is datacentric. If they are a telephony vendor, they are telecentric in their focus. By promoting their position they hope customers and prospects will buy more of their system offerings. Thus they try to justify their offering on the narrow basis of telephone or computer hardware efficiencies.

The point here, is that neither focus is correct as it should be a combination of the improved user environment through easier operation, lower training requirements and overall productivity gains. The real leverage is the seamless integration of telephone and computer functions with the application. One keystroke invoking a macro command that effects changes in both the computer and phone state, but also follows a specific scenario required by the application or applications session running. We will discuss this at great length when we move to advanced customer call center strategies in Chapter Fourteen.

Unsurprisingly the PC based telephone instrument is not a particularly good replacement for a telephone instrument. Particularly a device designed for high volume telephone call handling. The reasons are simple. The use of single telephone based function keys is simpler and more direct than addressing these features via a combination of CONTROL + QWERTY key strokes, a mouse or a keyboard based function key. However if this is how the comparison is made, the entire point of combining the voice and data functions of a call in one device is missed.

The integrated desktop PC call management scenario directly addresses workflow and application integration. As a result this goes to the core of customer call center productivity problem by streamlining the process and resources necessary to serve a caller. The technology combination is designed to reduce the time, effort and skill level needed by the agent to "navigate" the technology, in the processing of serving the customer. Rather focus at the customer as the system "delivers" the required tools and information, or places it "just one key stroke away." Application scripts can anticipate steps, deliver on-line tools and automatically gather call tracking and wrap up data.

In spite of real advantages that a PC based telephone instrument, the majority of customer call center ACD installations still use ACD telephone instruments.

The Agent Instrument

The success of an ACD system is particularly dependent on the design of the individual ACD agent instrument. The number, speed and intensity of the transactions processed by the agent is a major element in the success of the application. The agent manning this station will spend many hours using the ACD phone. The ease of use designed into the agent phone will have a significant bearing on your customer call center success. Agent ACD telephones are not transferable between manufacturers. You get what you get with the ACD you select. The agent terminal should be a major source of investigation and comparison. Some models are limited, though some manufacturers have done a tremendous job in agent terminal design.

In this chapter we will use of the word terminal refers to the any terminal device or agent instrument, and is not limited to a computer display or CRT device.

Agent Instrument Design Strategies

As ACD systems made their way into the market, the early agent terminals were nothing more than multibutton telephone sets similar to those used on electromechanical key systems such as the 1A2. It was not until the introduction of the first true digital ACD in 1973 that a manufacturer decided an ACD needed an application specific "industrial strength" terminal. Among other things, the use of a unique instrument increased the cost of the ACD on a per position basis. But it was clearly demonstrated the time to process a call was shortened, and customer satisfaction was heightened as a result of the ease of use of the instrument which allowed more focus to be placed on the caller's needs. This efficiency is now being taken to new lengths with the introduction of integrated applications terminals combining telephony and data functions.

If a call takes less time to process, the time and cost of handling the call is reduced, therefore, the number of calls an agent can serve is increased. The application specific design of the ACD system, and consequent increase in cost is more than offset in the favor of the user. As a result the market for ACD systems continues to grow.

Mechanical Packaging

In the high volume call processing world of customer call centers and automatic call distributors, poorly manufactured instruments wear out quickly. Weight and robustness of the instrument are important. Pushing the feature buttons on the phone so often causes the key contact mechanism to fail and the illumination source to burn out. The repeated insertion and removal of a head or handset plug into the jack can unseat and break the electrical connections in a poorly designed or manufactured instrument. If the connection is not cleanly severed, the deterioration of the connection will introduce noise, static or a loss of volume into the call transaction. The instrument will be used constantly, be moved around the desk intentionally and can be unintentionally pulled off the desk by an active agent. This occurs when an agent gets out of his or her chair to stretch, reach for a needed item or attract the attention of a supervisor. A properly weighted instrument is less likely to move and more likely to serve as an anchor for the retractable headset cord.

Discouraging movement in the agent work area, such as standing up and stretching while working the telephone, is less productive than allowing it. Many customer call center managers believe that providing a longer cord than normally provided with the telephone reduces wear, allows greater motion and less restriction of movement. The underlying issue is one of allowing the agent a perception of some control of their work life. The more active the agents are, the increase in wear and tear on the furniture and equipment. Given the big picture however, hardware is less expensive than "live ware".

Analog Or Digital Instruments

Today, typically the instruments provided with ACD and PBX/ACD systems are digital instruments. The audio signal arrives in a digital form and is decoded into an analog audio signal at the phone instrument. This means the instrument constantly needs power for the coder/decoder (codec) to operate and to generate all the command and control signals for simple call setup, breakdown and communicating to the system any expected system status messages. It also allows the instrument to have many features. It typically cannot operate if power is lost from the switch. To get around this limitation, (namely a catastrophe in the case of a power outage,) optional 2500 single line phones can be installed with duplicate wiring and termination devices.

With an analog instrument (i.e.. normal "black" phone), the signal arrives in an analog form and typically all call status signaling follows standard telephony voltage changes, (as found in a simple 2500 series set). This allows the use of line power to accomplish all functions. This means in a bypass mode the instrument can draw line power directly from the CO, thus continue to answer calls as if a single line subscriber set. No secondary backup instruments or wiring are required as these instruments operate in bypass on CO provided line power. Thus the telephone customer call center can be in darkness, but the phones can continue to operate.

There are "hybrid" instruments, which use digital status signaling and analog audio. These allow a feature rich agent instrument and the ability to bypass directly to the instrument in a power outage. These instruments provide the best of both the analog and the digital world, with default to bypass without a second instrument, yet providing fully featured operation.

There was a brief period when a number of instruments required power from an external power source. Here a separate transformer (like a desk calculator power module) plugged into the wall to provide local power to the instrument. Although a viable strategy to increase the functional power of the instrument, it also added to the complexity of the installation in increased power requirements, planning around failure, and expense. Occasionally this strategy resurfaces again when the instrument power requirements exceed what can be supplied on standard telephone cabling. Occasionally these systems show up in the secondary market.

The "other shoe" here, is that to stabilize and back-up the power to these commercial outlets, which supply power to instruments that have external power needs, you have to "bulletproof" the wall plugs. If the switch is backed up and the instruments are not, who answers the calls? This can get expensive.

Cabling

Ideally this should be standard three pair telephone wiring found in a typical telephone installation. Using other than standard "skinny" wire introduces an inflexibility and increased expense in planning and installation.

A new installation does not create a major problem as new cable must be run. Where the system is replacing an existing system, the old cable probably cannot be reused, and when this system is replaced, new cable will need to be run. Cable installation is a relatively expensive labor intensive and inconvenient exercise and installation occasions should be kept to a minimum by intelligently over cabling (i.e.. putting more cable in and more phone jacks than you ever dream you will need) at every opportunity.

If a vendor promises to reuse existing cable in a new installation, have them test the cable, check all the runs to be reused and warrant, in writing, that the replacement system will operate as specified using the existing cable. REPEAT-- GET IT IN WRITING. When nearing a critical deadline, it is most embarrassing to discover the installed cable will not support the new system. It is expensive and inconvenient to replace this while the center is in any state of operation.

Repeat: it is better, safer and you will enjoy a more trouble free life if you run new cabling. Insist you contractor label and document every cable run, origin, destination and termination point.

Ergonomics

As overused as this term "ergonomics" has become, it is still expressive in explaining the discipline of designing manufactured things to reflect the fact people are intended to use them easily. The relationship between a driver and an automobile includes using techniques to increase safety and reduce confusion and fatigue. Although the issue of safety is less dramatic in telephone instrument design, fatigue and confusion mitigation are not.

The instrument used in a high call volume application should not get in the way of the task at hand -- responding to a callers needs. The instrument should be all but transparent to the conduct of the transaction. If the instrument intrudes into the process, it should be minimal in impact.

a. Key placement.

It is important the keys on an instrument are logically laid out. Processing a telephone call can follow one of three scenarios. The designation of these events parallels the frequency of encountering the call type.

> a. **Simple call,**
> b. **Complex call, or**
> c **Exception call.**

The suggested frequency of encountering these call categories could be as follows;

> ■ **simple calls account for 90% of the day,**
> ■ **complex calls, 9%, and**
> ■ **exceptional events, hopefully less than 1%.**

These suggested percentages have been arrived at unscientifically. The point made however is to suggest the frequency of agent need for certain call processing functions and features. The features required by an agent fall into three categories, Primary, secondary or exception functions. Again, classed by frequency of use. The key layout and use should follow this form.

A dilemma faced by a manufacturer as ACD instrument features evolve, is how to addition of physical keys to an instrument. Because software is more flexible than hardware it is possible to "double up" functions of the various feature keys via a "shift" mode. This technique is typically encountered in PC software applications. As this occurs, confusion increases. So do training requirements. Enter the "soft key".

A trend that has crossed out of the PC business into telephone instruments and now ACD instruments, is the soft key technique. To dedicate a key on an instrument is an unambiguous strategy, but it also causes the key field to proliferate with every new feature. This undesirable from a manufacturing and inventory point of view. The redesign of hardware takes time, costs a fortune in reengineering and inventory management.

Later entrants in the ACD market learned from the PC software market and made extensive use of the dynamically assignable keys. These keys are located physically adjacent to a dynamic liquid crystal display (typically below the dynamic display line) that allows the current functions to be displayed and changed based on a predictable call processing sequence. A single key depression activates the necessary system steps to cause a feature to activate. This mirrors software use of application "function" keys that embed a series of keystrokes into a macro command. One key executes a complex function.

The placement of primary, secondary and exception function keys need to be logical and pay heed to the amount of movement required by the user's hand from the natural rest position. The natural rest position on a telephone instrument designed for high volume use is center bottom. Typically with the heel of the palm centered and at rest position on the work surface or on the frame of the device. On most telephone instruments this covers the 12 character dial pad. In an inbound customer call center this is one of the least used key fields, therefore an exception function. It also strongly suggests the proposed instrument was not specifically designed for a customer call center and began life as something else. The design and tooling for a telephone instrument is among the most expensive and inflexible aspects of building any switch.

From this home point the movement to the primary function keys should be minimal. The movement to the secondary keys a little further and so on. There is an arbitrary physiological barrier or "fence" established at each extra stage of movement from the rest position. This increases slightly effort and fatigue, yet reduces confusion and training if this is a functionally exceptional motion. Few ACD vendors have spent the time to research and implement the results with the goals of confusion and fatigue reduction. The underlying goal of all of this is to allow the instrument use to become "autokinetic" or second nature. A better yet superficially contradictory goal is to make the instrument so easy to use through unambiguous keys, labeling and layout. The more you customize the instrument to the application, the less generalized it becomes. With that goes flexibility. At the expense of this goal the dilemma remains for the manufacturers and the freedom to develop and evolve the instrument to accommodate new features and functions.

FIG. 11-1

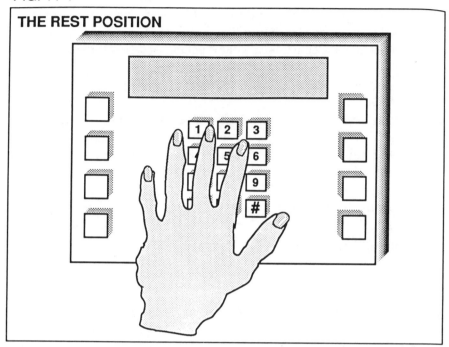

THE REST POSITION

Again with the introduction of PC based integrated workstations, many of the training or confusion based objections are minimized as more and more calls are "scripted" based on the complexity and frequency of occurrence. The issues of obvious and autokenetic keyboard use are not made less important.

b.   Key labeling

In key labeling, acronyms are undesirable. Do you know what a key labeled "HD" does? Or worse yet, "HLD?" High technology has an image of arrogance, partly brought about by the insensitivity to ultimate end users of the products and services spawned by the technology. It is assumed by a few, users have a responsibility for their own destiny. Idealism is great until it directly affects the market acceptance of a product. Users take the course of least resistance...if it is easy to use, it will be...if its hard to use it wont be!

The majority of ACD vendors appear to almost ignore this reality in system interface design, particularly at the agent instrument level. Function key labeling should use complete, plain language labels. If a "shift" function is used so the key has two or more roles, use of different colors for each function label are desirable and helpful to reduce agent confusion and accelerate training.

c.   Key labeling process

There are three or four ways to imprint the label on the key. The issue here is making the label robust enough to withstand many hundreds of thousand activations and still be readable. In a word, wear. The processes are in order of preference and expense; molding (the character/s into the plastic key cap), gas etching, printing or painting the label and finally use of a label decal. The higher the quality of the instrument the better and more expensive the process. The better the process, the crisper the key label is. They remain usable after five years. From a resale value, this is also important.

d.   Key Size

Key size is critical for three reasons. Agents move fast and are occupied with the primary process at hand; serving the customer. First, precision of motion should be a minimal requirement. They are usually interacting with a computer terminal and displayed customer and campaign data, so the ACD instrument is the least important device at hand. It also should be the least intrusive.

Secondly, Female and male agents have different hand sizes and many women have exceptional fingernails. Large male fingers and precisely manicured nails do not take kindly to precise key strokes and low grade feedback.

Thirdly, effective tactile range and "blind" autokinetic response does not work as well with small precise keys. For this reason "membrane keys" (smooth surface keys like those found on inexpensive paper thin electronic calculators) are less popular on ACD instruments. We do not recommend the use of flat membrane keys despite their moisture proof advantages when a beverage is spilled.

e.   Tactile Feedback

There is a great deal of need on the part of a user for some confirmation that the action just taken, worked. That's why typewriter keyboards "click" even when they don't need to. Its why touch-tones feed back to a caller dialing a call and any one of a number of other minor events provide confirmation to the user an action has been acknowledged. Without feedback, there is confusion and with confusion, a reduction in productivity.

f.   Display screens

There is an increasing proliferation of the information displayed on an ACD and administrative instrument. Despite the advantages information being available over no information, long term placing this on a telephone instrument is the wrong solution. The first reality is users do not look at this display screen if they are not obliged to. Doing so interrupts the current transaction. This transaction usually involves a computer terminal with a screen and keyboard. If there is a need to physically look at the instrument display, the agent must scan to the instrument display, refocus their eyes, read and comprehend the information, look back to the primary object (computer display), refocus and continue with the transaction. This is doubly complicated when you add soft keys that have dynamic functions as the whole concept of ergonomics and developing autokenetic behavior is diluted further. When the primary object is a CRT screen, the light intensity and distance is different from the low power LCD of a typical ACD instrument. Eye fatigue increases.

A solution to this is to closely couple the CRT to the ACD so all the functions and visual feedback/displays occur on the same device. This has been elegantly implemented on PC based integrated desktop devices with significant productivity improvements. Fatigue, particularly eye, is dramatically reduced.

When information is displayed on a phone instrument, a minority of ACD vendors   physically separated display devices associated with the agent instrument. These typically required separate cabling to carry the power and display message signals. The technology was fast being superseded by truly integrated display instruments.

g.   Call Type Identification. City of origin announcements or "whisper queues"

Call type identification, although a system based feature, rather than individual instrument based, appears as an agent oriented instrument level implementation. This has important implications as a "repersonalization" tool in the modern customer call center.

Call type identification may be a "whisper queue", flash announcement heard only by the receiving agent, or a visual identification display. The goal is to equip the agent with initial data so as to provide the caller with specific information and thus avoid the inevitable and time consuming caller identification questions of where and why are you calling.

With the growing popularity of dialed number identification (DNIS) and automatic (caller) number identification (ANI) services, voice response for account number collection and switch-to-host and automatic screen population ("screen pops") links, the need for the agent to ask who is calling and why is being reduced. Along with the call response now targeted to a particular caller's particular needs, the calls are shorter. Most important though, the agent does not have to look to the instrument for identification data provided the caller is recognized by your database.

Now with the integrated PC workstation, the whisper queue data can be directly sent to the PC and the necessary work script invoked automatically, thus reducing the required analog to workflow "agent translation."

h.   Head and Handset Jack Type and Location

The jack port on the instrument may range from a fragile modular (RJ-11 type -like your phone at home) plug to an industrial strength dipole jack. The tradeoff is simply ruggedness and size against lower cost and fragility. The repeated insertion and removal of a head or handset plug into the jack can unseat and break the electrical connections in a fitting not built for this purpose. The RJ-11 modular jack is plentiful, inexpensive but not designed for repeated connects and disconnects. When it is stressed or breaks, and if the connection is not cleanly severed, the deterioration of the connection will introduce noise, static or a loss of volume. The heavier the fitting the better, yet recognize the cost and size increases as you adopt increasingly   robust fittings.   These are normally associated with the older style of ACD instruments as manufacturers have increasingly adopted the less robust, smaller and cheaper RJ11, accepting attrition and wear as a fact of life.

The location of the jack may be on the front, side or back of the instrument. In a few instances it may even be dismounted from the instrument and mounted in the knee well of the workstation. Some ACD specific instruments are equipped with two jack ports, one on either side. This is for left- or right-handed operation and/or training purposes. A trainer may work with the trainee at the at the workstation and plug into the instrument simultaneously. The most desirable location tends to be toward the front of the device.

A cradle or handset rest is desirable for supervisor positions. Headsets do not need this as they generally remain with the wearer during the shift.

A word on headsets. I am a 48 year old male seller and writer. I effectively run a small business out of my home. I use the phone extensively and have at least two PCs running different tasks on my office desk. Databases, spreadsheets, correspondence and articles. I could not work without a headset. I don't feel like a "telephone operator," it is a trivial "inconvenience" and I guess it messes my hair up. My comfort and productivity are more important. I will never exclusively use a handset again.

i. **Instrument cable termination**

The cable termination is also a weak point on the instrument particularly if the instrument is going to be move about the desk as constant flexing stresses the connection. The big issue here is typically shoddy assembly as opposed to poorly designed connections. Make sure your maintenance contract covers the connection on the cable to the desk.

ACD Instrument Features

This portion of the discussion is organized to reflect the most used or primary features. This reflects also how frequently they are encountered in popular ACD machines. As ACD systems become less feature rich, those features falling into the secondary and exception categories tend to be less and less available.

During the ACD acquisition phase some of these seem relatively unimportant, and therefore appear to be features you can do without. A fact of life associated with the ACD system assimilation curve is this: as you become more familiar with machine and less intimidated by the complexity of operation, the "little" features that seemed unimportant during the acquisition process suddenly become very meaningful as their impact becomes appreciated. Even though it is easy to befriend a particular vendor during the buying cycle, listen to all the ACD vendors. Give them all a chance during the early stages of the ACD purchase process. The worst that can happen is time is spent to learn some clever new customer call center management tricks. The reality is these features were typically developed to satisfy a real user need. Take the time to understand the "whys" of the features.

With the advent of PC screen based telephone functions, the feature sets have the potential to be enriched again. Here occurs an interesting phenomenon. Many of the features that have shown up on ACD systems, particularly the standalone systems have been reactions to unresponsive data processing departments and systems. For example, wrap up. Wrap up is an ability for the ACD system to allow the impromptu collection of ad hoc numeric data or codes. This data can be sorted after the fact to identify calls by type, origin, disposition, revenue, etc. The fact this data was captured on a telephone system is relevant only because it was part of a call record or transaction type hash count. A better repository of such data would have been the customer information or order entry system. In the past however, this was not done easily. So the ACD vendors provided a fine interim solution. Now computer telephony both solves and complicates the whole picture again. These issues will be discussed more in Chapter Fourteen, The integrated desktop workstation.

Primary ACD Instrument Features

These are arranged in alphabetical order rather than order of importance.

Add-on or Conference (in a third party): This allows an agent to add another party, typically a supervisor, into the call for further help.

Asterisk and the Number (Octothorpe) keys: Or the "Star" and "Pound" key. I recently heard these called the "snowflake" and "tic-tac-toe" keys! These take on a special role in an ACD. They are used to signify key fields (such as a pause) when any data is entered at the touch tone pad. This may be wrap-up, call disposition or peg count data.

Available: This is either a individually identified key or a "tap" or "flash" plus key sequence, on a lesser featured instrument. Use of the "available" key by the agent identifies to the ACD system they are available to take the next call.

There are three ways to implement the feature on an ACD instrument;

1. **Manual identification to the ACD the agent is available for the next call.**
2. **Automatic identification of the agent available status immediately following the release of the last call. This is called "forced available".**

Release is "hang-up". The system is smart enough to understand the use of the release key to terminate the call and return to the agent to the available state.

3. **Managed manual identification; This is identical to 1. however, there is recognition by the vendor, the agent may need time between calls for "after call work" or wrap-up.**

Using the release key, ends the call and places the agent in the wrap-up condition. Upon completing the after call work the agent activates the key to return to the available state. During this period the system has tracked the three agent states; the incoming call time, the wrap-up period and the return to available.

There is now a fourth method made possible through the use of an integrated desktop workstation:

4. **"Scripted workstate management";**

Here, through the use of a "Windows" or OS/2 "script," the individual call/transaction can be scripted to follow a certain workflow, following predesigned steps, states and responses. At the end of the transaction, upon release of the caller, the agent is automatically placed in the wrap up state. However, given that a multitasking desktop operating system is in use, much of the need for post call work is eliminated as the system may be gathering wrap up data or performing wrap up tasks automatically! More later.

Behind the simple activating of the available key by the agent, is a philosophy that needs to be understood from a management point of view. It would be simple to allow the system to totally manage the agents and control their change from work state to work state in the normal and predictable course of calls. This however removes the perception on the part of each agent that they have some control of their destiny. Remove this and this accelerates "burn out". Manual control of the agents state by the agent, coupled with real-time management control to avert abuse appears to be a humane balance.

Hold: This works like any "hold" key to place the call in suspended state of silence, while some other activity occurs concurrently with the call being held. Redepressing the hold key reestablishes the connection so the conversation can continue.

Pound Sign or Octothorpe key: See asterisk key above,

Primary Extension or Call A: This is the primary line appearance, extension or directory (DN) number of the instrument. This may be a hardware address (station number or directory number) in a PBX/ACD or a logical resource location awaiting use by an agent signing on with their agent identification number. Once an agent signs on to this instrument/extension location, this logical ID number supersedes the hardware address once entered into the instrument as the agent signs on. All agent properties and class of service conditions are attached to this logical ID or address. Calls are now routed to the logical ID currently resident at this hardware address or extension number. Once the agent signs off the position returns to an inactive hardware address until reactivated by the next agent signing on.

Secondary Extension or Call B: This is the second line appearance at the instrument. This may be a second ACD extension number, administrative PBX extension number in a PBX/ACD system, or a DID circuit appearance.

Note: Most PBX based ACD require two different line appearances, one for the applicable agent group and one so any one on the same PBX/ACD system may call this agent position. This is also so the agent can make outgoing calls. These are physical port (extension) addresses. Most standalone ACD systems do not assign lines to physical addresses but separate call activity by combining transaction detail data by call type, assign the service necessary and collate the resulting data accordingly.

Ready: This key is used to signify to the ACD the agent is available to take the next call. This is used in the manually available mode described above.

Release: This is the equivalent of the switch-hook or "flash" key. Depression of this key during a call disconnects the call.

Status Advisory Tones: Different manufacturers use different audible tones and signals on the line to advise the agent of certain conditions. These may be zip tones preceding an inbound call and reorder when an incorrect or illegal dialing sequence is used.

Tone Dial Pad: Self evident as the dialing mechanism for internal and external call setup. The pad may also be used for data entry in conjunction with wrap up data entry.

NOTE: In the data entry mode, is the tone generator deactivated? If it is not the tones associated with the use of these keys will interrupt the conversation. The data entry mode therefore can not be used until after release is activated and the caller disconnected. More modern ACD systems allow concurrent conversation and data entry as they automatically switch on and off the tone generator based on call/instrument status.

Transfer: Depressing this key after an alternate station number is dialed, (e.g. a supervisor station), allows the transferring of the current call to the target station.

Secondary Features

Enter: Use of this key alerts the system to the fact the field of digits just entered via the touch tone pad is complete. Either a dial stream, an ID number or data. This key can be used independently or in conjunction with the * or # keys to indicate pauses, backspace/erase or field delimiters. It also introduces a human factors element long missing in telephony. The ability to "edit" a dial stream before "execution" by the switch!

Flash or Tap: The "Flash" or "Tap" key is used as an alternative to briefly depressing the switch hook to alert the ACD or PBX system to the fact the following key sequence is an operating instruction. The tap or flash key was introduced to resolve the dilemma created by the using the switch hook to terminate a call and to alert the system that the next dialed numbers were a command code. The length of a momentary depression meant different things to different users and many calls were unintentionally terminated, rather than transferred etc. Manufacturers solved the dilemma through use of the flash key. This key sent a fixed non-fatal switchhook flash message to the system that now placed the caller on hold and waited for the dialed command code.

Mute Key; This provides an ability to lock out the "talk" part of the instrument voice circuit so that the agent can hear the caller, but not the reverse. Typically this is a feature of a headset, though this has migrated onto the more popular agent instruments.

Prerecorded Automatic Announcements; This is a feature that places personal announcement capabilities with the agent. It may be inherent in the system or part of the instrument. This an ability for the agent to prerecord their personal greeting; "Thank you for calling XYZ Company, This is Andrew. How may I help you?" The argument in favor of this features is fatigue reduction and consistency of greeting delivery throughout the shift. This is now being dramatically expanded through the use of sound card options in the integrated desktop PC or outboard instrument device. Repeat Call Type or City of Origin (Whisper queue): Because customer call centers have the ability to serve different callers with the same staff, and do so with greater precision if the agent is alerted to the call type ahead of time, "whisper queue" announcements were introduced. This is a short audible announcement of the call type or city of origin. These are brief, often cryptic messages to alert the agent to a call type and subsequent handling and script considerations. They are often used in conjunction with or replaced by display messages. They still have a strong advantage in the fact the agent does not have to look at the instrument to get the message.

Again, this feature is progressively being rendered redundant with computer telephony links and scripted workflow at the integrated desktop workstation.

Sign on, Sign Off: This is an important function. No ACD system should be without this. This allows consolidation of management statistics by the identified individual and not the hardware position. Before the instrument can become active, the agent must identify themselves. In doing so class of service properties are extended to this position. Individual statistics are then collected and may follow the agent no matter which instruments, groups or splits they sign on (and off) and work during the course of an accounting period. This is a boon to management as there is no more need to separately track which agent was where for what shift, hour, etc.

Unavailable: Activation of this key alerts the system to the fact this agent is temporarily unavailable for calls. The condition should be tracked and reported on by the system. Returning to the available state is done through use of the available key.

Work: This is a key that formalizes the wrap up or work state. Activation of wrap up may be associated with use of release on some systems or upon release require the agent physically enter this status by using the "work" key. It may also be used to track a staffed agent position when they are reassigned into an extended non call related state, yet still being accounted for by the ACD.

Exception Features

These can be individual keys or keys that are dynamically assigned by the particular state the agent is in. These are called "soft keys" and while they are assigned that function, depressing this key gets activates the feature expected. This however means the agent needs to be able to follow the LCD screen and know which feature to activate while concurrently working at a data screen. This is an elegant solution to reducing instrument size while adding features, however it adds eye fatigue to the agent as they are constantly reading two devices with different display technologies.

Acknowledge: When the ACD system has supervisor to agent messaging capability, some systems allow a single key stroke acknowledgment of message receipt by the agent.

Bad Line or Trouble: As some line failures are not clear hardware failures (a "hard" failure) rather a subjective or "soft" problem, such as line noise or low audio volume, agents must detect and identify the calls (thus lines) effected. This is done by depressing the Bad Line or Trouble key. Administrative alarms and reports identify the components handling the call transmission that could be causing the problem.

Help: Use of this key is to provide the agent some instruction on the operation of the instrument. This is analogous to the F1 key in DOS or the Help button in Windows, but without the information depth possible on a PC.

Emergency: Use of this key typically activates a tape recorder, alerts a supervisor and initiates a time stamped hard copy error message. The airline industry introduced this to record threatening calls. Use expanded to other applications such as agent training and sale verification.

Manual Operation: In those systems allowing bypass operation to the usual ACD instrument, this key acts like a switch hook. By depressing the by-pass key, upon notification of the arrival of an inbound call, (ringing and/or flashing light), the agent was connected the caller. Upon redepressing the key, the call was disconnected.

Mute: Depressing this key cuts of the "talk" circuit on the instrument so an "in person" agent to supervisor conversation can be had without the caller hearing, yet allowing the agent to monitor the "listen" circuit for any caller comments.

Park: Like "hold", this allows the agent to put more than one caller in a state of suspense. This is done by activating the park feature and sending the caller into a particular park address, identified by a number. More than one call can therefore be simultaneously placed in this state by one agent position. To recover each caller, the process is reversed, again by using the "unpark" code and recalling each parked call by the assigned "parking address".

Ring Volume Control: This may be a rotary knob or slide control that allows the volume of the ringer to increased or decreased. It also may allow complete silence.

Supervisor: Depressing this key alerts the supervisor, typically via a console message only, the agent needs attention. The supervisor may join the call as a third party, monitor the audio only or physically come to the agent position.

System Speed Number: This allows the use of abbreviated or speed dialing by the agent. Frequently used numbers are entered as one, two or three digits.

Again with the advent of the PC based integrated desktop workstation, alpha speed number lists can be presented in one of two ways, straight alphabetic speed number lists or context sensitive speed numbers lists based on "account type," "call or case state" and "help." That is the system only provides services and numbers germane to the account, the state of the account or the type of services needed based on a combination of the two.

Test: Depression of this key allows a local diagnostic sequence to test the agent instrument functions, keys and lights for problems.

Time: Depressing this key displays the current time.

Volume Control: This may be manual or an automatic gain control circuit that can be used to keep the transmission volume at a comfortable level. This may be a rotary knob or slide control that allows the volume to be increased or decreased. Some agent instruments use a code then repeated pressing of the same key to incrementally raise or lower the call volume on the listen and/or talk circuits.

Plain Old Telephone Or "2500" Set

Most telephone instruments evolved from the plain old single line instrument, most commonly found in residential applications. Plain Old Telephone Service or POTS has birthed a thousand innovations and the evolution of the plain black "phone" or 2500 set in American telephone company parlance is the modern original. If you have ever used a phone, its probably been a 2500 set. A marvel of industrial strength consumer electronics. A single line desk set is called a 500 set. The "2" in front means it's touchtone.

The rotary phone evolved to the touch tone phone with its 12 key pad, 0 through 9 and its two special keys. Only recently have these special keys come into use with voice response and station user programmable PBX and CO feature sets.

The touch tone telephone has 12 keys which generate distinctive dual tone multifrequency (DTMF) tones and a switch-hook. The switch-hook amounts to a control signal. As the station user goes "off hook", or depresses it momentarily, the controlling system is alerted the following signals are system command instructions, that is the beginning or the end of a call. The placement of the switch-hook is traditionally in the handset cradle, away from inadvertent activation, because along with serving as a control signal, other than momentary depression, terminates the call. A momentary switch-hook depression or "flash" became a standard telephone system station user originated alert or command signal. Using the switch-hook to send other command messages to the switch was somewhat successful but lead to great confusion. "OK, I'll transfer you but if I lose you, here is the correct number to call!!!"

The layout of the touch tone pad is an inverted numeric accounting key pad minus the decimal point key. Consistent with a numeric pad is the fact the "0" key is at the bottom of the layout, though centrally positioned as a single key, versus the double wide "0" key of a computer or calculator numeric pad. This is flanked by the special # and * keys. (Octothorpe and asterisk). There are many stories as to the logic of inverting the numeric pad. The most popular is the impact the inverted key pad had upon slowing the number entry rate so the central office technology of the day could keep up with the tone identification and disposition tasks.

The POTS phone remains a basic instrument and the telephone terminal of choice for very generic telephone applications. The TAP or Flash phone is a minor variant introduced to do away with much of the confusion which arose as out of using the switch-hook as both a command alert signal and as the call termination "switch". Replacing the handset or holding down the switch-hook ended the call. After extended conditioning of users to end calls in this manner, the telephone industry introduced feature activation via depressing the switch-hook and dialing additional digits. Residential call waiting is a good example of a simple switch-hook routine. The accompanying comment became "...if I lose you (during this process) the number to call back on is 1234". User hostile technology!

To reduce this confusion and allow increased feature use by station users, a number of telephone system manufacturers introduced a 13th key on the instrument, known as the (switch-hook) flask key. This reduced confusion and restored some confidence on the part of station users that use of the flash key did not threaten to end the call inadvertently. Others committed to extensive use of proprietary telephone instruments. With this strategy came increased cost

A number of ACD vendors used these Flash or Tap key phones as ACD instruments. The main advantage to using "tap" key instruments is the low cost and universal availability of these instruments. The disadvantages occur in the relative complexity of feature use, and consequent impact on productivity. To mitigate this confusion, graphic templates are regularly attached to the face of the instrument so an agent can "join-the-dots" to complete a transaction.

To further increase usability, optional display units are provided with the instrument. These are typically a separate alphanumeric display of showing call type, instrument status, time in this status and in some cases allow supervisor to agent messaging.

There is a clear limit to the number of features that can be accommodated on a 2500 set. Very quickly a point of confusion occurs in the sheer number of steps needed to activate a feature. Training becomes increasingly arduous as the number of steps required to activate features expands. Fortunately most ACD vendors have avoided the 2500 or tap phone in all but their earliest implementations.

Those vendors who embraced "flash" phones have attempted to simplify agent operation through the use of "join-the-dots" dialing templates. In most cases this solved feature use confusion in all but the most complex of operations.

Most companies are evolving away from the generic instrument in favor of proprietary devices, rich in features, yet simple to operate. They have validated the experience of the standalone ACD manufacturers who chose to develop proprietary "industrial strength" high volume agent instruments in the interests of operator speed. To be absolutely effective these instruments must be supportive and transparent to the role system performs to support the agent in the business function they serve.

The Proprietary PBX Instrument

The PBX/ACD manufacturers have long used their proprietary feature telephone sets as the ACD instruments of choice. This allowed them to use existing devices, parts and proprietary signaling plans. The majority of ACD systems use instruments that began life as PBX instruments. Most PBX\ACD makers have pursued this course. The advantage accrued because manufacturing and inventory costs were only incrementally more, as opposed to the manufacture of a completely proprietary ACD instrument.

The disadvantages are relatively minor unless the instrument began as a poorly designed device. Everyone of us has sat at a telephone instrument that offended us. It was cheap, the keys and buttons were illogically laid out, not large enough, crowded onto a small space, cheaply housed, offered poor tactile or auditory feedback. An early proprietary instrument which won many industrial design awards due to its aesthetic appeal and manufacturing ease became a hated

ACD and operator console due to the design of the keys. These were perfect cubic protrusions, butting up to one another in a visually pleasing manner, yet an operator, particularly one with long finger nails found the "splash effect" when hurried operation caused the contiguous key to be struck inadvertently. This led to all sorts of unintended results. No serious professional keyboard uses anything but chamfered keys to minimize this problem yet to this day many telephone instrument manufacturers still seem to ignore this reality.

Another issue with proprietary instruments is the labeling of the key Typically high use keys should be clearly and unambiguously labeled. The labeling should be applied in such a way so as not to wear off with use. Molded or gas etched keys are ideal. Keys with removable cuboid clear plastic covers are generally too delicate for high volume use. These covers are removable so the key function can be assigned dynamically. It also certainly indicates the instrument began life as a generic instrument.

ACD Instruments

The leading standalone ACD systems manufacturers chose to build their own transaction intense ACD instruments. These rather neatly reflect the era in which the instruments were designed.

One provides a sturdy, well-designed instrument. It comes in two models, the agent instrument and the supervisor version. They have as few keys as was felt necessary when they were designed (1973) yet the vendor has continued to add features through use of a shift key mode. The increase in features and changes complicates the use of the instrument, the agent training cycle increasingly points up the need for a more comprehensive key field. This company added an external display to allow increased status information to be provided to the agent.

A 1977 introduction pioneered the use of an expanded agent specific key field with increased use of status lamps and special key fields. In 1982 this company introduced a display instrument that showed queue status, replaced many of the binary status lights with descriptive status fields and provided alpha-numeric descriptions of call type, city of origin and supervisor to agent messaging. There was an oversized three line by about 32 alpha numeric character low power LCD display. To be seen easily though the LCD display must be at the exactly correct angle, lighting and proximity to the agent. This oversized display attempted to bypass this problem.

In 1987, came the most recent ACD introduction. Along with providing hard key feature definitions, this instrument adopted many of the context control and soft key lessons of PC software development. They use advanced call context control and dynamically labeled soft keys which followed the call state and can be programmed to follow a "data script" thus force the agent to follow a certain wrap-up sequence and enter certain data. Dynamically labeled soft keys allow the dynamic reassignment of key functions based on call progress and the logical flow the transaction is following. The system will not allow illogical deviations from the call flow as well as bring up the next support key complement, displaying the redefined key labels on the LCD display above the associated function keys. Using software definable keys increases the flexibility of the manufacturer and increases the life of the instrument tooling. Coupled with call context control also decrease confusion and speed training on the part of the agent. This vendor also uses an audio on-line instrument tutorial via the system voice messaging feature.

The vendors PBX/ACD vendors were introducing some of the display features into their instruments, but again in a generic fashion.

Terminal Displays

ACD and PBX manufacturers added displays using two methods. First they added them as internal devices. The first and most pervasive was the PBX instrument. Early instruments used light emitting diode (LED) technology, but this proved too power consumptive and often required an external transformer and power source typical of a desk top calculator. Later models switched to low power liquid crystal display technology, typically found in wrist watches. This display needs abundant light and careful positioning to be effectively read by the agent. The viewing angle is absolutely critical. The size, content and use of these displays varied with the manufacturer.

Integrated Telephone And Display Devices

The next step in the evolution of the ACD instrument is the integration of ACD instrument functionality into on single desk top display device. The long awaited integrated voice/data terminal. Early examples of these devices are seen as display components of some dataprocessing system, rather that a fully functional CRT/volume call handling devices. Three strategies have been pursued.

First was a single proprietary applications terminal with concurrent data entry and instrument functionality. Examples of this are found in plug compatible replacement terminals incorporating basic PBX station functionality in the device. To use these devices means replacing the entire CRT, and in the case of one vendor, the terminal communications controller technology. This has not been seen as a necessity by most data processing departments. Early examples could not demonstrate the superiority of such a combined device. Good examples of this strategy are being used in outbound dialing machines but have yet to make it over to the ACD business.

A second strategy allows for the preservation of some existing CRT workstations as an external knee well box, with the instrument functionality and applicable hardware technology brings the station instrument capability to a data only device. The only caveat exists in whether or not the CRT device can accommodate the voice instrument key functions on the existing keyboard or an additional outboard key field is required.

The value of this integration means a closer operational linkage can occur between the applications software, data gathering and telephone operation control. Secondly only one footprint occupies the desk. Early integrated voice and data terminal (IVDT) vendors erroneously argued fewer cables with lower installation costs and less confusion, were a benefit. The missing link was compelling applications. These were still terminals and had little local computing power to run macros or functions locally.

The most important value though occurred in providing the telephone rep with a single integrated device to interact with. Less confusion, less refocusing at different display devices and less station to instrument hand movement and most desirable, less training. It was not until Windows (or OS/2) and client server architecture arrived and matured, that the integrated desktop really flourished.

The third generation has occurred with the adoption of Windows and OS/2 based PC application shells which can incorporate a screen based telephone. By using Windows or OS/2 as the standard operating environment, any number of standards compliant applications can run in the device along with all the telephony functions in a "window." This is essentially "first party" computer telephony. Provided the applications are all DDE or ELAHAPPI compliant, the windows can swap data and commands based on links that are established by the programmer building the desktop environment. When these are integrated with telephone and computer functions, and the customer applications that may run on existing host or "legacy systems," a great deal can be done to improve productivity. All this can happen without complex mainframe code rewrites. Again we will discuss advanced customer call center strategies further in Chapter Fourteen.

The PC telephone connection

At this point it is necessary to discuss computer telephony architecture. There are two ways of building this structure best call first party CTI and third party CTI.

Third party was the first iteration of CTI. This involved a computer running a CTI compliant application, a telephone switch and a link between the two. IBM's CallPath is an example of this on the computer side. Transaction Link (Rockwell,) Meridian Link (Nortel,) and CallBridge (ROLM,) are examples of the switch side link. It is called "third party" as the device requiring the "action" must speak to the device required to "deliver" the action via a third party. Typically this is a gateway or emulation system euphemistically known as a "telephony server." It really is a gateway or translation device that adds an additional layer (and latency) to the process.

First party CTI is the opposite. The device which requires the action "speaks" directly to the device. For example, a PC running a number of local client applications talks directly to the server housing the account database for screen pop purposes, then through PC terminal emulation software asks the mainframe for the master account file data. This requires no change to the host application to become CTI compliant as it still thinks the "party" it is requesting data is a standard 3270 or VT100/220 terminal due to the off the shelf emulation software.

We will talk more about the detail of this operation as we move into operation and applications.

PC Based Telephony

There are five considerations when looking at PC based telephony;

- **The PC chosen (size and speed,)**
- **the operating shell (Windows or OS/2,)**
- **the effect of loading all the desired applications,**

- how the hardware connectivity is accomplished, and
- what are the redundancy strategies followed to ensure operation in a revenue and mission critical call center.

The PC hardware:

First, if your company follows the rule of buying the biggest and fastest machine available at the time, for a decent price, you probably have a number of generations of machines, speeds, disk capacities and software features. The minimum size required to run a screen based telephone appears to be a 486 or larger, and a 33 MHz machine or faster. A minimum of 16Mb of RAM or more

is necessary and a decent sized disk, (500 Mb or more.) The key here is that the additional process introduced by a PC based telephone and integrated customer call center desktop tasks cannot increase call processing time or call length.

Second, most PC systems follow some recognized standards. After saying that, there seems there is no such animal as a standard PC, as each vendor adds particular features and design enhancements they believe to offer a competitive advantage over their peers. Some of these do deliver true advantages. Again, these conspire to defeat a true standards based approach in installing the telephony hardware interface to every conceivable telephone system. With Intel building more and more of the whole computer functionality into prepackaged motherboards, it seems PC are moving closer to a predictable "standard" configuration.

Any PC device selection involves the classic compromise of immediate utility and productivity gains, versus the device's inevitable obselesence. This book does not purport to give advice on PC selection other than to say that the writer's experience, buying a machine is like "never being too rich or too thin," that is your PC can never be too big or too fast, therefore buy the biggest fastest machine you can justify.

The impact of nonstandard machines on telephony interfaces means the designer of the hardware interface, must make a decision where to place the telephone interface device. There are two strategies that providers of PC telephony interface pursue when they "load" the PC with the hardware connectivity portion of this integration: an internal bus based telephone board deriving its power from the PC or an external telephony integration device, deriving its power from the telephone switch. The positioning of this hardware is significant for two reasons:

1. The compatibility with your PC hardware. If your vendor has chosen to take the external box route means you are not tied to one PC vendor over the life of your customer call center.

2. An external box is generally switch powered with which frees you from dependence on the uninterrupted PC operation for continued telephone instrument function. ACD telephone systems are typically built with a great deal more attention to operation in a power loss or other crises.

Those vendors of PC and network systems typically did not anticipate these systems being installed in mission critical revenue oriented environments. Most early PC based telephony solutions do not anticipate the impact of a network or workstation outage. This will change. Only one vendor the author is aware of anticipated this and engineered around a PC outage. It looks less elegant, but it is guaranteed to work in mission critical environments.

The telephone device replacement hardware is attached to the telephone system as a normal extension. The hardware must then emulate the functions of the actual telephone instrument. Remembering that there are no standards in purpose built ACD instruments either, so every device must accurately reflect the existing proprietary protocols required by the particular switch manufacturer.

There is also the issue of connection to the telephone system, the company local area network and the host or mainframe.

1. **Attachment to the telephone**

This occurs just as an ACD telephone instrument connection occurs today. The difference occurs if the device is internal or external. The headset may plug into the back of the PC along with the extension line on the special card. This is less preferred due to the issue of standards, redundancy and access to the back of the PC. Try plugging in a printer port to an active workstation. Now change an RJ11 attached device? Cumbersome to say the least.

With an outboard box the size of a cigar box, plugged into a COM port for control functions, and the switch for telephone service at least you can make this accessible, not dependent on a standard PC chassis, motherboard and power buss. Although it is not as tidy from an engineer's perspective, it is available during a PC outage.

2.   LAN connection

This is accomplished via a standard LAN card. However after saying this, industrial strength LANs are slow to make it into the marketplace and still expensive from a hardware perspective. If your business is mission critical or revenue intense, an outage may render the cost minuscule.

3.   Host terminal emulation and/or connection

This can be accomplished one of two ways; by direct connection via one of the serial ports on the PC or via the LAN. In both cases a Windows compliant terminal emulator can be used. One argument you will hear from MIS organizations that are hell bent on protecting the host is PCs are unreliable and difficult to maintain and update software currency. Therefore promoting the keeping of mission critical applications on hosts and dumb tubes and therefore dependent on third party call control. In both cases they are partially correct, but they ignore the success, flexibility and resilience of client server applications and first party call control.

Buy cheap, get what you pay for! PCs are as reliable as most consumer electronics devices and provided you buy decent brands known for quality the argument becomes illusory. As we discussed above some vendors can ensure the voice connection remains intact even with a PC or LAN failure. Today, LANs are reliable enough to be considered essential business technology.

Maintaining Desktop Workstation Stability and (Client) Software Currency

The difficulty of maintaining software currency and desktop system standards is simply a matter of unrelenting policy, both internally and as purchasing standards.

      a.)   Set a minimum PC configuration standard for the customer call center PCs.

      b.)   Rigorously enforce it.

c.)   Capture the desktop environment.

Eliminate personalized screen savers, (Batman Forever goes!) personalized wallpaper, personal software, (a bootlegged copy of Quicken,) access to Windows Control Panel and any other extraneous routines.

d.)   Ban Visual Basic production programs from your desktops.

The name "Visual Basic" should be a warning in itself! VB is an iconized version of basic, a rudimentary programming language. Microsoft pushes this as a "quick prototyping" tool to build small Windows routines and demos. It is ideal for this as you can quickly show the look and feel of a planned program. However any VB programs are generally sloppy code at best and consume far more resources than necessary.

Windows 95 solves the problem of resources but begs the question.   With Windows for Workgroups (3.11) being stable with a vast software library written for it, why go through the pain of an interim upgrade to Windows 95, when its planned replacement, Windows NT is significantly more robust and due in mid 1997.

e.)   Insist on Auto-deployment of all client software.

That is ensure the vendor provides a server based routine that interrogates each new client upon log on for software version currency. If the server detects an out of date version, the latest version is automatically down loaded to the client and documented accordingly.

The PC Software

This is a very significant issue as establishing a standard software PC configuration and "locking this down" is essential to the survival and sanity of you customer call center management. This is inexpensive and can be accomplished with about 8 lines of DOS code in the server and client autoexec.bat. The efficiency and payback is phenomenal. Sneakernet is all but eliminated but for basic PC reconfigurations.

Chapter Twelve

Customer Call Center Management Information

Background

The information collecting, processing, reporting and presentation capability of an ACD is its most important feature. With information from the present and the past, you can follow the progress of your business, understand where and when your business comes from and how to best serve your caller. You can tell who are your most productive agents, groups and supervisors. From this data you can make predictions about the future (short, medium and long term). Coupled with a good forecasting, staffing and scheduling program you can plan and organize your trunks, staff and ACD to optimally meet the business demand callers and your business campaigns place on your customer call center.

The success of early standalone ACD systems can be almost solely attributed to the power of their inherent management information gathering and presentation ability. One manufacturer's survival in the marketplace was because of their understanding of the ACD application and their provision of high quality MIS and ACD features. This manufacturer continued to successfully sell application specific analog ACD switches against generic digital systems because the those buyers using these switches realized the cost of doing business with focused technology (that is at managing the application and customer opportunities, staff and network resources,) far outweighed the technical inconvenience of older technology versus modern but generalized hardware. Understanding the uniqueness of the ACD application protected their customer base and margins from undue erosions in spite of fierce price and feature wars in the PBX and PBX/ACD marketplace. The first true ACD vendor eclipsed the Bell electromechanical technology of the mid-seventies, as much with their ACD MIS, as with digital technology. Today their are extensive advances being made both in the development of onboard MIS systems and in the availability of external data gathering and support packages for popular PBX/ACD and CO-ACD (CENTREX ACD) systems. These advances are being driven by the explosion in desk top computing and PC software world. Color graphics and display techniques have benefited from PC and computer game technologies.

These techniques are making their way into real-time customer call center management tools.

These same PC advances have bought complementary advances in the forecasting, staffing and scheduling systems business. No customer call center manager with more than 15 agents can afford to be without such a system now these are priced less than $7,000. Implementing a good service level and staff scheduling package is worth a 15% savings or productivity increase by more appropriately allocating staff or adjusting the hours you are open for business to meet caller demand.

New customer call center management applications are being discovered daily. These range from in-depth media sourcing analysis, staff adherence, customer call and status tracking to common cross platform database administration, diagnostics and reporting. Essentially the customer call center equivalent of network management.

Customer Call Center Management Goals

There are four facets of management reporting, the data gathering, the calculation and report generation, and finally the presentation techniques. Management style and use of this data is by far the most critical to the orderly management and long term operation of the customer call center.

There are four management goals in a customer call center,

- **To effectively achieve the business objective(s) of the customer call center,**
- **Provide a satisfactory response to the caller,**
- **Develop the long term business vitality of the customer call center, and**
- **Do all of the above, at as low a cost as possible.**

To achieve these goals there are eight areas to measure, some objective, others clearly, subjective. Objectively, the quantitative or functional elements are;

1. **The revenue or result of the calls, and deviation from these targets,**
2. **Individual telephone agent performance,**
3. **The service level provided incoming callers,**

4. **Network performance, and**
5. **System component performance, (that is IVR/VRU, ACD, queue, route and host response.)**

On the subjective level, the customer call center must be able to measure:

6. **The quality of the experience (results) or the goodwill impact upon the caller,**
7. **The accuracy of the information exchanged or delivered to the caller, and**
8. **The skill, attitude and morale of customer call center employees.**

These items are measured two ways. By gathering objective device performance data and consistent observation of and research into caller and agent actions and behavior. Quantitative and qualitative data.

Quantitative Data

True ACD systems, particularly the standalone systems have done an excellent job of the task of objective data gathering, storage and presentation. The PBX based systems have done, and still persist, in poorly emulating the class leading standalone ACDs.

There are a number of data gathering quirks in the PBX based systems that severely compromise the accuracy and presentation "spin" of agent data. For example; a call is counted from the time of answer, not from the time of appearance on the line. This means dynamic supervision and delaying the call in this state is not only not measurable, but not possible. Because PBX based ACD systems still insist on two line or extension appearances for an agent (one for ACD traffic and one for extension (DID, outbound or intercom traffic,) separate reports are kept for one agent and two classes of traffic. Though much is made of the ability to present combined reports, much complexity is added to the process.

Qualitative Data

In the last editing of the predecessor book, The Incoming Call Center, we maintained that this could be done through market research and monitoring. This is still the case but now one ACD vendor has applied automation to the monitoring process. That is the scheduling and gathering of agent call samples by a voice processing process so as to eliminate the need for a supervisor or auditor to be available to gather the samples. However the subjective aspects of this function still lie with a live auditor. The application of this technology mean a massive increase in convenience for management and a significant reduction in the chore of monitoring. The other major benefit is that the machine will keep trying to fulfill the monitored call sample until the planned call count is met. More on this later.

Justifying An ACD Through The Reports

When buying an ACD, much is made of the amount of money the ACD will save in trunk and labor costs. This is probably true. However, these are not the areas where enlightened management ends up finding the big returns. The ease and convenience of gathering and reviewing the customer call center performance data, allows time to be spent analyzing behavior rather than collecting it to determine what happened. This convenience and resultant insight is a most powerful justification factor. However the largest return arises from the business insight management can gain from this system information and the strategic and tactical changes to maximize business opportunities that can be made.

In review, potential savings are normally given the greatest weight in an initial return on investment calculation and justification. The secondary benefits of management convenience and insight into strategic business opportunities are initially given less weight as they are considered less tangible. In fact these are the things that ultimately justify the decision after the system saved minor amounts of money. The writer was involved in an ACD sale in the early 80's when the buyer was determined to justify the system on savings. The second day of operation showed him he needed to double the size of his call center as his service was so bad, he was not capturing most of the business offered his company! This business opportunity was less than apparent in the previous environment, and although the cost of processing an average call dropped his operating costs soared, as did his new found revenue.

Data Gathering

"If you can't measure, it you can't manage it." Today, it is universally acknowledged good data is necessary to produce meaningful reports. However the question must be immediately asked, what basic data is needed? Call records generated by a PBX, key system or CENTREX are a start, but they are generally inadequate. Why? The underlying philosophy behind call record collection in an administrative switch is to provide accountability for call usage and provide usage data for network management. Here, call records are collected by station and trunk.

The PBX business called this process, "station message detail recording". SMDR data was kept for every completed outgoing call. Sometimes counts were kept of inbound and internal calls. All this was designed to help the corporate accounting distribute costs to the responsible department and improve telecommunications management. This data was fed through a process called "call detail reporting" to price the calls and produce reports. CDR software is typically found on an external processor. This did a fine job for the accountants and telecommunications engineers, but almost nothing for customer call center management, particularly those with inbound applications. This direction was generally dictated by the original purpose for which the machine was designed. A PBX is generally less concerned about data as the main purpose for which it is designed is as a switching facility. A true ACD system never seems to gather enough data, because the system purpose goes beyond switching to serving a primary business goal.

Meaningful Data

The majority of ACD systems now provide agent sign-on/sign-off features that allow the flexibility to assign and move staff to any position during the day without compromising the accuracy of the data gathering. This ensures and agent's statistics "follow" the agent. The alternative is to manually maintain a "who's on first" list and then sort the station data against this in an attempt to obtain personal report data from hardware statistics. The last generation of customer call centers had many junior analysts, first to manually transpose this data on to accounting spreadsheets, then to enter them into a PC spreadsheet program. This should no longer be necessary due to most ACDs now gathering data by individual agent identity and the growing availability of onboard ACD, or closely integrated third party add-on, data processing capability.

One major handicap that still effects many PBX based ACDs is that a separate extension exists for outgoing, internal or DID calls, from or for this extension. Data is gathered separately, thus no consolidated reporting is produced to show the total session for the agent at that station. Add logical identification and agents moving from station to station, or multiple shifts with a different agent manning the position during different hours and data normalization and accurate reporting are a chore.

Peg Counts

Surprisingly, nearly every system, including some standalone ACDs collect peg count data only and not the detail of every transaction. Any report is only as good as the data displayed. Garbage in, garbage out. Incomplete data in, incomplete and misleading reports out. Peg counts are essentially stroke counts of a particular type of event. Inbound, outbound and internal calls. The time it took to complete these transactions can now be divided by these raw counts to create averages. From these counts and averages reports are then produced. This is the type of data the early electromechanical ACDs collected. The Bell System developed FADS (Force Administrative Data System) and BOFADS (Bell Operator FADS) used this data gathering technique. This is the type of report that gave rise to all the early controversy of customer call center sweat shops. Average and inaccurate reports being applied subjectively is no way to run a business.

There is a clear preference among sophisticated customer call center management, for more data rather than less. It is almost impossible to predict the next piece of marketing and customer call center performance data upper management will ask for, therefore complete call detail captured and stored constantly is the ideal. To this day only the standalone vendors provide this. One vendor calls this "trace agent," after the ability to be able reconstruct and agents workday after the fact. In many cases, days after the fact. It may be a trunk, an agent, a call type, ANI number or any logically identifiable record type. A successful PBX vendor has a feature they call "agent trace" that in no way operationally resembles or is even in the spirit of the "trace agent" feature. This illustrates the confusion and apparent misrepresentation when a marketing department gets involved in explaining how things work. "Agent trace" is merely a "before the fact" data filter that allows the user to identify a certain type of call, AHEAD OF TIME, and have the system track and record those transactions only! With every system comes a crystal ball!!!

Transaction Detail Records

Transaction detail recording is essentially the collection of every event down to the keystroke level, so a complete date and time stamped audit trail is available for every circuit, system component and every telephone rep working the system and every call processed by the system. A transaction detail record consists of events, when assembled together amount to a record, complete or incomplete.

Why would a manager wish to see incomplete records? Failed and incomplete call events identify all sorts problems. System, trunk, people and training inadequacies. A simple peg count or "tally" of events does not adequately identify the "choke point" occurring in the call progress. A peg count is a raw number. A quantity with little qualitative flavor. Little or no subsequent analysis can be done on these with these numbers as they are conclusive or final numbers. In contrast transaction detail recording does not provide an answer but it can identify where calls fail. It is the raw data needed to assemble an operational picture of call center performance. These detailed records can pinpoint where the responsibility lies and provide the insight necessary to solve these productivity eroding and business blocking factors. A basic comparison is that of a bank sending you a one line bank statement showing you your beginning and ending balance, versus the transaction detail that got you from the opening to the ending of the month. That is the difference between the way a PBX/ACD and true ACD collects data.

In a customer call center, personnel and circuit productivity is measured by successfully completed transactions. If a call fails to reach the desired conclusion it still occupied a trunk, used the switch and took the time of a telephone rep. It is important to measure the total impact all transactions have, good and bad.

Why?

> **Inadequate network facilities?**
> **Inadequate ACD equipment?**
> **Poor queue management?**
> **Poor manpower planning?**
> **Lack of training?**
> **Poor morale?**
> **Poor scripting of the business transaction?**

On the positive side, this detail can provide strategic insight into where staff assets lie so they may be used to company advantage.

From a personnel management point of view, transaction detail data is both individual and unequivocally objective. There is little room for management interpretation. There is no averaging at the employee level thus much less likelihood of arbitrary and capricious conclusions that are possible with generalized or inaccurate peg count based reports. Any Human Resources department, worth its salt, should insist on complete transaction detail as it is both objective, equitable and legally defensible. In both a merit or discipline situation a complete audit trail is vital to document the good and the bad.

What Are The Data Elements To Collect?

The relevant events making up call records and then the individual audit trail are;

- Telephone rep sign on/sign off times,
- all event start and stop times,
- Call disposition for all complete and incomplete call events,
- Holds,
- Transfers,
- Three way conference calls (supervisor assistance, etc.,)
- The trunk used, in and out,
- The position used (calls to or from,)
- The telephone agent identification,
- any numbers dialed (out, internal or wrap-up) for call accounting, account and list management purposes,
- any numbers received from the network such as DID (direct inward dialing) or DNIS (Dialed Number Identification Service) for "media sourcing" or other purpose.
- any ANI numbers or account or identification passed from the network or an IVR.

There may be other digits transferred to and from the telephone position to be recorded for management of data directed transactions. The less information we collect, the greater the handicap we build into our future. Analysis can only be conducted on available data. The system cannot gather too much data. To effectively measure productivity of available resources, all relevant states must be tracked. Without complete data, true productivity management is as incomplete and ineffective as inaccurate reports.

Inaccurate Or Missing Data

If you discover your reports contain inaccurate data, throw them away before your agents discover this. Acted upon or distributed to agents, these reports will cause more damage to management credibility than missing data or absent reports.

Once an inaccurate report is distributed and potentially acted upon, the loss of subsequent management or supervisor credibility can be great. The energy and persuasion needed to restore the system to a semblance of its former credibility is extensive. Do not oversell the data gathering, processing or report production of the ACD. No amount of computing can "make garbage, gospel out".

"State" Or "Record" Machines?

PBX systems tend to be "record" machines. That is, once a call is complete, a call record is assembled and shipped to the MIS gathering device. This is ideal for after-the-fact call accounting because the PBX only shipped completed call records to the call recording system. This also means the MIS system receives dated data. A standalone ACD tends to be "state" oriented. It communicates a change in a device state almost as soon as it happens. This is much more work for the ACD common control processor. A PBX system controller does not typically have the power to spare to manage call state data. Hence the data delivered from a standalone ACD system is almost absolute real-time and in much greater detail.

This is important from a supervisor's point of view. If the data is not presented in absolute real-time, the screen view of their agent group does not reflect reality. If you can see an agent talking on a call, yet the screen says available, there is a element of distrust toward the system. This happens frequently in PBX based ACD systems for two reasons. The processor that is running the switch relegates data gathering and presentation as a lower task priority to switching calls. That is quite an acceptable design decision if the standalone competitors had not designed their systems more robustly so as not to do this. On major PBX/ACD vendor has so underpowered their PBX/ACD to the point it stops reports during heavy traffic periods, when management needs reports most! Supervisor screens reflect what was happening 30 seconds to a minute ago.

ACD Data Collection And Storage

Some ACD systems, particularly the PBX based systems maintain the call data in volatile system memory. Should the machine "hiccup" during the day, this critical data can be lost. No reports will be available for that shift or day. If they are, they will have "lost" an hour or so of important data. Check how your potential vendors collect, store and write data to memory.

The answer you are looking for is that call detail is constantly and continuously written to disk so that up to the instant of failure, no data is lost. The three major standalone ACD vendors provide redundant MIS options, so that the MIS processing is never lost either.

Is storage of call records volatile (RAM) or more permanent such as tape or disk? In most ACD systems the production of scheduled reports does not interrupt data gathering. Can the ACD manager create ad hoc reports from the stored data on the ACD or is this an off line process requiring another computer system? Most systems require a separate system.

The Human Resource And Legal Implications

This is a big objection to every PBX based ACD system as they DO NOT capture every event in the machine and store it for later audit trail reconstruction. This is particularly significant when it comes to human resource reporting, merit; reward and discipline actions and challenging unfounded unlawful dismissal and unemployment claims.

The writer has always been surprised that the standalone ACD manufacturers do not actively pursue this feature against the generic report gathering capability of the PBX based ACD and older designed standalone ACD systems. Millions of dollars a year are lost to customer call center management in unjustifiable paid unemployment compensation or settlement of nuisance claims for unlawful dismissal. Historically most companies have allowed this to become a cost of doing call center business, as the most ACD system documentation has been indefensible.

Most of these machine report data in snapshot form from volatile memory, once the report is created and printed the data no longer is available. And it was summary data to begin with any HR policy would define as less than objective

With the transaction reporting and after the fact audit trail detail from the standalone ACD vendors, and the new qualitative reporting systems that are becoming available, customer call center management is beginning to particularly successful in their objection to and defensive of unjustified claims. This is money that remains on the bottom line, but only possible with complete, objective and accurate data gathering.

Integrated Data Gathering And Reporting

As an important aside, PBX based systems tend to require every position have a station appearance also. This is the station address an agent is reached by should a supervisor (internal call) or other party (outside call or DID) wish to contact them. The line which inbound ACD calls appear on is separate. A directory number (DN) or call vector number. The system collects statistics for the ACD directory number as ACD reports, and if any, separate statistics for the PBX extension as SMDR detail.

This is a definite disadvantage for customer call center management. The data is both fragmented and provided in a different form. Productivity management only applies to ACD work not the administrative extension traffic!! Most PBX/ACDs work this way. This is also true for DID calls which now account for a third category of transactions. Though this may seem a trivial limitation at the system acquisition stage, it adds real effort, confusion and cost to subsequent daily center management. Often to the point of deemphasizing this. It is important all call transaction data be integrated into one uniform set of data in one database. Managing multiple formats on multiple databases creates needless management overhead, not to mention muddles the objectivity of critical people management data.

Secondary Queue Reporting

Secondary queue reporting is another critical feature now that IVR or voice response systems make their way into customer call centers. Queuing structures are a great deal more complex. Typically in a call screening or prompting scenario, the caller elects to use the voice response system in lieu of a live agent. This may occur after the caller has already encountered a primary queue. For some reason the call scenario, following the voice response device, now requires the caller to be sent to a live agent group. This agent group is currently busy thus queuing all inbound calls. This caller has now encountered a secondary queue. In most cases this caller, although reentering the ACD from a functionally separate process, has already been queued and deserves some priority. From a management point of view the call needs to be tracked through the secondary queue state. If the caller abandons and the call is not tracked as a caller encountering a secondary queue, the call processing scenario can not be accurately measured. The primary queue statistics are inflated and the VRU data is fragmented. Few ACD vendors grasp this problem. If they do, even fewer have a coherent solution.

Skills Based Routing

One PBX based ACD has an even more confusing habit when the skills based routing feature is used. As an agent identifies themselves to the system as having certain skills, the system signs them on into a number of target vector groups as an "expert agent." For example, lets assume an agent is identified as being an operating system specialist for the MacIntosh Power/PC that speaks Spanish. The system recognizes them as three people, producing real-time screens and historic reports at three (count them....3) FTEs. Reports become garbage, forecasting systems don't work and the whole basic ACD MIS thrown into doubt.

Report Development And Presentation

The maxim, "if you can't measure it, you can't manage it" bears repeating. This is heavily reinforced by the fact "reports must be easy to use, or they wont be". Management style normally takes the course of least resistance because there are many other pressing tasks. The more readable, the less interpretation and the more self evident a report is, the more useful it becomes as it is passed up to higher management. This can be a powerful factor in ensuring customer call center management success. Computer generated reports have a certain, yet not totally justified, credibility.

If the obvious and readable, without assistance of an expert, they carry more weight. "Mr. Controller, as you can see by the graph, we are losing 25% of our calls, we are wasting enormous opportunity. We need budget approval for an increase in staff to capture the revenue potential offered by those callers. Our call to sale conversion rate is 45%, therefore those abandoned calls amount to $XX dollars!!" Seeing is believing.

If the reports are hard to read or filled with jargon, they will be ignored. Transposing them to alternative forms, a memo, a spreadsheet or a Lotus 123 or Excel report, erode the power and credibility of the ACD report. There is little reason not to use plain language (English) in ACD reports. Many machines do not and this has created the opportunity for the boom in add-on report packages which repackage the data in readable formats.

Add-On ACD Report Packages

These systems generally take the data already provided by the PBX/ACD system and present it in a more usable form. There is a great deal of activity in this market with no fewer than 14 companies providing these systems. There are two types of reporting packages:

1. **Management Report Enhancement**
2. **Staff Management and Service Level Forecasting**

The Report Enhancement systems all run on IBM PC or compatible systems and add real value to the system they are installed with. The machines they typically target are the most frequently encountered in the marketplace. PBX/ACDs and CENTREX based UCDs. Staff management and service level forecasting packages are found at both PBX/ACD, CO-ACD and standalone ACD sites as they provide critical value and management time savings. There is a increased blending of these functions. A number of PBX\ACD vendors in recognition of reporting and competitive advantages inherent these systems are endorsing software developers as partners in advanced customer call center systems, CO ACD vendors are establishing relationships with external MIS system vendors as a enhancement and competitive edge.

The Reports
Introduction

Report presentation offers another area for failure for an ACD developer. Traditionally switch manufacturers thought of producing reports as less important than switching. The switch system is the focus of the effort and once complete, report data gathering and presentation is left to the least qualified to develop. Almost as an afterthought.

Understanding the origin of most telephone systems, explains much of the philosophy behind switching applications. Technology drives the telephony business. Technology once drove the computer business also, until vendors found selling advanced technology only became a handicap. More time was spent explaining the technology, than the real business value the technology brought to a business user. Most telephone switching applications unconsciously consider end user management reports an afterthought. Designed and developed with little or no research.

Formerly the dominant aspect of the ACD application at many companies was queuing, prioritizing and switching of customer calls. This telephony bias caused the success of many standalone or niche vendors who have focused at customer call center management issues equally with switching. Fortunately there is a shift occurring in the telephony industry. This as a result of competition as much as a concern for the end user. Considering end user needs is still being reluctantly replaced by market research and response to business needs.

Reporting Capability

Good data first. This is a overwhelming priority in the design of any tracking and reporting system. Report effectiveness is based on the depth of data gathered. Building a data gathering, normalization and storage of a usable database is everything.

There are two basic medium to display data. Real-time via a display or by printing paper reports. These may provide tabular alphanumeric data or information in the form of graphs and charts.

Real-time displays present data "as it happens" or as nearly current as possible. There is a clear advantage to providing up-to-the-second data. Many systems, particularly the PBX based devices, claim to have up-to-date CRT displays. On further investigation these turn out to update anywhere from 15 to 60 second intervals. The data on the screen is a rapidly aging "snapshot" of the reported period. In a large and busy ACD, by the time the data is painted on the screen it is already out of date. In some of the PBX based ACDs, the "real time" displays and report become progressively dated or slowed down in a busy call traffic period as the switching of calls is made a priority over the administrative report functions. The standalone ACD systems build around this using dedicated dual switching and reporting processors that do not share tasks. A load on one does not impact processing on the other.

True real-time displays are not repainted or refreshed, rather the individual fields making up the screen display change and update as the individual agent status, service level or count changes. Real-time means real-time. What you see on the screen is indeed what is happening in the customer call center.

A CRT display that is perceptibly behind reality lacks credibility and becomes unimportant to a supervisor. It reports an agent as being busy, yet looking at the agent in the customer call center, the supervisor can see they are now idle, and vice versa.

Each manufacturer has chosen one of two processor strategies. One central processor running the switch and the reporting or a down line processor that runs the reporting system separate from the switching processor. There are two issues. First, how much horsepower does the processor have available for gathering, processing and displaying data. In the case of a second device, what is the processor overhead and response time penalty paid for the inter device communications and data processing and display. Modern technology and techniques have solved both of these problems but the telephony business has been slow to adapt these to switching applications. Again changes are now occurring. Many of these are being used to update older systems to extend their life and provide more information than ever before. The outboard PC MIS providers are the leaders in this change.

Each vendor includes different data in these real-time displays. The single most important consideration is doing away with buzzwords, acronyms and codes. Numbers and acronyms mean the machine needs experts, or highly trained personnel to use the device and read the reports. This retards acceptance, extends learning cycles and the use of the machine and reports by management. Demystifying the ACD is desirable. If it is not easy to use, it wont be. If it is not easy to understand it will remain remote from the mainstream and certainly will not be exercised to its full extent. Alphanumeric data is more easily offered in real-time than graphic data. The latter requires far more computer power and time so the real-time slows down. Anywhere from 2 to 10 seconds after the event. The tradeoff is the increase in speed and capacity in communicating information by using color versus the slow down in real-time. Most of the leading ACD vendors, particularly the standalone systems offer downline graphics reporting packages or interfaces to popular PC spreadsheet programs.

The Reports

The reports provided by the majority of ACD systems fall into three categories;

Primary Reports:
- ☐ **The service level provided to incoming callers,**
- ☐ **The call applications,**
- ☐ **The trunks, and**
- ☐ **The agents.**

Secondary Reports:

- [ ] System diagnostics,
- [ ] Component usage, and
- [ ] Alarm conditions.

Exception Reports:

- [ ] Call wrap-up or call disposition,
- [ ] Exception lists, and
- [ ] Ad hoc user reports.

Primary Reports

Service Level Provided To Incoming Callers

NOTE WELL

Most well managed customer call centers are staffed close to the optimal at most points in time. The use of service level reports aid in the "tuning" of this balance of staff to demand. When unanticipated demand arises there is little dramatic that can be done to solve extraordinary problems. One call center manager wisely observes that current staffing and operations policy reflect the last crisis.

The basic reason for the use of an ACD is to ration your precious staff resources, agents and interactive voice response devices, across a larger universe of callers. If callers believe you are not answering their inquiries in a responsive manner, they perceive you do not care. Callers may abandon their attempt to reach your customer call center. They are now considered lost opportunities. Lost revenue, lost goodwill, yet there were substantial costs incurred to encourage them to call, and to have them wait, yet not receive service. To understand how often and to what extent this occurs in your center, two report groups should be available.

Incoming Call Waiting Information

First, the real time CRT display should, among other data, display a count of calls currently being held in queue. This data, along with the status of individual agents (busy or not), allows a supervisor to make minor adjustments to the center to capture a few more calls. Ensure as many agents as reasonable are available to serve callers. Adjust the group to group call intraflow so as to optimize capture opportunity. The periodic reports provide the average delay and hopefully the longest delay encountered by a caller in the reported period. This data gives insight into how long the typical caller waits. A daily summary should give a spread of the caller delay encountered over the day and not simple daily averages.

It is important to understand delay tolerance by caller type, by business type and time of day. We are seeing increasing interest in analyzing call business type and delay tolerance based on simple geographical and chronological issues. The generalizations of a New Yorker being willing to accept less of a queue than a Midwesterner turn out to be fallacious. New Yorkers' accept orderly and informed queuing better than a laid back Californian. This gives rise to another whole view of reporting, particularly when you consider the business type and value of a call. Add a interactive voice response device and there is another view needed.

Repeating a "old sore", with one foot in a bucket of boiling water and the other in freezing water, on the average things are quite comfortable. In fact the tyranny existing with averages, is to hide the worst in a rather benign "averaged" number. The better ACD system designers realize this and give averages as a broad guideline only and provide the "worst case" delay hold data also. The fact transaction detail is available on line allows exception reports to pull out even greater depth.

Incoming Call Abandoned Information

This data is rather meaningless to display on a CRT. The event is over and there is little now that can be done to correct for that call. The data should be provided as detailed "after the fact" reporting providing the ability to determine what queue the typical caller will tolerate at different times of the day. Most desirable is a call aging profile showing at what point in the queuing process, callers abandon. From this data, agent groups can be expanded and contracted, announcements, script and timing can be changed, intraflow between groups within the ACD or interflow to other sites can be considered. A subtlety that cannot be emphasized enough is the necessity to track calls from supervision in, and measure the call from its appearance, not simply answer. This way you can tell if any inbound event is a call or not, thus measure true traffic occupancy and circuit health.

A third and increasingly encountered piece of information is the real time service level calculation presented on the supervisor screen. This is typical of the more feature rich standalone systems. A service goal is established such as "80% of the calls answered in 20 seconds". The system then calculates what percentage of total calls answered by agents, met that goal. This adds to an already intense situation when little dramatic can be done to improve the immediate call capture rate. Histograms and graphic report representation are a great advantage in clearly showing the relativity of this data, both the goals and to different periods. This type of reporting is becoming increasingly popular though has been available since 1977.

The Call Applications

It is important to treat callers with a similar request with consistent service. For this reason call type reports are broken out by application, group or split. These are typically overview reports displaying the data by the originating trunk group. If the system supports any trunk identification   services, sorting calls by the inbound identification digits, such as the DID   or DNIS lead number, is also advantageous.   The data provided should include   number of calls offered, handled, delayed and abandoned. These should be expressed as relative counts and percentages. All trunks busy data and average service levels are also handy.

The Trunks

Trunks are arranged in physical and logical groupings.   Trunk group reports generally report like trunks.   From an ACD management point of view, they should be reported as trunks carrying like call types, then arranged in like trunk types. This way the business responsibility is reflected first, then the engineering issues second.   A subtlety, yet critical from management   convenience and insight.

The line use data displayed on these reports, at minimum should include call count, in and/or out, totals, abandoned, average length, trouble data reported by the agent or hardware problems, time out-of-service, time in use. It is desirable for the system to collect and display this data as individual trunk   statistics and present it both as split or group reports and assembled it in   logical and useful time increments such as clock and calendar. If the system supports any trunk identification services, sorting calls by the inbound identification digits, such as the DID or DNIS lead number are also advantageous. Faith in this data is assured as in the event of some anomaly being identified, having the ability to go back and reconstruct call by call reports.

With the availability of Automatic Number Identification (ANI) there is now a need to analyze call source by geographic origin. The potential for advertising promotion, support and service level and market penetration analysis is significant, though the full extent of call source and marketing media effectiveness is yet to be realized.

The Agents

Agent productivity is held out as the largest single efficiency gain to be had from these machines. This was probably true before it was rediscovered most employees do the best they can while they are working. Give them better tools and they will do more. In fact the power of an ACD is in the ability to take an individual employee's average performance and make it better. Without burning out the employee. Move bell curve forward. The real power of agent productivity reports is the fact the machine tracks all activity, does it in a constant and objective manner, then provides clear, detailed and understandable reports.

In a good ACD no additional interpretation is needed. In this day of full disclosure, an agent is entitled to see these reports and will probably unheeded, act upon them. Most ACD systems today collect data by individual. Management labors under an enormous handicap of uncertainty if they do not have this feature. To review individual productivity without being sure the data reviewed is about the subject is fallacious. Ideally agent report data should take two directions. One, as overall performance measurement and the other as individual activity. The objective in separating the approach is to enhance overall management oversight, yet lighten the management load of tracking individual detail unless there is such a requirement.

These machines have the ability to produce "blizzards" of report data. This is undesirable. Management has little time and even less interest in this detail, **unless there is something wrong**. The collection of transaction detail versus peg count data now becomes incredibly important. A manager can only trust high level reporting strategies if they know, should there be a problem, they can recover the "blow-by-blow" detail. Literally, "unpeel the onion."

A manager can scan an overall agent force productivity report and determine all is well, or note any exceptional trends needing attention. Individual activity reports are critical. These have value in merit and disciplinary reviews, as they provide a complete audit trail of all activity over the period in question. One standalone ACD vendor feature is "TRACE AGENT." The system allows the manager, once a problem has been discovered, to reconstruct an audit trail of all the events an agent was involved in. It allows this to occur after the fact. A major PBX/ACD vendor has introduced a feature they call "AGENT TRACE" as a competitive answer. The not so subtle difference is you must anticipate the problem and "turn on" the data gathering "filters" to capture the expected information. Sadly, a crystal ball is not supplied with this PBX. The whole point of the ability to recover raw data is to reconstruct activity of a past time period after discovering there was a problem.

Agent performance reporting should include sign-in duration, count of all incoming, outgoing and internal calls, totals, average duration of all these events, and analyze the time the agent spent in the various work states while manning the system. Agent activity reports are the individual call or transaction records, for all events the agent was involved in over the studied period. Data should include the event type, the disposition, start time, stop time or duration, call origin, call destination and all digits dialed by the agent, delivered by the network or entered by the agent as call wrap-up or cataloging information. Again it is desirable for the system to collect and display this data as individual agent statistics and present it both as split or group reports and assembled it in logical and useful time increments such as clock, calendar and also shift periods.

Secondary Reports

System diagnostics and component usage

The system should watch itself and warn management of potential problem conditions. This is important from a trunk availability and quality point of view. Many conditions exist where a trunk is out of service, or the sound quality eroded to the point of effective failure. A hardware failure is clear to most machines and they will report it accordingly. A circuit quality issue however is more subjective and typically is only discovered when an agent receives or places a call. The agent should be able to report this via a "bad line" or "trouble" key on the instrument. A failed or poor quality trunk negatively impacts service levels. Other system components also should be tracked and reported. Both as to availability and adequacy of the amount in the system. As most systems provide a number of utility devices to support a given application (tone detection, recognition, generation, etc.) too few can lead to blockage. Tracking their operation and adequacy is important. The ability for a vendor to draw this data off the system via remote diagnostic capability assists in many ways to accelerate diagnostic and service action.

Alarm conditions

Most systems provide a series of one line alarm reports that are printed as they occur. Trunk out of service, failures to respond, "hung," all trunks busy, and line trouble conditions, to name a few. These ideally should be coupled with alarm notification at a supervisor CRT. This avoids constant checking of the printer which is often installed remotely from the supervisor consoles.

Exception Reports

Call wrap-up or disposition

Although these reports are gaining in importance they are not universally available from ACD vendors. These are increasingly useful to analyze the many categories and subgroups of calls and the many alternative call results. The key to the success of this feature is twofold. First, the ability to enter data at the telephone instrument that can be used at any time. No complex planning or programming is necessary to set it up. Merely notifying your staff they are expected to add some data (obviously uniform numbers (keys) and fields) for each call via the touch pad. Secondly, that the results can be sorted and analyzed at will by customer call center management without external data processing resources. This is an extremely desirable, flexible and powerful system feature. One standalone ACD vendor has gone as far as to "script" and validate this data entry so agents do not make mistakes or overlook this data entry.

Exception lists, and ad hoc user reports

Most ACD systems provide standard report formats. Also with the advent of PC systems, exporting call data has become increasingly popular direction. The advantage of being able to sort call records on some exception criteria allows greater understanding of the data. Few ACD systems include this feature as part of the ACD software. External systems bring this, provided the call transaction data was captured and is easily available to analyze. A number of recent announcements allow the call data to be exported in LOTUS, EXCEL or other standardized ASCII format.

Report Use And Management Style

Customer call center management is both a company and a personal style, therefore the only comments that can be made here, are to discuss a few simple success strategies.

The most important issue surrounding report use is how the personnel productivity reports are presented to customer call center staff. Are they a whip or are they a carrot? The most successful customer call centers tend to take the latter approach using the reports to chronicle success rather than poor performance. Reports can be posted or copied and distributed to the agents. It is important they be accurate, clear and self explanatory. It is important they be distributed without initial management comment. The perception should be, the first people to see and study reports, should be the people measured. If they are delivered to the subjects, with management comment, the reports take on the overtone of "a report card". Self motivation is generally acknowledged to be the best method of staff motivation. This is not a one time event or a sprint, but an ongoing juggling marathon. Using an agent's self image and peer acceptance in an enlightened manner is the least threatening method of having your staff meet your joint customer call center performance goals.

Human Resources Implications

Over the last few years the whole notion of employee productivity reporting has taken on more legal implications than was ever intended. The fact employees are evaluated, rewarded and disciplined based on data and reports produced by a switching machine can become legally significant. Human Resource departments are particularly concerned about precision in data collection and presentation because the process and the results can easily become the evidence in discrimination and unlawful dismissal.

This takes on significant implications when you look at the ACD offerings of various companies. None of the PBX/ACD systems collect precise call by call data, rather hash counts, time and therefore averages. This is heighten by the fact they adhere to physical data collection, then extrapolate to logical units, i.e. an agent! If an employee was to challenge this data in a court of law, and the employee's lawyer had any idea how bad the data is, (they deliver separate ACD and administrative data as an example,) the case would be decided in favor of the employee and the employer could be sanctioned for arbitrary employment practices.

The only reason this has not happened is no lawyer has identified call centers with these PBX based ACDs to be at risk or gone after apparent "industry abuses" with a class action suit. It will happen. The vendors of standalone ACD systems are deliver far more robust reports that are less questionable and therefore deserve to be considered more conscientiously based on the risk one accrues just doing business in such a litigious employment climate.

Developments In Report Provision

Recent developments in reporting strategy include greater use of graphics and color.   Although this is an obvious strategy in the PC world, this has been relatively slow to arrive in the ACD world. The cost of adding color was minor in the context of total system cost and minuscule compared to the impact. Originally however, switch designers reluctantly added colored supervisor screens because of the initial additional cost and the processing overhead added to the management report process!!!

Pictures allow more information to be communicated more quickly than columnar or narrative data. Hence the popularity of business graphics and charts. Color adds a further dimension in speed of communication and depth of information understanding Supervisors can make judgments about customer call center service conditions by looking at their screens from a distance. General appearance, screen hue and color can be scanned quickly and understood rather than reading and comprehending the individual screen detail. This can occur for a roving supervisor over a short distance.   This is even truer in historic reporting when a graph can show the immediate relativity of otherwise dry numbers.

By adding PC systems to do the actual supervisor or administrative data presentation functions, much of the reporting load was shifted off the switch to an outboard processor. But with this went the immediacy of a real-time picture. This is because of two added processes that occur when the function is moved out of the switch processors; transmitting meaningful data to another computer, the receipt and processing of that data into graphical reports. Every processing step adds time. It is important to note the difference between "state" reports and historical reporting even though that "history" is as recent as the last minutes. A state report should not tolerate any delay. You have a problem now, display it, and allow for immediate review. A trend or problem occurs over a period as it builds or declines. This can tolerate some delay in reporting and trend analysis. Again 30 to 60 seconds being about the most acceptable.

There is still much talk of arrival of "artificial intelligence" in the ACD world. That is allowing the ACD system to learn how to optimize itself based on prior successful treatment of similar conditions. Remember an old investment joke about the technology of "artificial intelligence." It was something you announce just before you take the company public! The new appearance of the term is "genetic algorithms," as in machine evolved code, that "promotes" success and "extincts" weakness, thus finding the best way to do things. This type of machine learning depends on accurate and "honest" reporting, thus further adding to the need for serious call centers to focus on ACD systems with significant processing power.

Here is a dichotomy. As ACD systems matured, customer call center managers wanted more and more reporting. This added a significant burden to the ACD system and vendors as they strive to answer all possible customer call center requirements. The obvious solution was to add relational databases, and ad hoc spreadsheet reporting tools like Lotus 123 or Excel or a data export feature to their ACD systems. But many customers remain uncomfortable handling their own data in this fashion and insist on packaged reports. Either way, access to your customer call center data is desirable even though your system can produce "101" different report formats.

Fewer Reports and Reconstruction of past call center data

As customer call center managers became more sophisticated and mature in their role they grew to trust the machine data more. At this point they need fewer but more comprehensive reports. Everything they need to know to manage should ideally appear on one report. This is the ideal for an insightful manager. Trust in these type of reports is only possible if management is aware they can go back to the ACD and recover past detail. Less is more, as long is more is still available if it is ever needed. This is a big objection to every PBX based ACD system as they **do not** capture every event in the machine and store it for possible audit trail reconstruction. This is particularly significant when it comes to human resource reporting, merit; reward and discipline actions and challenging unfounded unlawful dismissal and unemployment claims

Quantitative and Qualitative Reporting

More attention is being paid to the quality of the customer experience at the "hands" of voice response technology and live agents. This makes for a new generation of reporting opportunities.

Major New Customer Call Center Management Processes

1. Quality Assurance, Service Observing Or Monitoring

This leads us to the subject of monitoring, a greatly over-debated subject. The reason for this over-debate is past and rather dumb strategies employed to motivate large groups of customer call center employees. The old phone companies were known for running operators centers with the working conditions two or three degrees removed from slave ships of old. Unfortunately some of the fears of employee abuse and misuse of report information were not unfounded. Today widespread abuse and misuse is generally unfounded but as, there are always a few extreme incidents that trigger union and legislative reaction. The customer call center monitoring and privacy debate of the last decade is a product of this. A bad manager, will probably always be a bad manager and depend on subjective data, bias data gathering and interpretation to prove their point.

As we discussed previously, most ACD system reporting is completely limited to quantitative, not qualitative reporting. A market differentiator now becomes quality management tools. Most standalone ACD system vendors have rung all of the efficiency possible out of call application based switching. That is the efficient connection of the call. The next area is the content of the call. Hence the thrust in to analyzing and reporting the quality management process.

Positioning and Labels

Today tools exist to gather objective data and thus position your monitoring as quality assurance. The first point of positioning is the careful selection of the names and titles that are given to the process. In some companies, "monitoring" is the preferred function name. It eliminates any ambiguity in what the short term goal of the process is about - monitoring what is said between the caller and agent. It however gives rise to a significant possibility of "them versus us" management problem.

A better position is that of quality audits and ensuring customers get the quality service, the accurate information, in a manner consistent with the policy of the company and the mission of the customer call center. Call auditing or quality reviews are better labels and do not attract the attention of your legal departments like the term "monitoring." If Detroit can inspect their work product, why can't a service company, particularly a customer call center.

Maintaining quality is essential to profits and the survival of a business. Recruiting your agents to this cause is the best method of deflecting any criticism. "Why would we want our customer call center to do a bad job?" Back this up with objective data gathering and enlightened management use and their is little likelihood of problems.

It is critical to the monitoring process to have clear objectives. Any measurement process must be measurable, objective and repeatable. It also important these goals and the use the data will be put to, be clearly communicated to the agents to be monitored. This may be done at the time of employment, having the agent agree to accepting monitoring or service observation as a condition of employment. Informed consent is a sound basis upon which to begin this process.

The goals of monitoring are:

    1. Ensuring the quality and consistency of the contact the customer has with the company and the customer call center. Making sure the information exchanged is adequate, accurate and delivered in the manner intended. Training and customer call center script guidelines are important starting points for any monitoring strategy.

    2. Ensuring any orders taken, are genuine. Many customer call centers pay incentives to employees upon a customer order or commitment, long before the customer pays for the goods or services. Order "verification" is essential to prevent "soft" orders or outright fraud. Monitoring is a deterrent to this type of activity.

    3. The maintenance of agent productivity in a customer call center is an ongoing task. To monitor intermittently and give the agent force the impression this is a halfhearted effort is to invite an erosion of quality and productivity.

There are few secrets in a customer call center and as soon as monitoring stopped or was restarted, the entire staff will find out and react accordingly.

4.   Individual performance is the basis of most merit raises and compensation plans. The attitude the agent projects to customers on the telephone is a component of this review and cannot be measured without observing the agent on the phone.

Regulatory Background

There is a minor degree of uncertainty to secret or silent monitoring or recording. Each state has differing legal requirements which typically can be obtained from the American Telemarketing Association (818-995-7338) or The Direct Marketing Association (202-347-1222). The proposed or existing state and Federal legislation falls into three categories. Laws are based on concepts of privacy protection, preventing illegal wiretapping or interference with confidential transactions. Your legal department will probably do what most legal departments do, go and make a project our of researching the subject to justify their existence. They will come back with a resounding "maybe," when they find their is no clear prohibition of monitoring, but a suggestion that recording of review sessions might be illegal under laws, the spirit and intent of which, was to prevent illegal behavior, not prevent the measurement of quality customer treatment.

Typically your customer call center is affected by three different jurisdictions that have something to say about monitoring. They are;

1.   The Federal laws dealing with interstate commerce

The mooted Federal legislation originally promoted by The Communications Workers of America (telephone operators belong to this union,) has ground to a halt, mainly from disinterest. Prohibitive regulation got significantly diluted from the original union hope for blanket prohibition of draconian, or for that matter, any monitoring. When the issue of customer call center quality assurance was made known as the real objective of monitoring and not interfering with operator privacy, reasonableness became an issue and the original sponsors' objectives became significantly less important.

b.   The states have legislation with varying levels of restriction.   The state legislation varies:

- ☐   **from no regulation,**
- ☐   **requiring one party (to the conversation) to consent to the monitoring,**
- ☐   **two (both parties) party consent, or**
- ☐   **to absolute monitoring prohibition.**

In the case of "one party consent laws," you are required to seek consent of one party to the conversation. This is generally of the person to be judged by the monitoring session. That is your agent. This is easily done by making consent a condition of employment.

In the case of "two party consent laws," gaining consent from the caller is more troublesome. The simple approach is to add a initial announcement that may go something like this....   "to assure the information you receive from Acme Computer Company is accurate and given in accordance with company policy, we may monitor this call." This occurs at during the greeting announcement. Though this will please the legal department as it is an "active" statement and gives the customer the right to act then and there, that is hang up! However it is impractical and inadvisable because of two issues;

- **a.**   The additional time added to a call to give such notice, and
- **b.**   the "kill" effect it may have on your business.

Callers can make a decision to hang up, so you lose a prospective customer or alternatively, stay on the line then involve the agent in a discussion about the fact your customer call center monitors calls.

Alternatively, you may add a monitoring disclosure statement to any contract the customer may sign to do business with your company, for example a loan agreement.   This states that "for quality assurance purposes, calls may be monitored from time to time." Adding a disclosure to invoice language or other customer communication is also an option. The problem the lawyers have with this approach is that it is a "passive" disclosure and does not give the customer the opportunity to act on the information, short of discontinuing their business with you.

Either way, announcement or printed disclosure, if people don't like it they are going to go elsewhere with their business. The most logical strategy is to disclose the objective of monitoring is in the interest of customer receiving quality service and doing it in a written form. It has less of a "kill" effect on calls and it does not impact call length.

c.   **The state utility regulations and maybe, the state penal code** may also say something about illegally monitoring a confidential conversation.

Again the spirit and intent of this type of law was generally directed at prima facie illegal behavior, not quality assurance and consumer protection. Your legal department may trot this out as the objection.

Despite many legislative attempts to circumscribe this business right, no where in the United States is it banned outright.

Conclusion

In this writer's humble and impatient opinion, the point of monitoring is to ensure quality customer treatment and consumer protection. Being discouraged to monitor, based on legal confusion and uncertainty, is more of a business risk than a legal risk. The question becomes can you afford not to care and do something about quality assuring your customer call center's work product?

BIG WARNING!!!
Still, check with your lawyer!
Telcom Library made me write this.

The Process

There are three points of a call that observation and measurement can take place:

- ☐   **The call data as gathered by the ACD,**
- ☐   **the actual call audio, and**
- ☐   **the call data session as used by the agent to serve the caller.**

These should reflect the

- [ ] **quantity of calls,**
- [ ] **the quality (sampled,) and**
- [ ] **results of customer call transactions.**

As the transaction happens, numeric data is collected and reported in real-time (supervisor's or reviewer's screen) or with after-the-fact statistics. This comes from the ACD. The service observation or monitoring refers to the recording or listening to the audio portion of the transaction between the agent and the caller. The final element is the use of a mirror of the data screen session the agent is working from to serve the caller. Ideally the monitor or reviewer needs to see the state of the agent being monitored (the supervisor screen,) and the data session they are working from, while listening the call. In most call centers the last element, sales results or a service request outcome, or however your call center defines a "successful" call conclusion, is not included in this measurement or transaction. Consequently there is an incomplete "performance picture."

Manual Monitoring

If monitoring is done, manually, in real-time, concurrently with the agent receiving the call, a supervisor or reviewer can select the particular agent's data screen in a mirror form. They can also concurrently watch a supervisor screen so collection of status and time counts can be written down from this screen. The monitoring supervisor should keep a detailed record of who and for how long each agent was observed. Be extremely careful in giving each party fairly equal attention. If there is a problem and one agent is identified as needing further attention, document this before resorting to extended observation. More recently service observing this has expanded to include the supervisor or trainer watching a mirror image of the application data screen the agent is currently working.

Real-time Session Review

This means the call is being monitored in real-time. That is a supervisor or reviewer must be available as the call is being received by the agent. The problems with this real-time approach are fourfold;

- [ ] **Monitoring is no supervisor's favorite task,**
- [ ] **scheduling monitoring sessions is not simple,**
- [ ] **there is always a more pressing task that interrupts this chore, and**

☐ extensive manual documentation needs to be maintained to make the review worth anything, particularly if the review has merit, compensation or discipline implications.

There is a bank in California that has a policy of monitoring 12 x 3.5 minute calls per month per customer call center teleservices representative. There was no way they could do this for 1500 agents per month easily, so policy was seldom met. The agents knew this, and worked accordingly. The customer call center management realized they were doing a less than stellar job in this area, wanted to be able to add an incentive portion to their compensation plan, and instinctively knew their were opportunities they were missing in training. They were acutely aware of the haphazard state of their documentation procedures. More in a moment.

Recording a Call Session

Alternatively the call can be recorded, typically on tape. But this means the real-time view of the agent state is lost as is the real time mirror of the data session, unless this can be recorded and played back concurrently with the voice recording. This is not a simple technology.

Automated Monitoring Systems

Recently a new genera of call center quality assurance products have been introduced by a leading customer call center vendor. These products have been so successful in filling this niche that a number of this ACD manufacturers archrivals in the ACD switch business, have agreed to partner with this vendor to sell these products.

There are three products to the customer call quality assurance suite and these are:

1.) The sample scheduling, gathering and playback system (data or sample gathering)
2.) A companion, call template builder, scoring analysis and documentation subsystem, (review scoring and analysis system,) and
3.) A data session sampling and recording system that matches a call recording to the recorded data session (voice and data session synchronization.)

This product assures a scheduled call quality sample, and that all agents, provided they are scheduled, will receive similar sample. Predictability and certainty are two key elements to quality assurance. The system releases the supervisors to the immediate role of supervision, so that the review role can take place at some later and less pressing time.

i) Data Gathering: The call scheduling and sample gathering system is a cross between an intelligent "tape recorder," even though it is digital recording on disk and a voice mail system.   This computer based system allows management to schedule the agent session samples to be recorded and then played back at some later time by the reviewer. During this review, the reviewer can then "cut and paste" certain call segments into a voice mail like message to be played back to the agent as necessary. The result is to free the reviewer from being available when the agent is available, and then wait, listening to silence, partial calls or the wrong type of calls to conduct a meaningful review.

The advantages of intelligent recording are many;

1.   It frees the reviewers from the tyranny of having to be present to listen to an customer/agent call, then "catch" an eligible call, meanwhile listening to all the other things that transpire in an agent's day.   The net effect is to reduce the time taken to complete the review task by 50%. This is achieved by recording a session and then playing back everything, skipping or cutting out incomplete or inappropriate calls, with the silence eliminated.

2.   Any measuring and scoring system only works when it is perceived to be certain, objective and repeatable over the universe of subjects to be measured.   In many customer call centers, monitoring has been a policy that is intended to be carried out, but inevitably takes the lowest priority in a manager's day due to more pressing tasks.   Monitoring defaults to an expendable function when any customer call center crisis occurs, no matter how small. Suddenly the necessary notions of certainty, objectivity and repeatability are lost and the value of monitoring degraded.   Just as with ACD system reports, any error or inconsistency debases the principal of credible reports. So too with quality measurement.

3.   The use of such a system assures that monitoring and sample size policies are met.   The system will blindly gather the required session sample until the quota is filled.   Human resource policy is met.   This goes a long way to dissipating the flaw in most measuring or monitoring practices.   That of incomplete or substandard data samples.

4.   An old gardening adage applies; "just walking around the garden with a pair of hedge clippers makes everything grow better!"   So it is with systematizing the gathering of monitoring sessions.   This assures the agents of predictable and certain reviews.

5.   Market research: One of the largest benefits to any corporation is to have key executives close to the business so they can understand and run the business to reflect the needs, wants and perceptions of a customer.   Getting a president to come to the customer call center and listen to customer calls is nearly impossible, however giving them easy access to a customer call sampling system, can create real convenience and get the company closer to the customer base than ever before.   This is a major feature and benefit of this type of system

6.   Finally, schedules, samples and reviews are rigorously and automatically documented.   This is a key issue for any human resources review,   If you have a policy it must be adhered to and applied equally across the applicable employee universe.   Then it must be fully documented.

WARNING:
CAN THE AUTOMATED MONITORING SYSTEM
<u>UNEQUIVOCALLY MATCH THE RECORDING TO THE AGENT?</u>

There are a number of companies offering recording and scoring systems, but they cannot guarantee the agent being recorded is indeed the agent scheduled to be monitored. This again is this physical extension vs. logical identity of an agent. A system without "follow the agent" cannot guarantee accuracy and therefore should not be used for merit or discipline reviews. Bad ACD data falls into the same category.

In a recent case illustrated this most dramatically.   A large California bank which employs this technology successfully challenged a former employee's claim for unemployment compensation.   Historically this bank had not challenged these claims as their monitoring process almost never met the policy plan, so if challenged inevitably showed that the process was unintentionally unequally applied to all employees.   Such was the nature of a manual system. Now with a system that collects these samples with certainty, with time and date stamped sample, review, and the time and date the subject employee heard these annotated review sessions, the bank had documentation of equal application.

They were able to stand before the unemployment compensation review board and absolutely refute the dismissed employee who, based on past manual practices, claimed he was never reviewed, never counseled or disciplined.   The bank could show time and date of every recording session, management and employee review.   They could also play the board the recording sessions showed the employee violating policy.   For the first time in the history of the bank, the teleservices department won an unemployment hearing and did not have to pay the justifiably dismissed ex-employee.   This was not their stance prior to

employing this technology. The savings in unemployment compensation has been dramatic and more than paid for these systems in the first year of use.

ii)   Review, Scoring and Analysis System

The first component of this suite is simply a voice sample or call session data gathering system.   The second component is the review system.   The system allows the construction of a call review template for each call type or class of agent.   This template is basically a list of all the call or script elements your company deems important or necessary in talking with a customer or prospect, to achieve a particular type of transaction goal.   The issues may be the relatively objective, the presence or absence of a script component or a more subjective, value based judgment.   Binary values are assigned where a   "yes/no" measurement is applicable such as "did the rep use the standard greeting?" or "did the rep identify themselves?"   Other issues such as agent attitude and presentation delivery, which require a more subjective value, where degrees of depth are associated with the issue require subjective or value (1 to 10) judgment.   Different templates can be set up for different call types, customer applications, agent types or skill levels.

The reviewer may listen to the call session samples from any telephone anywhere, using a voice mail metaphor. As this proceeds, the call type template is applied and each relevant call milestone or issue is noted in the review for presence or absence or where more subjective, assigned a value in a range of values, typically a 1 to 10 score. The addition of the values, creates an overall score for the observed quality of this transaction or session.

As we well know, a busy agent may indeed meet productivity quotas, but at the expense of company quality, policy or sales objectives. The opposite may also be true. The charm of this type of product is to be able to rank the quality performance of the subject agent, draw productivity data from the ACD MIS and balance the productivity (number and average length of calls handled,) against the quality scores and even sales results. This results in the ability to develop an X/Y "scatter chart" to compare performance across agents, groups and even the monitors or reviewers.

By taking the calls, by agent or group, and placing the data on an X/Y/Z chart it is possible to determine where training is most effective or alternatively where shortfalls occur. After evaluating the quality of customer experience, the secondary goal of the reviewers is to find the "best practices" in the call center

from a script, objection handling, close or customer mollification perspective, and "clone" these best practices across the customer call center. Individual agents inevitably take company policy and intentionally and unintentionally modify this to get the best personal results. Ultimately they learn more about the call process than management. But typically most management does not have the time or tools to analyze this work process evolution. In most cases it remains transparent to or out of reach of management. This is where the real value of this system comes in. It allows a manager to analyze the strengths and weakness in customer request handling by agent, and determine the most profitable, effective and "customer friendly" way of reaching a conclusion that benefits the customer caller and the company.

Without a disciplined and automated way of gathering these samples, integrating these with ACD MIS call handling data, the review and analysis functions simply do not occur in a way that can be effectively reviewed and used to optimize agent behavior and productivity.

The benefits are overwhelmingly in favor of the technology. They provide agents to the agent, the reviewer and the customer call center owner with significant benefits.

Benefits to the agent are:

- ☐ Predictable,
- ☐ Objective and
- ☐ Equal across the agent population provided the schedule assures this.

Benefits to Supervisors are:

- ☐ Freedom from being on the phone concurrently with the agent and caller,
- ☐ Can review sample calls from any phone, anywhere, any time,
- ☐ Can speed the calls up to twice the speed of the actual conversation,
- ☐ Can skip forward, back and over call segments,
- ☐ Can annotate call segments and return to agent for informal review, and
- ☐ Can perform the monitoring function in 50% of the time it takes to perform manually.

Benefits to Management are:

- ☐ ensures equitable treatment of all agents,
- ☐ "Reviews the reviewer" to assure equal agent reviews,
- ☐ allows a complete record to append to personnel files,
- ☐ ensures any monitoring sample sizes and policies are universally met,
- ☐ Provides a documentable program to use in agent disciplinary disputes,
- ☐ Allows identification of individual and group strengths and weaknesses so training can be adapted,
- ☐ Allows identification of "best customer call center practices" for refinement and cloning across the customer call center, which can lead to call length reduction and significantly happier customers.

☐ One of the largest benefits to any corporation is to have key executives close to the business so they can understand and run the business to reflect the needs wants and perceptions of a customer. Getting a president to come to the customer call center and listen to customer calls is nearly impossible, however giving them access to a customer call sampling system can create real convenience and get the company closer to the customer base than ever before.

A major California bank has used these technologies as an aid to reducing call length in their teleservice centers. A year ago the Bank had an average call length of 188 seconds. Today, through "best practice" cloning, they have reduced the average call length to 144 seconds. Automated monitoring and scoring has provided the automated sampling and scoring ability to identify the best agent processes for various call types.

This is truly breakthrough technology as hardware vendors push more into software based value engineering in customer call center equipment. As of this writing, the vendors of this equipment are primarily selling these as yet another standalone call center management device that begins to deliver a more complete picture of the actual agent or group or "rolled up" performance of the complete customer call center in two of the three measurable dimensions. The quantitative (ACD MIS reports) and now qualitative, (monitoring systems reports.) exist. There is still no direct integration of the "results" of the call volume by agent or group.

Chapter Thirteen

Integrated PBX/ACD vs. The Standalone ACD?

Pleasing Customers, Call Center Managers and The Company Accountants

There is an ongoing debate amongst vendors and telecommunications departments about the best decision to be made here. For users it is clear.

What customer call center ACD system will provide the tools that will:
- [ ] *help guarantee customer service levels,*
- [ ] *conveniently,*
- [ ] *provide unimpeachable personnel review documentation,*
- [ ] *provide the greatest strategic insight to the business,*
- [ ] *at the lowest possible lifetime cost?*

And The Answer is....

Remember few people buy more than one ACD in their careers so they have little experience in this area. Most vendors have little experience in building true a ACD, so how could they be experts? The things you don't know about system operation can cost you a fortune in daily operating expenses, even though the PBX based system was half the price of the standalone system. An extra twenty extra agents can cost you $1,000,000 extra a year. Half a million more spent on a standalone ACD may pay for itself in six months if you have a customer call center in excess of 120 agents. That is a decision any accountant would love.

Here is why:

Doing an apples to oranges comparison of any alleged peer technology is not a simple task. Although 90% of the systems appear to be the same and the feature defined as being similar, implementation can be dramatically different. This can impact operational efficiency.

The Technical vs. User Buyer -- Opposing Goals and Mind sets

Remember the difference between capital goods and operating costs. A technical buyer will buy based on feature content (typically feature count) and cost. A user is left to manage operating costs over the life of the system with shallow features that do not address many of the daily customer call center management issues with incomplete tools (feature depth.) Add to this the way a technical buyer is judged, which is similar to the user buyer. How much money did we avoid spending to get an ACD? The truth is they have very little stake in lifetime costs, therefore are at financial opposites with the user buyer from the beginning.

The Differences

Standalone ACD systems are frequently benchmarked against other ACD systems by various end user customers and these are constantly rated as the most efficient and productive ACD type available. The test is in the percent of available time of position occupancy per agent. The best ACD system delivers 70 to 80% agent availability. The next best is in the mid sixties with the least efficient standalone being in the 50 percentile, as are most PBX based systems.

One customer call center in the cellular phone customer service produced this "before and after" data following replacement of a popular PBX/ACD with a standalone system:

	Before	After	Effect
Calls Handled per day	16,000	24,000	50% increase
% abandoned/day	13 - 17%	3 - 4%	300% decrease
Average talk time	160 seconds	149 seconds	saved 11 seconds
Service level (80x 20)	unmeasurable	86.6 %	exceeded goal
Customer callback %	57%	42%	149 hours of calls avoided per day!

The additional irony was that this cellular telephone division of a large Bell operating company can buy PBX based ACD systems from a sister division at a greatly reduced "family" rates.   The fact they do not speaks volumes to the modest weight to the cost of acquiring the technology versus the loss of operational efficiency.

A similar mind set was shown by IBM when they owned ROLM. Their operating units continued to purchase a competitor's standalone ACD rather than their own ROLM PBX based ACD for service and sales customer call centers. They understood the way their business and management would be compromised by the lack of user management features in a hybrid PBX/ACD.

This efficiency and ease of use is why standalone ACD users are extremely loyal. The standalone ACD vendors are still unique in a number of call center management and reporting strategies, keystroke level data gathering (only two vendors do this,) complete HR audit trail reassembly, productivity and quality management and inherent time clock and payroll interfaces. It is surprising that after having many of these business features for up to 15 years, the PBX/ACD vendors have still not copied these key standalone ACD call center management features.

Part of the problem is that a number of switches began life as generic switching machines and have been adapted to applications specific roles such as an ACD, without having the physical or logical architecture required to support true ACD operation. All of the PBX based machines trace their physical architectural and logic origins to the mid eighties. And as such they still reflect many of the limitations they were born with.

The best way to compare operation is to trace the path of a call and contrast call processing steps and alternative methods of making process decisions and measuring the processing milestone. A call has a life in time, even though it may be milliseconds in the case of an incomplete call. Nevertheless this is a traffic event that potentially displaces a customer call and the call center manage needs to know about it.

When is an inbound call a call?

From a customer's perspective it is the point of a call being dialed to a vendor's number. Beyond dialing a wrong number, the customer call center needs to know the call exists. Most machines do not recognize a call as a measurable call until supervision is returned to the CO and the call answered and billed for. However by taking this position an ACD vendor has ignored a number of operational realities.

1.   A call center does not want to answer a call until an agent is available or until a point of queue intolerance is reached by the customer. Using a VRU is

no different than an agent resource if they are all busy. If a call is only measured from supervision return, "spikes," "glare," premature hang-ups and failed calls are never recorded, or alternatively, answered by the ACD.

2. By using answer supervision (or supervision out) as the call start, you cannot dynamically retard supervision on the basis of appropriate agent or VRU port availability. This is because two issues are overlooked. First, you can measure the call or event from appearance, that is supervision in. Yet you do not have to answer the call immediately, thus you can retard answer and billing and use the inbound CO ring cycle as an active part of the queue process. A customer will accept up to four or five rings, (24 to 30 seconds) without hanging up. This assumes that the trunk card is "logically attached" to sort of resource interrogation sequence that says "if a call appears on trunk X, what am I to do with it?" "Then is the target resource available?" A PBX machine drives the answer decision into trunk based firmware, that answers every call on supervision in as there is no resource interrogation process attached to this firmware until after the call is answered!

A PBX based ACD vendor will reply that they can delay supervision to reflect one or more ring cycles. This however is a fixed cycle (time based) that still ignores the dynamics of call center resources. For example, an agent or VRU port can become available to serve the call in this preset delay cycle, but the call cannot barge out to an available agent because of the logically uncouple resources. This issue is brought about by architecture. It effects all PBX/ACD machines. The standalone systems from Aspect, Infoswitch and the Rockwell Spectrum are exceptions. This is one small reason the standalones get greater FTE time out of ACD positions than other ACD switches.

3. Because calls are measured from supervision in, the customer call center manager can actively use ringing as a queue factor. Infoswitch customers enjoyed this feature for a decade before anyone else added it to their system. The three major standalone ACD vendors now offer this. They measure the call from supervision in, and differentiates between pre and post (supervision out) answer for purposes of accurate abandoned call reporting and trunk diagnostics and performance.

Selecting an Agent

The next issue is selection of an agent. This is accomplished in one of three ways; top down, round robin or most idle. The addition of skills based and overflow routing are variations on these schemes, all of which have very appropriate application. Despite the fact that UCDs are held in contempt as old technology, their routing strategies (top down or round robin) are ideal in certain conditions and the standalone ACD systems reflect this requirement in route table options. Most PBX ACDs allow one or other strategy (round robin or most idle.)

PBX based machines originally accomplished routing by using call forwarding and overflow processes, with a freelist as an interrupt strategy. A true ACD uses the freelist first and uses overflow as an interrupt strategy.

Additionally, the standalone ACD systems originated the notion of expanding the available agent pool, no matter what group the system was addressing. The PBX/ACD use call forwarding principals, snap shots and loop back (a.k.a., a "branched GO TO.") The implication is to defeat economy of scale operation to not reduce the speed of answer and not optimize available staff resources.

Most systems allow overflow (intraflow or interflow) to secondary groups and agents, but are they SIMULTANEOUSLY looking at a group considered more ideal for answering the call? The goal is to expand the universe of agent service possibilities, not substitute another group. The impact is to stimulate traffic and workload in areas which are less desirable. PBX based systems claim overflow and lookback but is never true multistage, simultaneous list interrogation. This is because they are primarily designed as "event," not "state" machines. They take "snapshots" of the group as they do not have the processing power to manage all port states simultaneously along with the ability expand the polled port universe as a true ACD does.

Then if this overflow occurs, are the calls tracked across subsequent groups to determine if the call should go where they are desired, thus allow the customer call center to optimize group size and load management? This is limited to the three standalone ACD systems.

This doubly complicated when a caller is switched multiple times between VRUs, agents or transfers. In most systems, the call not is tracked throughout its life as a customer experience, but by device, target answer group and its discrete performance! The standalone ACD systems are unique in solving this problem in various ways.

Event vs. State Machines

This is a very key issue. An ACD call is about seven time more complex to process than an administrative call. This is arrived at by watching how many PBX stations are displaced when a busy ACD group is added to a theoretically full switch. Typically it ranges from 5 to 7 PBX stations based on the manufacturer. This is due to the traffic demands of call center resources (trunks, VRU ports and agents) and the processing horsepower required for the ACD SWITCHING and data gathering function only. MIS is normally performed down line by a secondary MIS processor.

A true ACD is a state machine, which means it manages the call state by scanning the ports and network setup much more frequently than a PBX based machine. In conjunction with state measurement, it must manage the call treatment route table for this call, unique and logical event identification, state, target, call age, condition changes, clock data for each call, and gather all of the milestone data for the call for real-time state reporting (supervisor console,) administrative and accounting reporting (historic reports.) This requires significantly more processor power and storage than most PBX based machine can be configured for. The impact in a busy hour is to have "slow" supervisor consoles and retarded reporting while the PBX switch is busy processing calls. These vendors have a "task priority stand down sequence" to protect call processing as the highest priority. Although this is a desirable customer oriented strategy with a "throttled" machine, building a machine with the required processor power is a better alternative. The standalone ACD vendors prefer this strategy, hence the higher capital cost of entry and lower cost of operating expense.

Call Data down to the Character

Most desirable is that every call state and "keystroke" character be recorded and written to the database for service and resource management. Infoswitch pioneered this in 1978, and today only Aspect and the Rockwell Spectrum have adopted this strategy also. The standalone ACDs, because of their complete data gathering, are generally acknowledged as having the best ACD reporting available.

PBX based machines generally only collect call hash counts and from this develop summary reports and averages. They cannot provide an after the fact audit trail of historic call data for a given device, agent etc., no matter how recent. One major PBX vendor does provides an alternative, known as an "agent trace" filter which allows the user to anticipate a problem and set a filter to trap call event meeting filter criteria. One standalone ACD vendor's "Trace Agent" (approach is to capture and write to disk every event character (port id, clock, keystroke, network derived DID/DNIS/ANI numbers, or agent derived dialed number out, or wrap up characters.) This is believed impossible on the current generation of PBX based ACD systems.

Now that Human Resources has gotten into the act and is looking more closely at objective, measurable and repeatable standards for call center employees, PBX based ACD systems fall far short of the mark in collecting or delivering accurate and objective reports.

Customer call center managers regularly use agent detail data to defend unwarranted unemployment compensation claims. At one California bank this is proving to save a significant salary expense. This would be impossible without transaction detail reports unavailable on any PBX/ACD. Other ACD vendors cannot do this, and no PBX vendor can warrant the accuracy of your reports. If a disgruntled agent ever understood the way data is gathered on a PBX or an ACD of older manufacture, they could have a significant action against any ACD user who rewarded or disciplined an agent on the basis of these inaccurate ACD reports. Most customer call center operators, in an assumed trust of their accuracy, blithely use these reports to review, reward and fire agents.

Conclusion

You be the judge. Because as business and service delivery systems demand more and more accurate data, and applications specificity, reporting detail cannot be sacrificed just because the purchase cost is a couple of hundred grand less.

How do you tell a sales vice president of a health maintenance organization the service performance guarantees and case tracking he is competing with from Insurer A cannot be delivered with the PBX/ACD technology your call center has. It is happening in leading edge industries now and will spread to all service delivery and customer call centers within the next few years. It is one of the compelling business reasons for considering an application specific customer call center ACD and computer telephony integration.

Acquiring An ACD System

Throughout this book, we have discussed the applications and issues involved in using an ACD system. We have spent little time focusing on the ACD acquisition process. The politics of buying a system are complex and unique in each situation. A hallmark of this book to this point has not been to show money saving techniques in acquiring an ACD, rather explaining why spending a little more money wisely at the outset, can save and win vast amounts of revenue and goodwill for your company over the life of the system. Revenue in amounts that far outweigh the few relative dollars invested in the system most appropriate for your application.

Strategic Buying

It is said today, buying is more difficult than selling. There are many potential antagonists in this process particularly if you are buying on the behalf of a modern corporation. There are political issues to contend with in the company. First, there is recognizing the need and gaining the blessing of upper management for the project. This itself may be a hurdle. Information exists in Chapters One , Two and Six to help you place the costs of not upgrading the call center and accepting poor service levels and losing business opportunities. The second set of antagonists are the other interested political entities within a company. These may be the telecommunications, data processing, administrative and financial departments all who may get involved in the acquisition process. This book is aimed at assisting the end user navigate their way through this process. Most sales or service managers typically have few opportunities in their career to acquire large capital items for their corporation. Conversely, few technical buyers have the opportunity to buy call center equipment throughout their careers also.

The customer call center management has to live with this system decision everyday. The results produced by this center are directly effected by the ACD. The reports which flow from this system document that success or failure of the customer call center mission. From their point of view, there are two, maybe three, prospective allies or "obstacles" to obtaining what the end user needs to get the job done right. The client department head (sales or service?) is the greatest ally. The technical departments (telecommunications and/or MIS?) will be involved because these systems involve telephone lines and computers. The financial and/or administrative departments who oversee capital expenditures and administer the buying process.

Expect to see any human resource group in you corporation begin to take an increased interest over the next five years. Quality, "quick response" and "high reliability organizations" all depend on well trained and responsive people. The issues of training, quality control, responsiveness, morale, incentives and compensation depend on management and their ability to gather and analyze quantitative (objective) and qualitative (subjective) data. A sales or service representative is a highly studied employee. This raises employee relations issues which human relations departments care about. The biggest thing they care about is equality of treatment and accurate employee review data. Reports and review processes must be beyond question.

The Politics Of Purchase

There are the user, technical and financial interests to be considered in this purchase process. Each group has their own set of objectives. Each contributes a different skill to the buying process. Each is goaled and judged differently. Traditionally these buyers have been the end user buyer, the technical buyer and the economic buyer.

The user buyer or user department often initiates the idea to buy an ACD. Often they are the recommender and often the source of the funding for the purchase. If the budget is under the control of the user the acquisition is much simpler. However, because this is incorrectly viewed as just a "phone system," the budget may lie with the technical buyer. The end user is the actual user but ends up living with the results of the purchase on a day-to-day basis. The big question for the end user is how will this ACD work for me. How much more business can we win and keep. How will it make my life more convenient and how much operating expense can it save.

The technical buyer is generally a telecommunications specialist, or more recently a management information systems manager. These individuals are under enormous pressure to keep costs under control and keep systems compatible. The time and effort spent keeping abreast of their respective fields leaves them little time to keep up with each end users individual tasks or problems. Technical buyers understandably have little time to really get into the customer call center application and buy the best solution for your day-to-day needs. The technical buyer is often the recommender or the technical "referee". Seldom does the technical buyer say yes to the purchase but may deliver an absolute veto due to the technical incompatibility with the companies technical direction. The questions asked by the technical buyer are;

1. **Will the system do the job?**
2. **Does it meet the quantifiable specifications?**
3. **What are they?**
4. **Are these compatible with our corporate technical direction?**
   a. **Vendor(s),**
   b. **Computer platforms,**
   c. **Operating systems,**
   d. **Applications languages,**
   e. **Communications protocols, and**
   f. **Local area network standard.**
5. **Do we know the vendor?**
6. **Does the vendor meet any corporate "selected vendor" purchase and support policy?**

These policies and specifications are heavily influenced by what the technical buyers know about particular applications.

If you have a "one vendor" telecommunications policy but that vendor provides a mediocre ACD, why blindly adhere to policy and compromise your business? Here is a major educational challenge. The end user buyer must intimately understand their business and business goals. Here there is an obligation on the customer call center user to learn what customer call center systems do. The better vendors are excellent at educating customer call center management. Build alliances with members of your technical departments. Get them educated. This can have great effect when it comes time to select any end user technology. The decade of the 90's has already see sales, marketing departments buy more technology than ever before. Become an applications resource to the technical buyer and provide intelligence and insight into the application so features and functions take on real meaning.

Many end users have been thwarted by failing to recruit the technical buyer early in the process, winning their confidence and assistance by understanding what the minimum technical standards are, then investigating within those guidelines. If your selection of vendors meet those company guidelines, your job is easier. The recommendation comes as with no fundamental surprises and the technical buyer cannot claim to be blind-sided. In the selection of call center technology, look beyond corporate guidelines as typically these favor big telecommunications manufacturers who don't tend to make robust technology for niche markets. ACDs are such a niche. None of the major telecommunications manufacturers offering "comprehensive solutions," have technical leadership in customer call center systems.

On the other hand the technical buyer may claim this area is their exclusive domain. Influencing their applications understanding is then the default tack. The financial or economic buyer is often the decision maker. At minimum, the deciding vote. This individual is aware of the larger issues in a corporation and applies this special knowledge to this and other purchase decisions being made in the corporation. What impact will this purchase have on the system generally and will it provide a return on investment within current corporate guidelines? There may be a fourth element in a corporation assuming the user buyer does not already be part of this power bloc. The sales and marketing element of a corporation has a tremendous interest in winning and keeping customers in the most cost effect way. Recruiting these groups as allies can greatly enhance the process of acquiring the most revenue and cost effective system.

The dynamics of this buying committee is the balancing of the end user getting what they need or wanting a "cadillac". The technical buyer blessing the technical acceptability of a number of machines and the economic buyer getting the "best deal for the money". There are three votes and they are loaded in favor of the "best technically qualified system for the money", not the best for the job. The end user buyer has the most to lose and the most to win by managing this process well. Good Luck.

The "Standards" Battle

Watch for the cry of "the proposed system does not meet corporate standards" therefore it won't fit. Standards are generally promulgated by some industry committee or are as a result of a dominant vendor, and these are just fine as a pure technical argument. The problem is standards are developed way behind the arrival of useful applications and vendor breakthroughs which your business wants to take advantage of. I have just spent three years watching a really major bank lose time implementing a really leading edge client server telephony integration approach to teleservices management, because client server was not something they embraced yet as they were insisting on all vendors meet their mainframe CT standard. Today the user still waits, while their competition has a already deployed the same technologies. Watch out for the standards argument. It is generally a last gasp of a dying elite, who are trying to hold onto a mainframe way of doing business in a fast moving era of PC driven developments. PC developers are less shackled with a past way of business.

The MIS Department of the 90's

There has been a dramatic restructuring and in the MIS departments of most corporations. This has come about by the arrival of the PC. This is a of great advantage to a user buyer. The reason is often it has lead to a factionalized MIS organization that fights amongst itself. One department blaming another for a system failure. The monolithic MIS department of the early 80's now consists of five or more major factions; the keepers of the host, host applications developers, The local area network managers, the PC and desktop support organization and telecommunications. They can be further splintered in a large corporation between operations and planning. This means the user has regained some importance as these departments are realizing they exist for their internal customers and if these departments are not functioning optimally they are out of a job.

Buying A PBX/ACD Or A Standalone Acd
Beyond Buying "Phones!"

Can you play a round of golf with only one club? The answer is yes, but you won't do a great job or have much fun.

As always there are two sides to every story. A vendor who tells you their solution has advantages over another, while makers of the other solution are enjoying robust sales, should immediately raise suspicion. If PBX based ACDs had such clear advantages, why are sales of standalone ACDs still so strong? PBX vendors forget the lessons of data processing. Mainframes did not provide all the solutions users needed at a realistic price. So began the minicomputer business and then the PC business. These offered limited solutions at lower prices. PBX vendors followed the same pattern, but began with unrealistically low prices. This meant they could not afford to build or support applications specific solutions like ACDs and predictive dialers.

Here are the arguments you'll get from the PBX vendor explaining why his solution is better. Remember he's selling a telephone system. A smart ACD vendor is selling a business system and a better way of doing business.

A PBX Based ACD System Is Integrated With The Administrative Part Of Your Business

The switching system of a PBX/ACD is integrated.

In all but a small application (20 agents or fewer) this may be an advantage. What is given up for the "integrated solution" is an ACD specific machine. If a PBX was designed as a PBX to begin with, you give up architectural, common control and database flexibility needed in an ACD.

The Dialing Plan Is Universal

This is true for administrative stations. An agent must have two extensions, one for production (ACD) calls, one for administrative calls. This requires two ports on the switch for both the ACD directory number and the extension. A different number must be dialed for an agent group than the extension. This can even be an outside line. Real messy.

There is no need for tie lines between the ACD and the PBX portion in a PBX/ACD

Tie lines are a commodity that consumes a port per end. Tie line implies ongoing monthly telco costs when we are only talking about a pair of wires in the switchroom. The trade off on a PBX/ACD is buying increased station capacity. A minimum of two per agent. This is not true of standalone ACD systems that allow logical addressing, therefore only need one physical extension per agent.

Calls flow easily from the ACD portion to the PBX portion

First, why is this happening? If this happens to most calls there is something wrong with your business flow. Five to ten percent is acceptable as there may be some non-production (call) reason. Beyond this your business is not flowing smoothly. A good ACD will show you this.

Administrative extensions can backup ACD groups

This is true and a valid reason to use an administrative group, but be careful this is not a crutch for bad planning.

Reporting is integrated

This is not true on most PBX/ACD systems. All ACD traffic is reported in the ACD group and station reports. Any outgoing calls or internal extension to extension traffic is reported on the SMDR (station message detail reporting and call detail reports) in the telecommunications department that has nothing to do with the customer call center. Reporting on logical entities (such as agents) in a PBX machine tends to be inaccurate because of a hardware based system design philosophy. How do you report on a changing entity that has no hardware address? Add shifts or dynamic skill or load reassignment and reporting is further complicated.

PBX/ACDs can grow easily

True, if the system has lots of capacity. An ACD call is five to seven time more complex to process and because it has revenue or goodwill associated with it is infinitely more sensitive (to blockage) than an administrative call. PBX systems are designed to ration trunk resources across a large universe of administrative stations. Ten or more stations per trunk. ACDs work the opposite way, not to mention common control (computer running the switch) capacity. When you take 20 or 30 ACD positions off a PBX you get the equivalent of 100 to 150 PBX stations freed up. Conversely putting 20 or 30 more ACD positions on your PBX dramatically changes traffic demands on the switch. Watch what happens if you are near a shelf or cabinet limitation and need to add racks. Large costs!

All the PBX features are automatically included

You don't want most of these in a customer call center. Most ACD stations are there to support production tasks. Fewer worthwhile features are necessary. Few keystrokes and no codes to distract from the business at hand. Remember most PBX user only know how to use five or so features easily and maybe speed dialing.

Below 50 agents you don't need a sophisticated standalone ACD

Maybe your business is not worth protecting. If American Airlines loses a customer call center they estimate they loose $16,000 a minute. They use a true bulletproof ACD. What's your business worth?

There are also the cost containment aspects of a standalone ACD. Queuing theory is poorly implemented by most PBX/ACD vendors. If they do not use "multistage queuing with simultaneous lookback" you are hiring extra staff to compensate for this. Three extra bodies for every 20 positions. How do they sense and answer a call? If they do not dynamic answer, retarded on a call-by-call basis and if no agents or VRU ports are available, they are costing you 10 to 20 seconds of billed 800 time per call. And you thought you got a great deal when they included ACD software with your PBX at no charge. What you don't know can hurt you badly.

Every 20 agents on your ACD will cost you $1,000,000 a year in expense. Up to 15% of that is avoidable with the correct management tools only available on the standalone ACD systems.

Winning Concepts

A clear business mission can a focus to buying process. Focus on a common business goal can keep the political dynamics at a level that avoids feature requirements and necessity battles. The buying committee is kept to a mutual goal. Examples of these goals maybe solving poor customer service, meeting a new challenge represented by increased call volume. It may be doing more with existing resources. Providing the same level of service with less resources. Reducing costs of operation.

Justifying An ACD

In reality there are three justification issues and these occur at different levels. Each is harder than the next to prove in the acquisition phase yet becomes clearly the justification for making the purchase in retrospect.

1. **The system can save money?**
2. **The system will allow increased ease in getting information about business performance and allow convenient insight into the business.**
3. **This insight will allow strategic and tactical decisions to be made to allow the customer call center to become an even more effective tool for winning and keeping customers.**

The system may cause you to spend more money as once it is installed it may graphically demonstrate how poor service really was and how much money and opportunity was being lost.

All the major ACD vendors have extensive experience in building detailed financial justification models for you. Accept at least three and scrutinize them extensively. There will be bits of all of them that will provide help to this process.

Chapter Fourteen

The Future of Customer Response Centers

Background

The state of the switching systems business, PBX and ACD systems, look awfully like the computer business in the late 1970's. Then the need for applications specific functionality gave rise to minicomputers that satisfied business and user needs far faster and more cost effectively than generalized mainframes. The result was a hugely successful generation of minicomputers that grew in size and power to the point they also became mainframes. The next generation has been the vastly successful and ubiquitous personal computer. Switching systems are beginning to undergo the same transformation but at a far slower rate.

Standalone ACD, Predictive dialers, external voice mail, auto-attendants and voice response units are all examples of this deconstruction of "mainframe PBX." The desire for the mainframe and PBX vendor has been to keep all computing or switching applications in the host or the switch, thus retard any loss of market share. Many aggressive users realized there was little hope of achieving the same application richness or staff productivity on these generalized switching machines and have rejected PBX and CO systems as their ACD platforms. This accounts for seven healthy standalone ACD and outbound dialer systems vendors. This does not include two network based call center server products that enhance distributed customer call center operations.

"Back to the Future"
Future ACD Switching Systems Developments

There is a significant trend in customer call center environment, and that is the deployment of client server applications. After saying this, there should be a great deal of skepticism leveled at any vendor who believes switching voice will become a server on the LAN application in the near future. The one thing that has defeated every major computer company foray into the telephone switching business has been the distribution of voice connectivity within a building. That is cable management. Have you ever wondered why computer rooms have raised floors? Maybe to hide the hideous cable mess! As an example of the different disciplines and biases of the two businesses, look at the cable management behind your mainframe or computer system and than that of your telephone vendor.

There is no financially compelling breakthrough switch technology that is coming in the next five years that should cause the switch manufacturers concern. Major technologies such as optical switching, continued miniaturization and reliability will continue to reduce hardware purchase and lifetime costs. Iconosynchronous switching is running on an Ethernet LAN, switching voice on top of data, however the added expense of phone cards in PCs, plus a phone software, the trunk interface technology make the conversion moot. The switching software is unproven and to date the reliability of LANs and PCs no where near meet the stability of telephone switches. As stated before, there have only been two major new switches aimed at the ACD market introduced since 1987. Building these is capital and time intense. Manufacturers tend to value engineer these platforms for as long as they can. The Nortel Meridian, ROLM 9000 and The AT&T Definity PBXs are nearly a decade old! Many installed standalone ACDs are beginning their second decade of service.

Though never, say never. There is probably "a guy (excuse me "person") in a garage" working on the next breakthough. Problem is seldom the technology but the process of documenting, stabilizing and supporting the product. Then marketing, gaining sales channels and a significant customer base to provide the product with a future.

So what is expected? PC based ACD systems are available but limit their application to the common control function. There is still a physical "switch matrix" card or external switch that is controlled by the PC. These systems are generally aimed at the low end and because they are PC based tend to be inexpensive. On the mid to high end, expect the mainstream switch vendors to progressively add features to compete in the computer telephony market till they collapse under their own complexity. Already this is happening with the leading PBX/ACD vendors. This is demonstrated by their current inability to provide accurate MIS following adoption of skills based routing and other "me too" features.

What is needed is a big dumb switch. Dumber than a box of rocks, that can be completely controlled by external server based applications. The model exists in the long distance network with the network control points (NCP -- databases and routing instructions) and network action points (NAP -- switching sites.) In the customer premise business expect to see are large voice connectivity matrix or switch, attached to the LAN for control and reporting purposes only. All the voice will most likely remain on existing or new voice wiring. Putting voice on a LAN is extremely complex, expensive and capacity consumptive. Most current LAN technologies and protocols do not have the bandwidth or control signaling for voice.

What is expected to happen is to see standalone ACD vendors start to deconstruct their switches. Take off the skins, disassemble the MIS and common control from the switch system and place these components as servers on the company LAN where they can more effectively participate in enterprise wide applications. This makes particular sense for IVR and computer telephony applications. The big switch vendors will fight to keep their switches an associated applications monolithic. Their market share in these applications will be static compared to the growth of the deconstruction and LANable switches.

Customer Call Center Database Administration And Reporting
Consolidated Systems

"A customer: Arriving with a history and leaving with an experience."

The arrival of computer telephony in call centers adds a new level of database administration and reporting confusion.

Database Administration

The first major opportunity in ACD MIS systems is the consolidation of database administration and management. If you take a look at the average customer call center, there are a minimum of seven separate databases that need to be updated and precisely cross-referenced for these systems to work in concert. They are:

☐   **The ACD switching process**
☐   **The ACD MIS**
☐   **The VRU system and reporting**
☐   **The CTI Server**
☐   **LAN workstation node and addressing system**
☐   **The desktop workstation, (sign on and system configurations)**

❑ **Any host customer account database**

This can be further complicated by the addition of:

❑ **more than one VRU,**
❑ **additional desktop applications,**
❑ **additional host applications**
❑ **any multiple LAN access systems**
❑ **any quality measurement system**
❑ **any staff forecasting, staffing and attendance adherence system**

When you add computer telephony plumbing to this mess, things must work in absolute ultra real-time precision or the whole exercise fails. Particularly the synchronization of databases just from an address point of view. Add staff management, quantitative and qualitative, and a whole raft of personnel, compliance and legal problems demand absolute database accuracy.

Reporting

Manufacturers of specific devices all read "In Search of Excellence," or at least remember one important principal espoused there; "stick to the knitting." That is focus on the business you know and very become good at that. Do not dissipate invaluable corporate focus on indirectly related businesses. True to this, the ACD manufacturers delivered ACD reports, VRU manufacturers produced VRU reports and host applications developers produced their applications reports.

The problem now is a customer arrives at the customer call center as a single call transaction, unrelated to past history, and passes through a number of processes and devices. The caller "leaves" information and valuable business data each step of the way. This is further complicated by the fact a customer call is merely a "waypoint" in a much larger customer relationship continuum. No one device has a global view of this or the overall customer experience. A big opportunity exists to deliver a system for call tracking (that is the immediate transaction experience,) data or customer relationship management information, where the continuum of this particular call is tracked, then recognized as part of a larger picture.

First by allowing the caller to identify the customer account before they reach an agent means we have identified an individual entity; most likely a customer or prospect! The caller may first encounter a VRU, complete a series of VRU steps and may get transferred to an agent who accesses a customer information system database. In most cases, none of this interaction or process is accounted for in one reporting suite. It gets further complicated if any workflow applications are involved and written communications result from a call. The reporting of the customer experience as a single event across the various components and processes of the customer call center is a major opportunity.

There is only two places all the call, the systems and customer data come together, first at the incoming switchpoint as the switch acts as a traffic control point, then at the agent desktop workstation. This means that the data must be gathered in real time, normalized, stored and matched to build a complete "customer experience record."

The call gets delivered with or without a screen pop containing the caller experience to date (any ANI and DNIS digits, VRU entered ID and applications choices.) This all comes from the ACD as the VRU is typically managed by the ACD as "virtual agent."   The agent now follows a task script to satisfy the callers request, whatever. As a LAN participant, a server can be gathering relevant data about the caller's "experience." One of the immediate benefits that flows out of this is the ability to track the call as a "case." Remember, seldom is a call request complete as a result of answering the call. Some fulfillment function has to occur. A database updated, service or goods dispatched, etc. Now we are back to workflow and task queue management. More later. The point is today there is no one place all this data is consolidated to allow customer experience (with your company) tracking.

The position proposed by the writer is exactly the same as was proposed almost ten years ago. When we stop looking at calls as "traffic," and start seeing these as customers and reporting on that entity, we have made achieved a breakthrough in customer call center reporting.

Today, there is little being done to build a customer experience database as the callers arrive with a known history and are brought to a point of satisfaction, thus leave with a god experience.

Required Data for Relationship Management

Relationship management has long been promoted in the banking industry. There was perceived to be a need to relate all the accounts and individual or business had with the bank, so any transaction could be viewed in toto, rather than as it applied to that single account.   The nightmare the bank wished to avoid was bouncing the personal check of the financially sloppy wife of the chairman of some Fortune 500 customer.   Today, the banking account management software typically links these accounts together.   Nevertheless, although the accounts may be linked, little is done to follow the day-to-day interaction with the account holder, particularly if there is a problem or ongoing dialog.   A caller arrives at the your customer call center and typically has to begin the transaction by identifying themselves or worse, in the case of a transfer, retelling a whole new teleservices representative of the reason they are calling.   That takes time and does not serve the customer or your business well.   This need now exists in most businesses, though some have a more immediate need than others;   for example managed care and health insurers versus airlines.

The problem is presented in two dimensions.   All of the devices in a customer call center collect transaction data.   That is raw call data; some as detail, some as peg counts.   These are the ACD, PBX/ACD and IVR systems.   Now we have added CTI links with applications that also gather "results" or outcome data. The net effect is to have lots of data, in unlike formats and in different databases about the same transaction.   Further this data is granulated to **the** transaction with no heed for past or related transactions with the same customer. This represents data.

The mainframe or host customer information system (CIS) has individual account records but these are normally at a much higher level or more global in their perspective. This represents customer information.

There is no cohesive view that brings together data and information to provide context specific account, inquiry or customer case state data.   This is truly customer knowledge.

Call Tracking And Relationship Management

What is currently needed is a management information gathering system that crosses all customer call center devices, gathering and normalizing data to present a complete view of the immediate customer call experience, then relate this to past calls and customer history to provide the agent with call context knowledge.   Before we reach this point though there is a real necessity for the makers of these devices to recognize more data is needed in an easily exportable form so that external applications can run these call tracking consolidation reports. The majority of switches available on the market today cannot do this. thus may cause a call center to upgrade to newer switching technology sooner than they require.

By delivering an inquiry management or a case management system, much of the necessity for skills based routing is reduced as now nearly any agent in your customer call center can serve the caller by virtue of case related knowledge. This returns the ACD to one of its original goals of optimizing staff resources by using statistics and queuing to have as few staff as possible serve as many customers as possible.

Further there are many other compelling business reasons for call tracking or inquiry management. The obvious one is discouraging "shopping" for an acceptable answer. In the managed care or health insurance business, callers will call more than once to get the most desirable answer from an agent.

Agent interpretations may differ, as may be the way the caller poses the question. By providing a case related record with the computer telephony based "screen pop," CTI prevents the same caller "shopping" for the most desirable answer, as all previous call instances are delivered to the current agent, with the outcome or answer given on the last call.

There are many exciting applications and uses growing for this technology and the writer expects this to be a commonly used tool in most customer call centers by the end of the decade.

Major Customer Call Center Fallacy

The average inbound call center understates the number of outbound calls that are made. There is marked irony here in that original ACD design was focused at high volumes of inbound calls. Outbound calls were treated as "business as usual." As the ACD found its way into more diverse applications, outbound calling became a more significant issue. Now the predictive outbound dialers are looking more like ACD systems and ACDs are adopting interfaces with dialing and database systems.

When computer telephony is introduced and call types, processes, task cycles and applications are analyzed, inbound customer inquiries via correspondence vehicles (mail, fax and E:Mail) end up just being a different medium that may have more intense implications but are nevertheless inquiries that need to triaged and responded to much the same as a customer call. The other consideration is that integrating a correspondence unit into the customer response center allows greater staffing flexibility, task mix and balancing. Also add the fact that often a call back as a response to a customer letter is often cheaper and a more immediate solution for both the enterprise and the customer.

No customer request is ever completed by simply answering the call. There is always a database update, a letter, dispatching a service or shipping a product. Take a look at the average customer call center workstation and you will see a pigeon hole system full of a variety of forms and most likely a person pushing a mail cart. This cart distributes work and picks up work from agents desk. These are typically forms based requests to other departments, outgoing mail to customers, etc.

Correspondence Integration

Customer call centers are no longer just call centers. There is a real need to have these centers more balanced in term of staffing and work load. "Boom and bust" call volume cycles require precise forecasting and staffing to avoid poor service levels or over staffing. Integrating other customer communications events to mitigate this is a real opportunity. This becomes critical, especially if the result of a customer call results in a written instruction or response, whether this be in the form of a mail, fax, package or E:mail fulfillment result.

The customer call center is often divorced from any company correspondence unit the business may have. Traditionally complaints and other communications have arrived at a business in letter form. Indeed before the advent of 800 services, this was the dominant form of communication. The mail order business derives its name from this fact. Today many companies still receive a small, but significant portion of customer communication by mail. They typically build a correspondence unit to triage, process and respond to these letters. For example the ratio of letters to calls may be 1 letter : 20 calls, yet the effort involved may amount to ten to fifteen percent of the companies total response cost.

Basically it takes longer and costs more to respond in writing than by placing a call to the potentially aggrieved customer. The correspondence effort is disproportionately higher than it is to respond to telephone inquiries. This is complicated by the fact that a customer who has written a letter has the perception that their letter deserves to be directly responded to. There is more emotion attached to a letter than a telephone call.

Here is both opportunity and a problem for most businesses, where the customer call center has both peak, shoulder and low traffic periods. Integrating inbound, outbound and correspondence functions in the customer call center allow

additional staffing, functions and flexibility. The other opportunity is to make a cost analysis of the most effective means of response and then make an intelligent decision about the handling of the customer.   Assuming a letter deserves a written response may not always be cost effective.   Now another element has be added to the customer communication process that needs integrated reporting.

Using an intelligent desktop workstation with telephony and correspondence functions such as a letter generation or automated forms completion tool for process fulfillment steps, also allows the customer call center to track, trigger customer communication events (much like a personal information and appointment manager) and maintain case state information.

Workflow Management

What is now being describe is a full desktop workflow management system that tracks the completion of a customer event. Task queues should be developed and managed on line at the agents workstation so the customer inquiry or case is actively managed to completion either in the course of the call or subsequently. Letter generation and automated forms completion can be developed to be driven from key host screens and field using standard Windows or OS/2 compliant terminal communications and word processing software. The document can be electronically routed to a mail room for printing and stuffing for mailing. Alternatively sent to a FAX or E:Mail server.

This market is only just awakening and the future looks extremely bright for any company in the integrated agent workflow workstation business. Sadly, none of the major computer or switch manufacturers seem to grasp this as it too far from their core businesses. One standalone ACD vendor offers such a tool and three startups offer PC based telephones with some level of agent workflow management. Only the ACD vendor will commit to prime contract management.

A significant fact that cannot be ignored by anyone developing these processes remains the ability to track a customer experience across all the systems, through the complete customer satisfaction cycle, whether it be a customer sales, support or help desk event.

The Future Of Audio Archival Systems

As a sideline to recording applications there may be a need to track the audio of every call for audit, archive or compliance purposes.   In high risk or high value transactions like electronic funds transfer, sequential recording devices have been used to record the audio aspect of every call.   The 1995 furor over the Bankers Trust tape recordings involved just such a device in their bond trading and derivatives departments.   These systems have typically been non-interactive tape oriented (analog or digital) in either audio or video cassette format.   The problem is that these recordings are seldom time stamped and cannot be easily recovered in the event of a question without manually listening to the tapes where the subject call is likely to be.   The writer is unaware of any "digital match" to the ACD call reporting or any hard copy record of the audio transactions on the tape.   To date this has not changed.   Expect this to become of greater significance as more companies recognize a requirement to maintain more complete records of customer contact.   This is driven by increased legal exposure and the increased opportunity for error as customer call volumes grow.

Reporting The Complete Picture

The major change that has happened in call centers over the last eight years has been the growing recognition that they are now the primary "front door" of most businesses.   Based on the title of this book, "Customers: Arriving with a history, leaving with an experience." we are trying to recognize a shift from the classic structure of the customer call center being a secondary or fall back customer contact strategy, to a primary customer focused marketing, sales and support strategy.

One of the big changes we predict will be a shift to consolidated customer contact process reporting.   What we mean by this is best explained by making the statement that most systems vendors report on the domain they control.   If it is an ACD telephone switch it reports on the "calls" it processes.   A VRU, the voice transactions that "pass through" it.   A host order entry system, the number of orders and status inquiries made.   The result is that most vendors of technology simply report on the "domain" they address and control.   Add a monitoring system, and the picture gets even more cloudy.   Telephones, or VRUs, or staff, or applications even though they generate disparate reports, only address one common denominator; **a customer and their experience with your business**. But no one addresses reporting from this perspective.

Most machines develop three types of reports and screens; usage data, administrative reports and diagnostics for maintenance purposes. However these reports are restricted to the operation and application of this machine only! As more and more customer call center management tools become available, the greater the number of reports. The management data gathering, normalization and analysis burden increases. As expected more reports produce less attention to critical areas as they disguise important trends in more data. Expect developments in this area.

Performance Guarantees

"We serve 80% of our callers in 20 seconds" has been a touchstone of the customer call center business. Now the marketing departments of competitive businesses such as managed care, are writing this or similar standards into their customer contracts to cover telephone and written inquiries. If the vendor does not meet the standard, they reduce the group premium by significant percentages. Medicare has long had a standard by which they expect seniors to be treated. Should an audit show a health plan failed to meet this, they had to return a portion of Medicare payments to the federal government.

Problem is no one knows how to measure this. Few ACDs track the actual customer or caller experience by call and certainly do not provide that level of data necessary to track an health insurance employer group experience. Add VRUs, database, workflow and the problem is massive. Basically there is no caller experience audit trail.

In the few cases where the data is available, none of the device use a develop or are compatible with an external data correlation record. That is a unique call identification number that travels with the caller across every system so that each devices data contribution contains a unique call sequence number so all the data may be assembled to provide a measurement of the callers experience. This then can be "rolled up" to report on group experience and other issues for the marketing department.

Computer Telephony As A Solution

The vendors of host based computer telephony have claimed they solve this problem but frequently they do not get all the data so the reports are not as robust as they would have you believe. Also the time to install host based computer telephony interfaces is long, tedious and expensive. A client server screen pop solution can typically be up and running within three month of the decision to do it. But this is often an illusory exercise as screen pops alone cannot justify this type of automation. Task integration and workflow is the big win.

A good rule of thumb to go by is that the average agent cost to install computer telephony, after you have installed the ACD switch, the host and the PC is approximately $3000 a head. Screen pops cannot justify this. Because the PC is present, ideally with the phone function in the PC, the whole nature of work begins to change.

Workflow and systems integration inevitably require some enterprise specific software development. This takes longer and adds to the expense. But here is the real win in computer telephony and the integrated agent desktop.

Computer Telephony Justification

Screen pops seldom save the time they are expected to. Any vendor selling screen pops and coordinated data transfer as a justification is missing the point or has never really done a real integration project. Computer telephony integration does not stop at installing CTI and screen pops. This is no more glamorous or compelling than upgrading from Windows 3.X to Windows 95. CTI is merely an telephone to computer integration protocol. Plumbing! In the big picture not more significant than an operating system upgrade.

Workflow and process improvement is the win. The datacentric or telecentric vendors seldom understand this that is why they are not heavily promoting this. As long as they perpetuate the justification of CTI making shorter calls they avoid reality.

Longer Calls To Reduce Call Volume

One of the basic discoveries in any workflow project is the opportunity to do more with the caller on line so a greater degree of satisfaction can be delivered, more data gathered, more product or service sold and basically amaze the customer and maintain their loyalty. The goal is to increase sales revenue first, cut costs second and reduce call length last. Often the result of these initially longer calls results in fewer subsequent customer calls or a change in the nature of those calls.   But the more complete customer transaction was designed to reduce cost and increase revenue.

Selecting a Workflow Vendor

Selecting a vendor as a partner in a large formal customer call center and workflow project is difficult. First there are few companies that have really done a full computer telephony and workflow project. Those that have are typically not household names. The large vendors like IBM or AT&T typically stop at the "plumbing," and as discussed does not begin to justify itself. Often, they are also selling goods and services to protect their mainframe or switch position which may not be the best solution for your application.

The most important skill the vendor must have after the products and development and test ability, is project management. This is an acid test. These CT and workflow projects are messy and political. The buyer must also be prepared to put together a team representing the different disciplines and technology domains that will be affected in your enterprise. They are:

- ☐ **The Users,**
  - ☐ **A strong manager,**
  - ☐ **An agent advocate and focus group for subsequent workflow and process validation.**
- ☐ **Management Information Systems,**
  - ☐ **Host and terminal management,**
  - ☐ **Applications,**
  - ☐ **LAN manager,**
  - ☐ **Desktop/PC management, and**
  - ☐ **Telecommunications management.**
- ☐ **Project Team Leader with a high level of project management skill and authority.**

Ideally your customer call center needs access to some in-house test, validation and acceptance process to ensure quality code is delivered and deployed into production in an orderly manner. Skimp on these skills and your project can be a disaster.   Your vendor needs to understand these skills and have a complementary team on your project.

Any solution is probably going to be a combination of existing or legacy systems, hosts and switches, LANs and desktop devices. There will be packaged code from the vendor partner, or other vendors chosen on a "best of breed" basis or systems that maybe developed uniquely for your business. More than one vendor will be in the partnership, but one side or the other (vendor or customer) should take prime responsibility for project completion because even your in-house disciplines need to be managed as vendors who must meet time, budget and quality targets for all this to work.

Conclusion

By opening up the issue of workflow, we enter a whole discipline that exceeds the scope of this book. Correspondence, imaging, on-line policy and procedure manuals, scripted tasks, skill and decision support and on. We have just begun to scratch the surface of where this market is going and the benefits that will accrue to aggressive call center managers. This business has just begun and is bringing another whole crop of skills, opportunities and players. Enjoy and Prosper.

Sample ACD Request for Proposal

1.0 Introduction

1.1 Background Information

This Request for Proposal (RFP) provides the prospective vendor Acme Screw's requirements for an automatic call distributor system(ACD). This document also provides the format in which all vendors must respond. Acceptance of a proposal does not obligate Acme Screw to purchase any system. Acme Screw reserves the right to change any specifications outlined in this document prior to the signing of a contract.

Critical Needs

    Integration with existing system
    Call Center Support Systems
    Phased Cutover
    Technological Growth Path

1.2 Customer Contacts

1.3 Proposal

1.3.1 Time Table

Request for Proposal sent to vendors	February 23, 199X
Customer Site visits	February/March 199X
RFP due to Acme Screw, Inc.	March 20, 199X
LifeScan decision	March 31, 199X
Target installation date	September 1, 199X

1.3.2 The Proposal Format

All responses must be received by March 20, 199X. The package must include 5 copies of the proposal and the original RFP with signatures.

Cover Page
The proposed system manufacturer name and model; lead contact name and phone number

Table of Contents
List each topic and corresponding section and page number.

Requirements Overview
This section provides an overview of how the manufacturer addresses Acme Screw telecommunications needs.

Manufacturer Profile
This section must include an overview of the manufacturer. The manufacturer needs to provide answers to the questions posed in section 3.0.

Technical Specifications
This section provides the evaluation team information on whether the vendor can comply with Acme Screw requirements. This section must directly address the requirements described in section 4.0.

Proposed Implementation Schedule

This section outlines tasks, responsibilities, and timelines necessary to complete the suggested configuration. The implementation plan must include installation of secondary systems (i.e. CDR, call reporting systems).

Line Item Pricing
In addition to a net price for the suggested configuration, the vendor must include a pricing breakdown of hardware, software, installation cost for the ACD system and secondary systems.

Maintenance and Support
In this section, the vendor must describe how it intends to maintain the proposed system. The manufacturer must also describe how support, complaint, and resolution issues will be handled with the manufacturers business partners.

Financial Options
The vendor must list the payment options available to Acme Screw.

Appendix
The vendor may choose to add any marketing and sales literature within this section.

3.0 Manufacturer Profile

The manufacturer's responses to this section will provide information on company background, critical contacts, references.

3.1 Manufacturer Overview
The manufacturer is requested to provide an overview of the company. Include in your response, the following considerations:

• Describe how has the manufacturer made advances in the ACD industry within the last two years.

• Describe how the manufacturer partners with other companies to provide solutions to customers.

• Briefly describe the manufacturer's market share of the installed base of ACD systems by industry.

• Provide site locations of customers with similar configurations to the proposed system.

• Describe how the manufacturer partners with the customer to devise solutions to problems or needs.

3.2 Critical Contacts

Provide the following information for each principal:

Company name:
Individual name:
Address:
City/State/Zip:
Phone:
References and work history (for Project Manager only):
Principals:
• ACD System Manufacturer
• Sales Contact
• Technical Contact
• Service Manager
• Secondary System Manufacturers
• Service Managers for Secondary Systems

• Project Manager (for the Acme Screw project)

3.3 References
• Provide the company names and contacts of the 3 most recent customers whose business your company has acquired.

• Provide the company names and contacts of the 3 most recent customers whose business your company has lost.

4.0 Technical Specifications
This section details required configuration and integration issues. Desired functionalities are listed as well. Note that Minimum Requirements are headed by the notation (MR); Extra Requirements begin with an (ER) notation. An extra requirement describes a function/feature that is not critical to Acme Screw business but is a desired feature which will help increase efficiency and productivity.

Unless otherwise noted, the term *user* refers to call center agents or other station users. *Agent* is in reference to ACD agents; a *SA* is a system administrator; *supervisor* is the lead for a group of ACD agents.

4.1 Required Equipment

Listed under the 'Current' column are the system equipment configurations for our ACD system. In this section, the vendor is asked to provide data on the capacity of the proposed system and the capacity limitations of the proposed system.

System Equipment	Current	Desired Capacity	Proposed eqp'd for	Proposed wired for	Max Capacity
Digital Voice/Data ports	150	400			
Analog Voice/Data ports	30	100			
Voice Announcement ports	16	100			
Basic rate interface (BRI) ports	0	100			
PRI spans	6	10			

4.2 ACD system capacity

Listed under the 'Current' column are the system configuration items for the current environment. The manufacturer is requested to provide capacity limitations for the items listed.

Capacity Item	Current Limits	Desired Capacity	Proposed eqp'd for	Propose wired for	Maximum Capacity
ACD agents	300	400-500			
Outbound calling agents	10	100			
Agents per ACD group	504				
ACD groups	255				

4.2.1 Traffic Capacity

The system must be capable of sustaining 2,000 call transactions (about 20% outgoing) per hour while maintaining voice messaging, music on hold, queue messages.

4.3 Current Integration Issues

4.3.1 ROLM 9006 Model 50

Possible integration solutions are described under each bullet point. Describe how your proposed system will comply under these scenarios. Include performance factors, maintenance issues.

• All T-Spans connected to Model 50. The proposed system must receive and utilize D-channel information and ACD group ID from the Model 50. Proposed system must send ISDN information to the Model 50 for outgoing traffic. The proposed system (link) must handle the simultaneous traffic capacity of the ACD queues, outgoing, and other incidental traffic.

• Both outgoing and incoming T-Spans split between the Model 50 and proposed system
(see comments above)

• All incoming T-Spans connected to proposed system and all outgoing T-Spans connected to Model 50. Proposed system must send ISDN information for outgoing and pass D-channel information on incoming calls to Model 50 for non-ACD applications.

4.3.2 Octel Voicemail

(MR) The Acme Screw campus currently utilizes the Octel Maxum system for voicemail service. ACD system users need to have voicemail service that is tightly integrated with the Octel system. Users must have the same VM features i.e. system forwarding, message notification.

4.3.3 Front-end Call Processing

(MR) The system must satisfy one of the two options:

1) The system must have a built-in call processor feature.
2) The system must interface with the ROLM Phonemail which is currently used as a front-end call processor.

4.4 Survivability
In the event of a system failure, describe how the proposed system architecture can recover.

4.5 Processor - CPU

4.5.1 Redundant processors
(MR) The system must have redundant processors.

4.5.2 Blockage
Provide information on the number of voice and/or data connections per shelf, per bus and per CPU before blockage occurs.

• Describe factors leading to service degradation i.e. will data calls have a greater effect on systems than voice calls ? do ISDN trunks have a greater effect than T1 ?

4.6 User Features

4.6.1 Required Station Features

Feature	Standard	Option
Automatic Callback		x
Definable Status Buttons		
Call Forwarding		
Station display - ANI		x
Station display - destination name	x	
Station display - call origination		x
Station display - length in call state	x	
Station display - real time agent stats	x	
Station display - real time call queue	x	
Recall data	x	
Call Park	x	
Call Transfer	x	
Distinctive Ringing		
Park call indicator	x	

4.6.2 Required Station Equipment

Feature	Standard	Option
Support Head and Hand set	x	
LCD Station display	x	
Definable feature buttons		

4.7 System Features

4.7.1 ID based agent station identification
(MR) The system must recognize ACD agents by login ID instead of by extension. Login ID based routing will provide agents the ability to pick up any ACD phone and receive ACD calls based on their respective agent profiles.

4.7.2 ACD states with Configurable states
(MR) The system must contain the standard ACD states: ACD-IN, Work, Available, Unavailable, External, Internal, Other. (ER) The system must provide the user the capability to configure different ACD states: i.e. Start of Day login button, Break unavailable vs. Lunch unavailable

4.7.3 Phonemail boxes recognized as ACD objects
(MR) The system must recognize Phonemail boxes as ACD objects. This feature must allow summary statistics to be collected on each box. i.e. number of times entered by hour, day, selected time/date interval

4.7.4 Agent Status in Park, Transfer Attempts
(ER) When an agent attempts to transfer/parked a call to another agent, the system must provide the target agent an option (via beep and LCD display) to take a parked call.

4.7.5 Recall ANI feature
(MR) An agent must be able recall the ANI data after the call has been ended. In the event of a disconnect, the agent must have means to retrieve the ANI data in order to either enter the ANI data to a route table or call the dropped caller. (ER) The system must provide a button to dial the ANI of the most recent connected call.

4.7.6 Silent Monitoring /Tone Monitoring
(MR) The system needs to allow supervisors to monitor calls within the call center via a supervisor station set.

4.7.7 Call tracking

(ER) This feature would allow an agent to flag call topics (types) to a call event. As a caller begins discussion of new topics, the agent would hit a button associated with the topic. The system would then store the responses as data elements of the call event.

4.7.8 Audio Call Center Status

(ER) The system will provide any user the capability to call into Acme Screw and retrieve desired call statistics, work schedules, or message via a voice response unit.

4.7.9 Voice Announcement of Call Source

(ER) The system needs to provide a pre-recorded announcement prompt of a call source i.e. if a call comes through the Technical Services queue, a voice prompt will announce to the agent "Call for Technical Service". This should be configurable by DNIS table or front-end processing.

4.8 Call Processing Features

4.8.1 Routing

In this section the manufacturer is asked to describe how route-programming functions within the proposed system. The manufacturer should describe the limitations of the routing feature i.e. What are the maximum number of routes for each group ? What are the maximum number of steps per route ?

The system must provide the standard features of route programming i.e. wait, music, conditional routing, overflow, queue messaging. conditional defined as: length of time in queue, no of calls in queue, time of day, agents available/not available, customer ID.

The system must have the following added features:

4.8.1.4 Calendar storage of route programming

(MR) This feature allows route steps to be stored and executed on a prescribed date. Example; on Christmas Day, the Technical Service department - normally open 24hrs a day - is programmed two weeks before for a 5 hour closure.

4.8.1.5 ANI route table

(MR) This feature allows calls with a ANI entering the center to route to a specific group or agent. (ER) The system must allow an interface for agents via desktop computer/supervisor terminal to enter the ANI routing tables without access to other vital system functions.

4.8.1.6 Supervisor temporary route control
(MR) This feature would provide a supervisor in the call center to initiate temporary route-programs. Likely, uses for this feature would be in emergency situations when calls would need to be re-directed to another site or to a temporary down-time message which could be announced to callers in queue.

4.8.1.7 Test and Production programming environment
(MR) The system must be able to maintain a test and production environment. The test environment is an area where the code can be created and then tested without affecting the call center. There must also be a function to easily port the tested code into the production area.

4.8.1.8 Music on Hold
(MR) The system must allow multiple queues to access multiple MOH channels.

4.8.1.9 Non-interruptible programming
(MR) The system must allow route program changes without interruption of service.

4.8.1.10 Skill-based Routing
(MR) The system must provide a means for a supervisor to define the skill profile and level of each agent. Calls must then be routed based on these definitions.

4.8.2 Queuing - The section below describes some of the required queuing features.

4.8.2.2 Incoming Queue Priority
(MR) The system must allow a SA to set priority parameters. Calls must then be routed based on the set parameters. Priority must be configurable based on the following parameters:

DNIS table
ANI table
Front End Processor dependent
Internal transfers
Overflow

External transfers

4.8.2.3 Queuing to Multiple ACD groups
(MR) The system must have the capability to place a call in multiple queues. Real-time and reporting systems must peg situations where the call originated from another queue.

4.8.2.4 Outgoing Queue Priority
(ER) The system must be able to prioritize calls in the outbound queue.

4.8.2.5 Intelligent Queuing
(ER) The system must allow a caller in queue to access voicemail boxes which provide training/informational messages to the caller without losing their place in queue.

4.8.2.6 Queue announcements
(MR) The system must allow each queue to receive numerous queue messages. A queue announcement must be accessible by multiple queues simultaneously.

4.8.2.7 Call Status announcements
(MR) The system needs to announce relative call queue status to callers in each queue. The status selection types must include: age (in seconds) of the oldest call in queue, the number of agents currently available, the number of callers currently in queue, the average speed of answer (in seconds). To derive queue status information, the system must segment information coming from priority calls versus overflow calls.

For example:
Two agents are logged-in to receive calls. There are two ACD queues. Queue 1 receives calls for health care professionals. Queue 2 receives calls for rebates. Agent 1 only receives rebate calls. Agent 2 can receive rebate and health care professional calls.
The queue announcement for both ACD queues provides average speed of answer to the caller waiting in queue. The system must provide average speed of answer of all rebate calls to the rebate queue. The system should also provide the same for the health care professional line.

4.9 System Administration Features

4.9.1 Multiple Logon
(MR) The system administration features (command line) must be accessible to simultaneous users.

4.9.2 Control Logs
(MR) The system must maintain activity records for SA logins, queries to critical tables, and changes to any system parameters.

4.9.3 System Administration Profile Tables
(MR) This feature would allow a 'master' SA to set a profile table for other SAs. The profile tables need to limit views, change, delete, and create functions.

4.9.4 Critical System Function Access
(MR) The system must allow SAs to query and view error tables. The system must also allow SAs to begin first aid fixes until a service technician arrives to the campus.

4.10 Call Center Support Systems (CCS)
The call center support systems are used by Customer Services management to monitor real-time and historical call center activity. Real-time systems provide information to the Customer Services management team to correct problems as they occur. Historical data is used to evaluate individual agent productivity, the behavior of the call center as a group, call patterns, and staffing. Customer Services is committed to improving the call reporting systems to better manage the department by integrating new system capabilities described below.

4.10.1 Hardware

4.10.1.1 Supervisor Terminals
(MR) The real-time reporting system must provide the supervisor a means via a terminal to monitor agent activity and query current status (less than 15 second delay). (ER) The system must provide the supervisor a means via window on the Macintosh (or PC) desktop to monitor agent and call center activity.

4.10.1.2 Message Boards
(MR) The reporting system must route real time (less than 15 second delay) call center status and messages to the message boards. (ER) The system must provide real time call center data, agent data and

applicable global, group, individual messages via window on the Macintosh desktop of each agent.

4.10.1.3 Historical Systems (and other CCS Systems)

(MR) The system must be able to store a minimum of 3 years of call detail, 3 years of agent event records (assuming 1 minute detail). Provide performance specifications when specific relational database operations are performed i.e. joins, intersects, correlated sub queries - provide the number of records used to compile the performance specs.

4.10.2 Software

The data must be stored in a database scheme. This system should allow the customer to create ad hoc reports using SQL tools to read against the database. The system must also provide a means to maintain standard reports by storing desired SQL statements. Listed below are some of the desired data elements, parameters, and features of ideal support systems.

4.10.2.1 ACD Agent Activity Reporting

(MR) The reporting system needs to provide data -(time of day, length of time, associated ANI activity, extension number) for an ACD agent in an ACD state - (ACD-in, Work, Outgoing (ACD) , Internal (non-ACD) , External (non-ACD), Other, Unavailable, user-defined states).

4.10.2.2 Programmable Productivity measures

(ER) The system must allow new standards for productivity measures to be calculated and displayed via terminal, or window on Macintosh (or PC). i.e. Percentage of (ACD-in + Work + Other) by each agent.

4.10.2.3 ACD group reporting

(MR) The reporting system must provide multiple definable fields to group and summarize agents - and thereby their data - in various ways. i.e. Joel Bockrath is an agent under Harry Abe but he is also a Data Management team member, a Blood Drive member, etc.

4.10.2.4 ANI to Agent report (Call Detail Report) system

(MR) The system must provide storage and retrieval of data which lists by agent and extension the external-outgoing and incoming traffic (ANI) . (ER) The system must store and retrieve data for internal station to station traffic.

4.10.2.5 ANI Routing Report

(MR) The system must be able to capture the routing events of a particular number(caller) once entered into the system. For example, this report would show that a number entered pilot 1234 at XX:00 am; it was then overflowed to ACD group X at XX:15 am; it was then transferred to the pilot of ACD group Y at XX:30 am.

4.10.2.6 Migration from CallStat system

(MR) The manufacturer of the proposed ACD statistics system must provide the means to migrate the existing historic data from the ROLM-Affinitec CallStat system to the proposed database. Once migrated the data should be accessible by the database tools of the ACD statistics system.

4.10.2.7 Forecaster

This system needs to capture relevant historical call data, allow input of independent variable data i.e. meters sales by month (by day) and correlate this information to call history. The system should then provide linear model options to apply. Forecasts should then be performed based on input of independent variables. Forecast output must include call volume, agents required, and projected call handle times by the half hour for each 'typical' day of week of a given month. The system should also provide the total required headcount for a selected time parameter. This information should be portable into the scheduler system.

4.10.2.8 Scheduler

The Scheduler system needs to accept automated inputs of the required headcount from the Forecasting system. Based upon the forecaster inputs (with a user-defined variance tolerances) and user-defined parameters, the system must generate date specific schedules for each agent. Unlike typical call centers, Acme Screw does not have a pool of agents to draw upon to cover unexpected peaks in call volume. To a certain extent, the Customer Services culture supports a schedule which revolves around the agent; as opposed to a culture where the agents revolve around the schedule. In other words, a system must favor the input parameters set for each agent over ideal schedules based on optimization. This section describes some of the desired parameters and features.

4.10.2.8.1 Agent Definition Tables

4.10.2.7.1.1 Agent Database
(MR) The system must maintain agent information within a database. This portion of the system would include non-scheduling related data i.e. home address, phone number, (ER) photo-image. Schedule related data would also reside in the database i.e. pay-rate, logon id.

4.10.2.8.1.2 Agent Schedule Parameters
(MR) The system must provide the user the capability to enter agent parameter inputs and schedules based on those parameters:

Example of agent parameters
-Lynn Sauta works 9 hour shifts and is available during the time range 9:00am to 7:00pm Tuesday through Saturday.

-Harry Abe works 4 hours on Monday from 10:00am to 2:00pm, is available for 9 hours on Tuesday-Thursday during the time range 6:00am to 6:00pm.

4.10.2.8.2 Global Agent Parameters
(MR) Global agent parameters are rules which limits or defines the use of a group of agent resources.

Example of group parameters
-All agents within Desi Difraia's group must have back-to-back days off.
-All agents cannot work more than 40 hours a week

4.10.2.8.3 Definable Activities
(MR) This feature would allow the user to define at least ten different off-the-phone activities, i.e. hour off the phone. The activities can then be entered as a schedule item.

4.10.2.8.4 Group assignment of activity
(MR) This feature will provide the ability to assign an activity to a pre-defined group of agents. i.e. set a one-hour meeting for Harry Abe's group from 11:00am-12:00pm. The system should also flag possible schedule conflicts with existing schedule request changes.

4.10.2.8.5 Schedule Analysis

(MR) The scheduling system will provide analysis and recommendations to maximize fixed resources while balancing requests. The balance request feature needs to provide best-time-to-schedule recommendation. i.e. what is the best time to hold a one hour meeting for 10 agents on December 12, 199X; the scheduling analysis must take as-of-date requests into consideration.

4.10.2.8.6 Storage of Change Request and Change Control Log

(MR) The scheduling system must be able to store all immediate and as-of-date requests. As-of-date requests are recurring schedule changes (i.e. permanent schedule, weekly activity schedule) which become active on a user-defined effective date. All changes to the scheduling system must be recorded as within a retrievable control log.

4.10.2.8.7 Ease of use and administrative support

(MR) The interface to enter parameters to create schedules, perform analysis must be accessible to users with limited computer knowledge.

4.10.2.8.8 Graphical Representation

(MR) The system must be able to produce graphical representations of the schedule for a requested day. This will provide easy to read format for any person - especially agents - to review (see Appendix B for a sample).

4.10.3 Scheduler Adherence

(MR) This feature will allow supervisors to observe real-time and historical agent adherence to 'posted' schedules. Through the supervisor terminal (or window) the supervisor must be able to view the scheduled activity against the actual agent events in real time. An indicator (audio/visual) flagging non-conformance must be an available option to allow supervisors to easily/immediately pin-point potential problems. The supervisor should be able to view their respective group in entirety or on a selective basis. Historical reports providing detail and summary data must be available to the supervisor.

4.10.3.1 Timecard

(ER) This feature will accept agent input of timecard information i.e. vacation, time worked, sick time, etc. This information should be reconcilable to the schedule.

4.10.4 Multi-Session capable

(ER) This capability will provide to all agents the capability to query and view data from various reporting systems. The agents would benefit from having LAN accessibility to scheduling, scheduling adherence, agent performance, call center status systems.

4.11 Growth/Technology Expansion

This section includes the listing and description of applications which may be implemented in the near future. The manufacturer is requested to describe how the proposed system can be implemented with each application listed below.

4.11.1 Interactive Voice Response (IVR)

The Customer Services department intends to utilize IVR technology for various applications described below. The manufacturer is encouraged to suggest other applications for this technology.

4.11.1.1 Interactive Survey

(ER) After a call is completed, the agent must be able to 'connect' the caller to a Survey system. This system will ask the caller questions about Customer Service quality and provide multiple responses for the caller to choose. The system must be able to accept touch-tone or voice as input to the response.

4.11.1.2 Voice Response to menu selection (for rotary dialers)

The system must be able to accept voice response to menu choices.

4.11.2 Computer Telephony (CTI)

(MR) The proposed system will need to link to the CPQS system (client-server based system) and to the MOMS system (host based system) to provide screen pops. Provide alternative methods to implement CTI i.e. host link or desktop link like AT&T-Novell's PassageWay.

4.11.3 Computer Desktop Phoneset

(ER) This is a feature which would eliminate the need/use of a physical phone. A headset is attached to a device which is attached into the computer. Software on the client system provides the interface for users to receive the same (or more) functionality with standard phone station sets.

4.11.4 Intelligent Monitoring Systems
(ER) The proposed system needs to be able to integrate with an intelligent monitoring system. Intelligent monitoring systems provide the capability of recording or viewing(real time) simultaneous voice and data transactions. Off the shelf systems by Witness Systems, Inc. provide seamless recording and playback of an entire call event.

4.11.5 Remote agents
(MR) The system must be accessible to implement remote agents (both voice and data.) The agent must have the same functionality as agents in the home office i.e. same queuing behavior, share in call distribution, provide information on call state.

4.11.6 Remote site
(MR) The system must provide a seamless and cost effective solution to implementing a "second call center". Provide detail for remote shelf or networked (public or private) solutions. Describe how the proposed solution integrates with other PBX/ACD as a remote system - particularly with Mitel, Northern Telecom.

4.11.7 Modular expansion
(MR) Future expansions must not involve significant changes to the "base" system (i.e. forklift solutions). The manufacturer must provide detail on how the system can be expanded beyond the full capacity stated in 4.1.

4.12 Outbound Calling
(MR) The proposed ACD system must be able to accommodate outbound call capacity. The system should be able to utilize outbound call center technologies i.e. sales and marketing databases, contact managers, preview dialing, predictive dialing. The system needs to provide the same

5.0 Implementation

5.1 Proposed Implementation Schedule
The manufacturer is requested to provide a general task outline to install the proposed system. The task outline must include the concurrent custom

development of call center support system features. The Proposed plan must also include provisions for how uninterruptible service will be provided.

5.2 Technical Training

The manufacturer needs to provide a list of recommended training classes for the SA roles (both ACD and call center support systems). Any training required before/during implementation of the ACD system must be included as a task item in the proposed implementation schedule.

5.3 Hardware/Software Diagram of Proposed system

The manufacturer will provide a hardware diagram of proposed connection configurations. Software configurations i.e. Data flows, Call Queue flows should also be depicted.

5.4 Environmentals

What is the power consumption of the ACD system when fully loaded ?

How much AC (in BTUs) does it require to maintain optimum operating temperature ?

What is the optimum operating temperature and what is the safe operating range ?

Does the system have any distribution frame needs ?

What are the grounding requirements?

What are the floor loading requirements at maximum configuration?

If the battery backup comes with the system, what are venting requirements?

Please provide specifications on the cabinet (i.e. dimensions, weight, foot print, elevator accessibility ?)

6.0 Maintenance Support

Define major and minor system failure.

Provide your company's response times for major and minor system failures.

What is the worst case guaranteed response time

Provide details on some historical problems with the proposed ACD and call center support systems.

Provide the MTBF for the proposed systems (include Call Center Support System hardware).

What are the terms of and pricing for maintenance support? Are there varying levels of support ?

Provide the proximity of the closest parts depot - particularly for T-1 cards, ISDN cards, analog   cards, phone equipment.

What is the case load of a typical service technician ?

Computer Telephony Request for Information

1.0   Introduction

1.1   Purpose of request for information

First National Bank of Axxum (FNBA) is soliciting information about potential teleservicing vendor solutions to enhance its retail Customer Service Department (CSD) systems with the intent of:

*   Increasing the speed of transaction access and execution.
*   Reducing transaction complexity.
*   Reducing the amount of training required for FNBA Customer Service Representatives.

The response to this Request for Information (RFI) must describe features, equipment, software, vendor services, and expected FNAX accountabilities to complete the project.

The intent of this Request for Information is to describe the various attributes required of the new or enhanced Customer Service system. Responses will be used to select finalist vendors. Finalist vendors may be requested at a subsequent time to formalize their responses and bids for final selection.

1.2   Type of proposal solicited

FNBA would prefer to not undertake a large scale development effort using internal resources. Ideally, few changes to FNAX Mainframe and Voice Response Unit (VRU) applications will be required. FNAX is looking for a prime contractor for all software integration and customization outside of current FNAX systems. However, it is imperative that potential vendors clearly identify how their product and services allow FNAX to be more efficient at implementing or maintaining a Customer Service teleservicing solution than using internal tool sets. Thus, responses should clearly indicate both whether a vendor can support a specific feature or requirement and <u>how</u> that function would be customized and implemented.

Vendors must make a clear distinction between requirements and customization which will be satisfied by their standard package or tool set and those which require modifications/development. In each instance where modifications/development will be needed to satisfy a mandatory requirement, vendors must indicate a completion time frame to provide the new function. In addition, vendors must clearly identify where co-development on FNAX systems (e.g. Host or VRU) will be recommended to satisfy a specific requirement.

It is suggested that vendors review Section 5 to gain an understanding of the different scenarios and options to be estimated in vendors responses. Note that in addition to the scenarios involving a vendors participating as prime contractor, a response is also requested from vendors regarding how they would be willing to work in partnership with FNAX and other vendors should we choose a 'best of class' approach for the different components of a CSD automation solution (especially the Computer Telephony Integration portion).

1.3 RFI Format

Section 1 -   Contains background information and sets forth instructions for participation in this RFI process. This section also includes background technical information on FNAX's current environment.

Section 2 -   Defines the various high level functional requirements of the Customer Service System.

Section 3 -   Sets forth preliminary minimum FNBA contractual expectations.

Section 4 -   Is a questionnaire which solicits vendor information regarding a variety of topics.

Section 5 -   Identifies the financial and resource information required for financial analysis and sizing of vendor responses.

Section 6 -   Are the appendices which contains specific information, including:

* Transaction volume data
* A description of the top 15 transactions to be re-designed
* A document describing 'key concepts' which will be the basis for developing detailed business requirements
* A detailed set of preliminary requirements for a representative transaction
* A sample Terms and Conditions document which is typical of FNAX technology acquisition contracts.
* A glossary

1.4 Format of response

Vendor proposals are to be submitted with materials arranged in the same order and sequence as this RFI. Identical numbering schemes should be used as in this RFI. Instructions for each section precede the material and should be read carefully to insure that the type of response requested is fully understood. **Failure to follow instructions may result in disqualification of the vendor.**

• The vendor should provide FNAX six (6) copies of their response materials.

- Proposals are to be submitted on standard 8-1/2 x 11 inch paper (8-1/2 x 14 inch is permissible for charts, spread sheets, etc.)
- Proposals construed as proprietary should be so marked.
- FNBA will not be responsible for any costs attributable to proposal preparation or submission.
- Responses are to be received by 5:00 p.m., 02/27/95 in the office of:

Phillip Smith
Senior Project Analyst and AVP
First National Bank of Axxum
12 Main Street
Axxum, ZZ 12345

1.5 Current operational and system environment
1.5.1 Current processing environment

FNAX primarily operates two mainframe environments for on-line and batch processing. The IBM environment handles the majority of traditional applications. The Tandem environment is the processor that drives our ATM / POS system as well as the Wire Transfer application.

IBM Environment:

- 288 MIPS configuration provided by;
  IBM 3090 600S
  IBM 3090 400S
  Amdahl 5990 - 1400
  (Plans are to upgrade to a 350 MIPS configuration in 1995)
- DASD of 1 Terabyte primarily on HDS and IBM devices

- MVS/ESA release 4.3
- IMS release 3.3
- CICS release 3.3
- DB2 release 3.1
- VTAM release 3.4
- TCP/IP release 3.1

Tandem Environment:

- Six Cyclone processors for ATM / POS processing
- Eight processors for Wire Transfer.
- ACI Base24 release 4.0

Front-end Network Processors

- Four IBM 3725's (NCP release 4.2)
- Two IBM 3745's (NCP release 7.1)

Enterprise Processing Volumes

- 1,500,000 IMS transactions per day supporting Branch On-line, ATM/POS, CIS and Hogan applications.
- 1,200,000 CICS transactions per day supporting eMail, Credit Card and Retail Loans.
- 3,000,000 paper items processed per day of which 60 % are on-us transactions.

1.5.2   Customer Service Department environment

The Customer Service Department is physically divided into two sites; one in the Xzzum and one in Axxum. The Axxum site is open 24 hours a day, 7 days a week. The Xzzum site is open from 7:00 am to 9:00 PM and is closed on Sunday's. Of all calls received 43% are handled by the Axxum VRUs , 32% are handled by the Xzzum VRUs, 16% are handled by the Axxum CSRs and 9% are handled by the CSRs in the Xzzum . 800 numbers are primarily routed to the Xzzum site. The Axxum site handles all local western Washington calls. In both sites the VRUs are the initial point of customer contact. In December the CSD VRUs handled 75% of all calls. Workstations for CSR, training and managers are divided as follows; 120 in the Xzzum and 173 in Axxum.

Multi-queue call handling

Agents are organized into three groups:

1)   The primary queue answers and responds to 90% of general information and account requests.

2)   The special queue handles all customer requests requiring research or additional customer assistance and takes calls transferred from the other representatives. Special queue also handles queue overflow when there is heavy volume.

3)   The business queue responds to calls from business clients for such things as check verification.

Note: There is also a Reference Center that provides support for all of CSD. The Reference Center performs Teller functions such as not on-us credit card advances, G/L functions such as fee reversals, letter writing, research, microfilm requests and a number of other support activities.

1.5.3   Telephony

- Two Teknekron Series Three Infoswitch ACDs, one located in the Xzzum area and one located in Axxum.
- The Infoswitch ACDs are currently running on software release 3.22 (proposal in process to move to release 4.11).
- The ACDs are linked together by T-1 lines so that they can balance calls between the two CSD sites. (a T-1 equals 24 lines)
- Since the ACDs in both locations are linked together they can support each other during scheduled or unscheduled downtime.
- Each ACD has independently programmable "routes" that control how calls are handled. An example of "route" flow would be:
  1. Call comes in to the Axxum ACD
  2. ACD checks for available VRU in Axxum
  3. After a specified time (perhaps 3 seconds) the ACD will look to see if a primary queue representative is available in Axxum.
  4. The ACD continues to check for an available VRU or primary queue Customer Service Representative (CSR) until another specified time period passes.
  5. Next, the switch will start looking for an available special queue representative (all the time continuing to check for a VRU or primary queue CSR)
  6. A search for a business queue representative would start if VRU, primary CSRs and special queue CSRs are not available.
  7. At this point the route might tell the Axxum ACD to contact the Xzzum ACD and make a reservation in its queue. (This starts a "route" on the Xzzum ACD that will also have a programmed series of attempts to find a VRU, primary queue, special or business queue representative)
  8. Finally, (and this may be as little as 12 seconds later) the ACD finds an available special queue representative in the Xzzum area.
  9. The call is routed over the T-1 lines from Axxum to the ACD in the Xzzum and then to the available special queue representative.

Note: The "route" also includes information about the type and timing of announcements or music to be played while the client is on hold.

- There are currently 190 programmed "routes" in use by the two ACDs, each "route" can have up to 48 steps.

- All representatives are defined to the ACD by userid. These id's are attached to defined groups. Each group has a class of service, it is the class of service that determines what function (e.g. primary or special queue) is performed by the group.
- A representative can sign-on at any station. The sign-on tells the ACD which group the CSR belongs to and therefore which class of service to allow the CSR to perform at that station.
- Each ACD provides detailed reporting about the calls handled. The information reported each day includes but is not limited to: calls offered; calls handled; calls abandoned; calls transferred; average delay time; agent minimum, maximum and average call time; and wrap up information. These reports are produced in both half hour increments and daily summaries. Samples of one of these reports are in Appendix A.

1.5.4   Voice Response Units (VRUs)

- The Infoswitch communicates with 9 VRUs dedicated to CSD teleservicing functions (7 are CSD and 2 are Pay-by-phone which is a CSD function) of which 55% reside in Axxum and 45% in Xzzum.
- The VRUs operate from three servers, IBM PS/2 models 80, 57 and 95.
- The servers operate under OS/2 1.3 software.
- The servers and the VRUs run Intervoice IFORM software release 5.0.8.
- There are approximately 60,000 calls per day processed by the CSD VRUs.

1.5.5   Host network

- CSD connects to the IBM Host through an IBM 3174-1L Token Ring Gateway Controller.
- The Token Ring Controller connects to an IBM 3745 Data Communications Controller which interfaces with VTAM on the IBM mainframe.
- There are a total of 300 IBM 3270 type terminals in CSD.
- Each terminal has a four session capability.

1.5.6   Applications

Access
- The Access system is supported by the Stairs/VS Release 4 Level 3 application.
- Access contains information on:

1. Branch location, hours, phone numbers and other miscellaneous information;
2. ATM locations;
3. Automated Clearing House (ACH) transaction activity.
- There are more than 50,000 Access application transactions performed each month.

Bill Payer (PBP)

- A FNAX developed application which allows customer to direct the payment of bills through a VRU session.
- Bill Payer is an IMS DB/DC application developed with a Telon code generator.
- There are approximately 1000 Bill Payer sessions each day resulting in about 6000 payment transactions.

Branch On-line (BOL)

- BOL is the IBM host portion of our Branch On-line system. It supports both teller and admin (platform) transactions. BOL is the repository for most current day memo-posting activity. Eleven BOL strip files, which are files created daily based on information extracted from the various systems of record, are used by Teller, Admin and CSD areas as the primary source of customer account information. CSD sessions are part of the BOL on-line application. Each processing night BOL sends paperless memo-posted transactions from CSD and other areas upstream for posting to the system of record.
- BOL is a FNAX developed COBOL II application using IMS DB/DC (Fastpath) Release 3.1.
- It supports 157 transactions, 62 Teller, 70 Admin(which includes the CSD transactions) and 25 support functions.
- There are eleven application strip files plus 29 other data bases supported by the BOL application. The eleven application strip files are:
  1. INV - Investments - mutual fund, Annuity, Brokerage
  2. RLS - Retail Loans
  3. SBS - FNAX Bankcard Services
  4. RET - Retirement
  5. TSP - Trade Services
  6. SDB - Safe Deposit Box
  7. CDA - Certificates of Deposit
  8. SAV - Savings
  9. DDA - Demand Deposits
  10. FLP - Lease
  11. OTP - Outstanding Transaction Processing (overdraft and NSF history)
- BOL interfaces with 25 other production applications.

- There are 10 million BOL Teller transaction per month and 4 million BOL Admin transactions per month. (CSD transactions are a subset of these BOL transactions)
- It is linked to an Electronic Journal archive of 62 days of on-line monetary transactions. (See below Host Electronic Journal for more detail)
- Accounts in Jeopardy (AIJ) is a subset of the BOL system that acts as an account closing warning system. It is an in-house developed IMS DB/DC, COBOL on-line and batch processing application. AIJ records account closing information that is then passed onto personal bankers for follow-up. There are 2 on-line transactions that are used by the AIJ sub-system.
- The Inbound Telemarketing (ITM) application is also a sub-system of BOL. It contains product information. This is an in-house developed IMS DC application. The product data is stored in DB2 tables. ITM contains updatable product information and simple scripts to support the sales effort.

Customer Information System (CIS)
- This is a Hogan Release 8306 IMS DB/DC.
- Customer Information file (CIF) containing 4.8 million records.
- Account Information File (AIF) containing 7.9 million records.
- Address Information File (ADF) containing 3.5 million records.
- CSD performs approximately 20,000 IMS transactions to retrieve CIS each day.

Automated Teller Machine (ATM) / Point of Sale (POS)
- The switch and drive for the ATM / POS application is resides on the Tandem mainframe.
- Host authorization, logging, network settlement and ATM balancing all reside on the IBM mainframe. There applications are FNAX developed, IMS DB/DC applications.
- Currently, ATM / POS transaction detail comes to the mainframe through a batch process. The detail is stored in multiple flat files daily processing.
- The ATM / POS environment handles over 11 million transactions per month.
- CSD does not directly access either application at this time. The limited ATM / POS information currently available is viewed through the BOL application.

Credit Card / Merchant System
- Cardpac Release 5.0 CICS / VSAM application.
- Personal account volumes of 1.1 million, other account volumes in excess of 150,000 accounts.
- CSD does not directly access the Cardpac application. Credit card transactions are processed through the BOL application.

Host Electronic Journal (Host EJ, HEJ)

- Host EJ contains an on-line record of all BOL monetary transactions.
- It is a FNAX developed COBOL II, DB2 application.
- The application load to Host EJ is performed in the IMS environment, the on-line inquiry capability is through CICS /ESA.
- The application process approximately 400,000 incoming transactions per day through IMS.
- Currently, CICS transactions are running at approximately 20,000 per day.
- There are approximately 70 different screens used by the HEJ application.

Demand Deposit Accounts Application (DMS)

- Hogan application Release 8603
- IMS DB/DC
- 967,000 DDA accounts
- Information for this application is stored on BOL strip files. Inquiries are processed by the BOL system. Updates from CSD are sent through BOL to the system of record each night in a batch process.
- Each day after batch processing BOL strip files are updated account by account.
- BOL keeps memo-post information for DDA accounts on the strip files.
- Memo-posts that occur after the batch processing cutoff are reapplied to the strip file account records after an account is refreshed.
- OD protection via credit card or line of credit, on-line exception processing and restraint processing for stops, hard holds and reserved/pledged funds are all sub-systems of the DMS (DDA) application..

Savings Application (SAV)

- Hogan application Release 8603
- IMS DB/DC
- 910,000 open linked savings accounts
- 364,000 open unlinked savings accounts
- Information for this application is stored on BOL strip files. Inquiries are processed by the BOL system. Updates from CSD are sent to the system of record each night in a batch process.
- Each day after batch processing BOL strip files are updated account by account
- BOL keeps memo-post information for SAV accounts on the strip files.
- Memo-posts that occur after batch processing begins are reapplied to the strip file account records after an account is refreshed.
- CD processing, on-line exception processing and restraint processing are all sub-systems of the Hogan Time deposit application..

Microfilm Services Automation (MSA)

- FNAX developed IMS DB/DC (Telon generated)COBOL application.
- Interfaces with the Procars a PC based microfilm application.

- MSA passes requests to the Procars application three times a day using a batch process.
- MSA keeps a record of requests made but not the detail for the request.
- Procars operates in a standalone DOS environment. It is not tied to a LAN and communicates to the host through 3270 emulation.
- Procars groups the requests in batches, creates pull lists and detail pick lists, contains status information about each request, and contains three months of history of each request at the detail level.

Clarke American check vendor information
- FNAX is currently developing a pass through access to the Clarke American check order on-line application.

Electronic Mail (eMail)
- CA eMail release 3.2.
- Application runs in the CICS environment
- Support the X.400 protocol (note: the product as installed at FNAX does not support this protocol even though the vendor product does)

TCS Telecenter workload projection and scheduling system.
- A windows application written in FoxPro running on a PC resident in CSD.
- Schedules over 500 individual staff members.
- Interfaces with the Teknekron ACD and uses call volumes to project future staffing needs.

1.5.7   Application processing cutoffs

BOL, the primary application supporting CSD, is a 24 hour, 7 day a week application. Batch processing for most applications occurs on a Monday through Friday schedule. To support timely batch processing applications have standard times to cutoff that day's work. After a cutoff the transactions for the application are recorded as transactions for the next day. For example, the credit card application may cutoff work around 5:00 PM while BOL transactions may not cutoff that day's work until after 10:00 PM. That means that throughout a 24 hour period applications will be processing work for different business days. It is possible that the data source for application information may change throughout the day due to business day cutoff criteria.

In addition, account refreshes are performed on an application by application, account by account basis. It is possible to inquire on a checking account that has been refreshed or updated from batch processing yet inquire on that customer's savings account that has not been updated. For that reason, refresh dates are stored at the account level. It is important to track the work-of date for each application throughout the day when providing customers with account activity and status information.

1.5.8   Session concept

There are two aspects to the session concept with regard to CSD. First, each 3270 type terminal (the basic CSD workstation) has the capability to handle four host based sessions or logons. Second, each customer interaction is considered a session.

3270 sessions

- Each station or terminal has the ability to handle four separate host logons.
- As configured, the first session (session A) is the only session defined to IMS and therefore is the only session that can access the Branch On-line (BOL) application. This also means that to access any other IMS application the CSR must log off of BOL and onto the other IMS application. CICS applications can be accessed in any session but cannot be accessed through a session already logged onto IMS. All four sessions are used. The applications most commonly in use would be:

  1. BOL - Branch On-line, this is the application under which CSD functions.
  2. eMail - The electronic mail system, a CICS application originally the ADR eMail, now a CA product, is used for written communication throughout the bank.
  3. Access - is the FNAX application that allows the CSR to locate information about staff members, departments and branches throughout the bank.
  4. Host EJ - this is a record of the transactions performed by the branches and the memo-post transactions performed by CSD.

Customer event session

- A customer session originates with the TS07 CSD Identification screen.
- The account number entered for identification purposes is carried and pre-filled where appropriate throughout the session. (Only one account number is carried throughout the session)
- Sessions can contain a number of individual application transactions. A session continues as long as the CSR is dealing with activity for the same primary account. If you want to perform transactions for a different account number you must begin a new session.

- At the end of a session, the decision is made to charge or not charge the client for the activity requested. Either charge choice brings the session to an end.
- The decision to charge or not charge is up to the CSR in most cases. (Some microfilm requests result in automatic charges, some items such as statements are manually charged). The CSR is provided with guidelines to follow in making the decision which is processed by pressing a function key for "charge" or "no charge".

1.5.9   Host applications and userids

Each CSR has a Host defined userid. All userids for IBM mainframe access are defined through the RACF security application. This userid is used to logon to a Network Director screen with pre-defined CSD appropriate applications. IMS and CICS applications can be entered by screen selection or using the appropriate function key, an additional userid is not required. eMail requires a different userid and password in order to be accessed. The same userid can be used to logon to each of the four sessions but each of the four sessions can have a different user logged on. CSRs may logon to multiple CICS applications but only one IMS application since only one session is defined to IMS.

2.0   Requirements

All requirements listed in this Section must be addressed. The vendor is to respond to the contents of this section in the same order, and numbered in the same manner, as set forth herein.   Where a list of requirements or questions occur, the vendor should respond in the same sequence. Functionality is listed in either the form of a description or a question. In either case, the vendor should indicate how the feature is supported and avoid 'yes' or 'no' answers.

List any ways in which the vendor product(s) exceeds the requirements or has capabilities not directly addressed by the questions. Include these additional capabilities directly after the most closely related requirements listed below.

The response must clearly indicate which functional requirements are:

1)   Deliverable on a turnkey basis (no development or customization required)
2)   Deliverable on an end-user definable basis (no technical resources required to adapt to FNAX requirements). Differentiate between functionality which can be implemented by the end-user without technical support and that which requires more formal procedures or control for implementing.
3)   Deliverable using standard vendor provided tools and pre-built modules which can be adapted. List which tools or modules will be used and/or what modifications must be made to pre-built modules. The level of effort to adapt the tool or module to the FNAX requirement must be described.
4)   Deliverable only with new development.
5)   Is a deliverable of a planned release not currently in production.
6)   Not deliverable.

Tools and pre-built modules which are identified in this Section should cross reference to full descriptions of those specific tools/modules in Section 4.2 (General Package Information).

Vendor must indicate specifically if a requirement can be supported but is not being used in production by any clients at this time. Vendor must be prepared to provide references, including contacts, for sites who are using any functionality which is in production today.

If the vendor considers a requirement to be a future enhancement which will not be deliverable with the current product(s), then the proposed availability date must be specified.

The vendor may propose various alternative solutions for meeting any of the requirements. The determination of the suitability of an alternative will be solely at the discretion of FNBA.

The appendices contain the following documents which will assist you in understanding our direction and system requirements.

*   Appendix B contains a 'Key Concepts' document describing some of the major issues that we are facing and our high level approaches to solving those problems.

*   Appendix C contains a description of the 'Top 15 Events' (most frequent) which occur in the Customer Services area and the types of changes we would like to make to the way those events are handled today.

*   Appendix E contains a description of one particular event and a detailing of the requirements for one specific path down to a fine level of detail. This is intended to provide vendors with a sense of the relative complexity and functionality that are likely to be built into final requirements.

Where 'Supplemental Information' is requested, the questions do not indicate requirements for that section but indicate an interest in understanding the vendor's ability to support the functionality or feature discussed.

2.1   Functional requirements

2.1.1   Event and activity tracking

Event and Activity Tracking must be supported.

2.1.1.1 Contact History Database

1.   A Contact History database must be maintained for all customer calls. The file would contain a record of all events and transactions which occur during a call. Information maintained in this file must be accessible by customer, account, or reference number (a unique number assigned to each call which is provided to the customer on monetary transactions).

Logging of all key data required to trace which individual performed a transaction needs to be supported. Logging may be selective based upon the transaction or event being performed. Logging should include information on the operator ID, a time stamp, etc. As this is required for audit and control purposes, logging must be performed with a high degree of data integrity.

2.1.1.2 Activity Tracking

1. During the course of an event with a customer, specific follow-up activities may be identified which need to be tracked. For example, microfilm copy requests, statement copy requests, closing account checks mailed, etc. may occur during a customer call. Each of these action items may require work be performed after the call is completed. The ability to track, update, and manage these tasks from initiation to completion needs to be supported. Specifically, describe how you would support each of the following capabilities:

2. Provide on-line status of any follow-up activities which are required due to an event.

   Allow viewing of the items in a 'tickler' file by each CSR or by their supervisor or surrogate. Should allow the viewing to be filtered by date so that only today's events are reflected.

   Allow reporting of overdue activities to Supervisors for their group.

   The ability to review the history of an activity including who updated the status or completed various portions of the work associated with it.

3. Scheduling of future activities (e.g. a customer callback) which may occur.

4. Automatic entries based upon call events. For example, should a photocopy of a check be ordered (this would also apply to a referral), an item should be entered into the activity file on the expected day of arrival of the photocopy. The expected day should be calculated by the system based upon standard lead times.

5. The initial status (e.g. "Copy requested") of an activity generated by the system should be automatically entered into the Contact History database.

6. The ability for a CSR to exit an event or transaction before it is complete (e.g. a customer letter, a photo request, etc.) and have the transaction automatically logged to a pending file for future completion must be supported. CSRs must be reminded of open activities requiring completion from the pending items list (e.g. when logging on or off). Recall of the transaction in its stored state must occur when that item is selected from the pending list.

7. Allow updates of transactions from different customer events or transactions. For example, should a customer call result in the resolution of a pending activity, the ability to note that the activity is complete during the call should result in the activity being updated and dropped from the active list. Essentially, we do not want to perform separate maintenance of the status of customer events and the outstanding activity files.

8. Automatically remind CSRs of current items in the tickler file. Reminder could be by a message which pops up on their screen during the day or at logoff times.

9. Allow updating of the status of activity items by the CSR or their supervisor. Activities marked as complete should be dropped from the tickler file.

10. Restrict access to certain types of activities, i.e. fraud research items.

11. Identify 'surrogate' CSRs who can access and update the Tickler file should the primary CSR not be present.

2.1.1.3 Workflow management

1. Activities which are currently manual such as printing Cashier's Checks, ordering microfilm copies, or creating time cards may be automated in the new environment, as note elsewhere in this RFI. Describe overall workflow management capabilities supported by your system and the process for tailoring those capabilities to our environment.

2. Open activities may result in work being performed by persons other than the CSR. This would include the Research department in CSD. Research personnel are responsible for processing the activities from all CSRs. To support this, the following capabilities must be supported:

3. The ability for a CSR to forward a 'form' to a research area for action needs to be supported. This 'form' would need to include all relevant call and action data so that the research area would know what action to take and have the information they need to process it. Content of this 'form' could be generated automatically by the system in some events while in other situations the CSR would manually enter information such as the task description and customer data. Describe how you would support this capability. For example, this could involve:

- A message being generated from the event and placed in a 'Research Queue'.
- n file being created during the event and placed in a 'Research Folder'.

4. Allow open activities to be prioritized by the personnel in Research based upon activity type or an indicator set by the CSR (such as a date or 'high priority' indicator).

2.1.1.4 Event recall and correction

1. The ability to recall data about specific transactions for a customer from the Contact History database must be supported. Recall may occur based upon customer name, representative ID, time of day, reference number, or account number. The system may return a qualifying set of transactions (e.g. all transactions for a customer) and provide an ability to select one for research or processing. Once selected, the system must support the ability to 'delete', modify, or 're-enter' the transaction; this may require host updates.

2.1.2 Computer/Telephony Integration capabilities

FNAX is currently uses a Teknekron ACD and does not intend to switch ACDs as part of this automation effort. In this section, note any features or capabilities which would be available to FNAX (or be substantially easier to deliver) should FNAX switch to another ACD and specific switches these additional features apply to.

1. Screen pop with call, customer, or contact history prior to CSR receiving call must be supported. Customer identification will be based upon the entry of an account number and privacy code by the customer onto the VRU which is validated by the host mainframe.

2. Describe the different options which you support for controlling what screen appears on the recipient workstation. Criteria must include, at minimum control over screens based upon what group the receiver is in, source of call (e.g. a Bank of America, Idaho customer versus a FNAX customer), the call event.

3. Upon attempting to transfer a call or contact an individual within CSD, should they not be available, return the status of that person to the operator, e.g. on phone, on break, not at work (see Section 2.1.12, Schedule Adherence). Provide options to forward the call to a

surrogate CSR or to add a message to the original CSR activities file to return the customer call.

4. Ability to control phone from PC including:

* Answer call
* Select phone number from context sensitive pick list
* Transfer calls
* Conferencing others into call
* Other phone commands such as wrap-up, take message, etc.
* A single sign-on to the workstation which automatically enables a sign-on to the ACD.

5. Support of coordinated voice/data for call conferences or transfers. This must include the capability to:

* Provide the receiving person with the active screen from the senders workstation.
* Provide the receiving person with a different screen. For example, when transferring a call to the Sales area on a referral, the initial screen may be the client relationship screen regardless of the original event.

6. When a call transfer is performed, the current status of the customer event in progress must 'transfer' with the call to the new representative. For example:

* If a customer has already been identified to a specific level, then the system should continue to manage the event and screens for that transaction as appropriate.

* The screens appropriate for Bank of America, Idaho customer must be presented to the new CSR if the call originated from an Idaho 800 number and screens appropriate for FNAX customer must be presented to the new CSR if the call originated from a Washington 800 number.

7. Support for conferences with VRU while having visibility to what the customer does on the VRU (e.g. have customer entry of numbers displayed on the CSR screen).

8. Calls may be transferred back to VRU.

9. Multiple screens or windows may be brought up as part of screen pop. List any restrictions you may have on the number of windows.

10. Describe capability to perform call blending during low volume call periods such as the ability to mix inbound and outbound calls. Include discussion of:

* The ability for the system to control whether call blending occurs based upon incoming call queue volumes.
* The ability to select which CSRs are selected for alternative activities (e.g. CBT) based upon flexible parameters.
* The ability of the system to provide Computer Based Training (see Section 2.1.11) to selected staff (as opposed to making outbound calls) during slack periods. Must include the ability to identify to the system who is eligible for CBT and which modules they should review.

11. Support of electronic FAX direct from workstations to client FAX numbers.

Supplemental information

S1. Describe your capability to determine call routing based upon previous customer contacts? Parameters should include option for alternatives should primary receiver be busy, date of last contact (if old may be irrelevant), how busy the current queue is, etc.

S2. Can you support multiple switches or switch types simultaneously (e.g. Teknekron and Northern Telecom)

S3. Can the end of a call (e.g. a hangup) result in the system automatically providing the CSD the session ending screen (e.g. call wrap up, whether to charge the customer or not, etc.)?

S4. Do you support 'expert agent selection' to help select the recipient of an incoming call based upon CSR skills, customer profile, source of call, queue volume, etc?

S5. Do you have the capability to intercept customer calls when the queue is heavy and provide an option for the customer to leave a message?

S6. List ACD switches that your software currently interfaces with in production at this time. List additional ACD switches that your software supports although not in production at this time.

S7. Do you have a 'Snoop' feature allowing supervisors to view the screen that the CSR is viewing, including any data entry and updates the CSR may be making, in conjunction with listening to the client phone call, with or without the CSR being notified?

2.1.3   Check vendor interfaces

1.   The system must include an interface with Clarke American, Deluxe, and Harland for check ordering and performing inquiries as to order status and history. Describe the interfaces and functionality supported for each of these check vendors.

2.   The check vendor screens may be reformatted to present within the standard Graphical User Interface (GUI) look and feel that will be built for this project. In addition, the ability to capture information about check ordering transactions into the Contact History database (see Section 2.1.1.1) needs to be supported.

2.1.4   Letter generation

The capability to generate customer correspondence must be supported.

1.   Standard letter templates will be created for various call types. These letters will include the ability to:

   *   Pre-fill caller/account information from current call data
   *   Limit staff from editing the letter except for specific 'comments' sections for CSR input to the content. Staff editing of letter must be controllable by user class.

2.   Access to letters will be imbedded in the event flows. Depending upon the event, the letter may be either required or optional for the CSR. More than one letter option may be available for the CSR for specific events.

3.   Once a CSR has created a letter and is ready to send it to the recipient, the system must control the output. Based upon the letter selected, one of the following scenarios will occur. Describe the development necessary to support each scenario.

   3.1)   The letter is immediately printed on a central printer.
   3.2)   The letter is batched (and sorted by type of letter or zip code of the recipient) for printing on special paper stock. The ability to include supplemental materials to be printed with the letter must be supported.

3.3) The CSR may automatically fax the letter to the customer from the workstation. The ability to restrict faxing to specific correspondence must be supported (e.g. correspondence not requiring enclosures).

3.4) The letter is electronically routed to the Research area along with notification of a request for off-line information. The Research area prints the letter, provides the appropriate enclosure(s), and forwards to the customer.

4. The ability to incorporate graphics images such as the corporate logo into documents must be supported. Describe embedded graphics capabilities including what type of graphical objects may be included.

5. Non-technical (user area) staff must be able to create or modify standard letter templates and to place templates into production without a systems outage. The ability to change or create letters must be limited to appropriate staff. Describe how staff would perform maintenance to correspondence.

6. All customer correspondence must be maintained on-line for an archiving period of approximately two weeks (and reprintable during that period).

7. The batch processing capabilities of your tools must include the ability to:

* Reprint specific letters which may have quality problems upon output (e.g. wrinkled paper)
* Restart production at the point of failure upon print failure, etc.
* Automatically update a central customer database that the letter has been printed and sent

8. The system must support multiple fonts including multiple fonts on a single letter.

Supplemental information:

S1. Describe how you would provide the ability for CSRs to enter text while keeping the method simple.

S2. Does your software permit the use of Microsoft Word for Windows to create letters and correspondence? Are there any other standard word processing or forms packages which can be used? How would an external letter creation package interface with your software?

S3.   How would you support automatic spell check for all CSR entered text
        (e.g. it is automatically invoked when they update correspondence)?

2.1.5   Screen navigation and context sensitive events

2.1.5.1 Event control and transaction paths

1.   Each event may take diverse paths being taken depending upon
        customer input, data received from the mainframe, contact history, or
        CSR judgment. For example, the 'security screen' described in Key
        Concepts (Appendix B) identifying the customer should be skipped if a
        CSR has already performed a security check on the customer at the
        appropriate level for the current transaction. Describe the manner in
        which event and transaction paths are created and controlled.

2.   CSRs (or other users) will not be expected to input all data to complete
        events or transactions. If the data is available on the Contact History
        Database or from the mainframe and does not need modification or
        validation by the user, then that data should be used to complete the
        transaction (e.g. with the mainframe) without user involvement and
        with or without display to the user.

3.   The system must be able to complete a series of automated transactions
        or activities based upon a single CSR action. For example, a CSR
        completing a particular screen might result in the system automatically
        executing multiple host transactions, performing updates to the contact
        history database, and generating a customer letter.

2.1.5.2 Automated context sensitive actions

1.   Pre fill of data onto screens or forms must be supported. Data must be
        available for pre fill from earlier in the call including VRU or CSR
        input, the Contact History database, or from the FNAX mainframe.

2.   Should a call be received from a customer regarding an account which
        has certain pending action, e.g. an outstanding photocopy request,
        then a 'pending action' flag may be set in the initial screen provided to
        the CSR about that customer or account (see Section 2.1.1.1, Contact
        History Database).

3.   A customer indicator may be set which results in a specific message
        being presented to any CSR who accesses that customer's data on an
        incoming call. The message could be generic or tailored for a
        particular customer.

4.   Where possible, call wrap up codes should automatically be determined based upon event path. The option of having the operator override the codes or add their own input where automation is not feasible needs to be supported.

5.   The ability to translate data from other sources such as the VRU or host into different presentation data (e.g. in a more friendly form) must be supported. For example, account type codes might be converted into easy to understand account descriptions.

6.   The ability to identify the results of a host update transaction to a CSR needs to be supported in easy to understand terms. For example, was the transaction accepted on-line or off-line? Was it rejected? The response format such as highlighting, flashing, color, etc. may vary based upon the result.

2.1.5.3 Navigation

1.   Standard tools should support:

      *   The ability for a user to navigate among different screen fields via the forward and backward tab keys.
      *   Full point and click Mouse capabilities
      *   Function buttons and icons must be accessible via the keyboard, i.e. function keys or key stroke combinations (two keystrokes maximum).

2.   Transactions, field values, pick lists, and product or sales scripts should be variable based upon:

      *   The source of the incoming call (e.g. origination city or state); or
      *   Call data from current or previous customer calls and mainframe data (e.g. customer account list based upon our Customer Information File data)

3.   Two different paths for the same event must be supported: 1) 'Fast-track events' for senior representatives who understand transaction requirements and can utilize faster paths even if it involves more complicated screens. 2) 'Walkthrough' events for novice staff who may need assistance in completing transactions. Describe your support for the following:

        *   The ability to control the set of screens and transaction paths a CSR utilizes based on user class.

        *   Requiring supervisor approval for changes to user profiles (e.g. which class they are a member of).

        *   Development of the event paths that are assigned to user classes, e.g. specifically outlining which screens will be viewed in which sequence for which events. Describe how this control is provided to the user area.

4.   The completion of a transaction by a CSR (e.g. by pressing the enter key or clicking on a 'complete' icon) may occur while the cursor is in any position on the screen.

2.1.5.4 Miscellaneous

1.   The ability for CSRs to dynamically sort and filter a list needs to be supported. For example, checking account activity may be sorted in check number order, date of posting order, and/or may not include specific transaction types. Each option may be selected through menu lists or on-screen icons.

2.   The ability to select multiple items from a list to be acted upon needs to be supported. Items may not be contiguous in the list. This may require host updates be made for each item selected. For example:

        *   Selection of multiple checks and a photo command could result in multiple mainframe photos requests being generated.

        *   Selecting multiple overdraft fees to be reversed may results in all fees being reversed (conversely, the selected fees may be aggregated and reversed as a group).

3.   The ability to recall (and fill into the 'active' field) previously used account numbers such as:

        *   The session account number
        *   Last used account number
        *   Previous session account number

4.   The ability to easily develop different sets of screens and scripts based upon which state a call originated in. Can scripts be developed with variables which are dynamically changed in real time during the call based upon source? Differences could include:

* Different identifier for the source in all screens, e.g. 'Bank of America, Idaho' or 'FNAX'. The identifier could be text or graphics (e.g. a corporate logo).
* Different product scripts or product information.
* Different event flows based upon state requirements.

5. FNAX may choose to not re-engineer all transactions and activities performed within CSD. This would likely be true of small volume transactions where there will not likely be significant savings due to redesign. Thus, many current mainframe transactions will be 'passed through' to the CSR with limited or no modification. These transactions would have to be seamlessly handled by the CSR as part of a customer call without having to 'switch' to another host session or 3270 emulation. Describe alternatives, involving minimal development effort, for:

* Incorporating these 'passthrough' transactions into the standard look, touch, and feel of the overall CSD system that you would provide. This could involve insuring that similar keystrokes and navigation techniques are used by the end-user as well as providing them with a similar visual feel.

* Including statistics and information about these transactions into the Contact History database.

2.1.6   On-line user help or reference information

1. User help and reference information such as procedures manuals or product information needs to be available on-line.

2. Describe how the following user help capabilities are supported:

* Context sensitive help dependent upon event, transaction, or the active field.
* Placement and size options of help windows at user area discretion.
* Instant 'pop up' of help screens (e.g. avoid the slow speed typical of MS Windows help screens).
* Automatically invoke user help, e.g. through CSR errors, based upon specific events or transactions, etc.
* Control by supervisors as to who automatically sees help windows based upon user group parameters and the ability to assign staff to different user groups.

3.   For help and reference screens, describe the following capabilities of your system:

* Alternatives for accessing help or reference information which minimize keystrokes.
* Help or reference screens content and parameters that are maintainable by end-users.
* Quick access to help or reference screens by topic.

2.1.7   Scripting (dialogue)

1.   The ability to provide CSRs Scripts which help them service or sell to customers must be supported. Include descriptions of how your software supports the following features.

* The ability to create context sensitive scripts which are context sensitive, event specific, or dependent upon the customer data from various host or CSD databases.
* Displayed optionally or automatically based upon parameters.
* Indicating to a CSR that a script is available for their use if not automatically displayed.
* Placement and size options of script windows at user area discretion.
* Linking multiple, interactive script windows together and support of multiple screen paths available to the CSR based upon their input or selection.
* Supervisor control over who automatically sees which scripts screens based upon User Group parameters and the ability to assign staff to different user groups.
* Maintenance of script screens content, flow, and parameters by end-users.
* Alternative formatting options for script text or windows such as automatic scrolling across the screen, flashing of script, etc. must be available depending upon call or customer data. Describe options.

2.1.8   Screen design capabilities

2.1.8.1 Menus

1.   Menus must be customizable by user class.

2.   The ability to ghost menu options based upon event or call data must be supported.

2.1.8.2 Pick lists

1.　　Describe your software's ability to support the following regarding pick
list options:

* 　　　Ability to vary content based upon prior call data
* 　　　Function key activated
* 　　　Error activated
* 　　　Scrollable/pageable
* 　　　Size options
* 　　　Placed by program at user discretion.
* 　　　Minimal key strokes to select value
* 　　　Easily maintained and modified in production by end-user.
* 　　　Automatic display based upon prior call, customer, or
　　　　mainframe data,
* 　　　Long pick list. Identify any limits.
* 　　　Describe methods for easing navigation of a long list.
* 　　　Embedded pick lists within a hierarchy.
* 　　　Ability to assign specific keystrokes (e.g. numbers or letters)
　　　　to allow Pick List items to be selected.

2.1.8.3 Fields

1.　　Describe your software's ability to support the following field
alternatives:

* 　　　Highlight or change field format (e.g. highlight, bold, flash,
　　　　etc.) based upon call or customer data, information received
　　　　in a response from the host, or whether data had been entered
　　　　in error, etc.
* 　　　Blocks or methods of showing CSR the field size by a visual
　　　　clue.
* 　　　Ability to ghost fields, determined by event selection and
　　　　customer or call data.
* 　　　The ability to AutoTab to the next field upon completion of
　　　　the current field.
* 　　　Edits based upon co-dependent fields.
* 　　　Edit against pick list.
* 　　　Defaults can be determined by other field entries.
* 　　　Default position of cursor varied by customer data, call data,
　　　　or event path.
* 　　　Ability to place cursor in first field in error if multiple errors.
　　　　Tab should result in cursor placement at next error field.

*   Ability to edit each character of data entered into a field, e.g. use the mouse or standard edit keys such as arrow, delete, insert, etc. to change any character in a field.,
*   Varied fonts and font sizes within same window.
*   Field protection permitting specific fields to be blocked from change. Protection may be dependent upon customer data, call data, or event path.
*   Provide an indicator to the user, such as an auditory signal or flashing, when the maximum number of characters for a field as been entered. Retain the data entered in the field when maximum characters entered.

Supplemental Information

S1.   Describe cursor options supported which enable the cursor to be easily spotted (e.g. varying sizes, blinking, the active cell, etc.)

2.1.9   Department message broadcasting

The following department messaging capabilities are required:

1.   The capability to broadcast messages to CSD groups (or sub-groups such as 'special queue' personnel) or individuals which 'interrupts' call flow and forces staff to review before proceeding with calls. Note: messages should be targeted at specific CSD groups of personnel, not workstations.

2.   The message system should be easy to use. Describe what makes your message system easy to use such as easy editing, easy to understand commands, etc.

3.   Capability to broadcast to only those currently logged on (or scheduled in the current shift. (See Section 2.1.12, Schedule Adherence)

4.   Alternatives for placement and formatting of messages when received such as flashing, scrolling, etc. Ability to create these different formats must be easy to develop by the user area based upon standard formatting selection options.

5.   Store and forward of messages (e.g. should the recipient be logged off or the Workstation is off-line).

6.   Standard template e-mail messages must be available for either repeat messages or easy modification before broadcasting.

7.   Supervisor review of routing list and whether CSRs have reviewed messages.

8.   The ability to 'pace' messages so that not all CSRs receive the message simultaneously.

9.   Directory of past messages for retention, review, and possibly re-send.

2.1.10   ATM and branch location capabilities

1.   The ability to present CSRs on-line maps of ATM and branch locations needs to be supported. Verbiage would be presented with the map such as:

    *   Cross streets and nearby landmarks
    *   Directions from major freeways or arterial routes.
    *   Addresses

       *   Unusual hours of the ATM
       *   Branch phone number.

2.   There must be an ability to search the location database by alternatives such as zip code, street name, town or city, branch name, etc. Maps will be supported for three or more states.

2.1.11   Computer Based Training

1.   The ability to develop on-line training and skill certification courses is desired. Capabilities of the authoring tool and training environment must include:

2.   Support of automated scoring logic for tests, certification, etc.

3.   Tracking of results by user (by group, supervisor, site, total) including:

       *   scoring
       *   completion - partial or full
       *   certification
       *   module use
       *   error statistics by module for all students
       *   clock time spent in the training and individual modules.

4.   Remedial pathing, i.e. the ability to affect pathway based upon results of test. For example, if a student answers one or more basic questions incorrectly, force them to return to a more remedial section.

5.   Computer Based Training (CBT) availability 24 hours/day without impacting system performance of live operations.

6.   CBT deliverable to CSR workstations.

7.   Visual development tools appropriate for course designers, not technical staff. Describe the tools.

8.   Ability to run two versions concurrently, e.g. training modules based upon upcoming system changes versus modules based upon the current release.

9.   Ability to assign modules to specific staff by supervisor.

10.   Support of multimedia including sound, video, etc. Describe multi-media tools.

11. Ability to utilize production screens and business logic from the CSD automation system (including functionality such as access to production help screens).

12. Ability to simulate the production environment including VRU input, responses from host, field edits, etc.

13. Specific mainframe user ID's have been reserved for training. These IDs, when used, allow full navigation among system screens used by CSD but result in no changes being made to our production systems. They are 'dummy' IDs. Use of the CBT system must use these IDs when communicating with the mainframe. In addition, no logging to the production Contact History Database (logging may occur as long as it is clearly separated from production data and not included in production reports and statistics) should occur.

2.1.12   Personnel schedule adherence

FNAX utilizes the TCS Management Group's TeleCenter workload projection and scheduling system in CSD. This system generates a daily schedule for all representatives including start and finish times and break schedules. These schedules are distributed to supervisors at the beginning of each shift. Based upon this data, FNAX would like a 'schedule adherence' system which helps insure that customer service representatives work according to their assigned schedules. Functionality would include:

1. The ability to generate warnings for CSRs of upcoming breaks. Warnings would include flexible parameters as to the amount of advance notice given, the number of advance notices provided, the wording to be used for each notice, where and how it appears on the representative screen.

2. The ability to automatically log a CSR off the system at the beginning of each break period. If the representative is on the phone at the scheduled beginning then the system will log the CSR off at the completion of the phone call. The representative will only be able to continue phone calls during the scheduled break if they 'override' the logoff with a special logon sequence. The originally planned break period for a CSR should be adjusted if delayed due to a customer phone call which was in progress when the break was scheduled to begin (this would allow proper reporting on exception reports).

3. Tracking of all CSR time which is listed as breaks, lunches, research time, etc. This could be captured via specific logoff codes or the

selection of a logoff type from a screen. Exception reporting should be made of each adherence exception.

4. The ability to dynamically change break periods for each representative. Access to this function must be limited to supervisors and managers.

5. The ability to import the scheduling data from the TCS scheduling system into the CSD automation system to update staff scheduling data must be supported. This file must be uploaded daily at user request. The PC containing the TCS software will be connected to the CSD network. All weekend days may be uploaded on Friday before close of business. This file may be uploaded more than once, should updates occur. The system must be able to override previously entered data without interrupting functionality to representatives who may be already at work and logged on. Note any assumptions you make in your ability to support this and alternatives for importing the file (e.g. can you read the native TCS DBF files or would you need us to create a special export file of the scheduling data).

6. Provide ability for CSRs or supervisors to interrogate specific CSR schedules.

2.1.13   Time card system

Current time card system: Time cards are currently completed manually by staff. Both the staff member and their supervisor must sign the card. Cards indicate time at work, absence reasons and hours, date of absences, etc. Time cards are scanned into a corporate time card system which calculates payroll hours and overtime and interfaces with the Payroll system.

Automation of the CSD timecard system should be supported including:

1. Data generated from the Schedule Adherence system (see Section 2.1.12) regarding when staff log-on and off the system should be used as the basis for time cards.

2. An on-line substitute for the time card should be developed to allow staff members to review and approve their hours worked. Employees should be able to indicate times which are in error (e.g. perhaps they forgot to log on or off as appropriate on a particular day) and note the correct hours or time.

3.   The supervisor must review and approve the employees on-line time card. Supervisors can override hours as logged by the system and approve employee corrections.

4.   A electronic file equivalent of the time cards should be created weekly for input into the corporate time card system.

5.   Complete audit trails of all actions taken in conjunction with creating electronic time cards including any changes or updates made. This must include the user ID of whomever made a change. Audit trails will be either electronically archived or offloaded to Fiche as it ages for long term storage.

6.   Viewing of time cards must be limited to appropriate staff. The ability to affect the on-line file of time card data must be limited to appropriate staff.

2.1.14   Telemarketing/sales specific requirements

Describe the use of your system to support a telephone sales organization or branch platform sales system. Clearly differentiate between functionality which has been implemented at a current site and that which has not. Include aspects which support:

1.   Maintaining detailed customer call and history information including customer financial profiles.

2.   Tracking sales, sales vs. goals, and who referred the sale.

3.   Interfacing with automated dialing systems

4.   Building and maintaining complex sales and product scripts which have alternative pathing possible based upon customer responses. Scripts should be maintainable by end-users.

5.   Ability to download data from other sources including the mainframe such as client data, competitor rates, FNAX rates, etc.

6.   Outbound sales calls such as:

      *   Building call lists based upon flexible criteria (such as customer income, product interest, etc.) and using those lists to automatically dial numbers. Include the ability to track the outcome and effectiveness of use of these call lists.
      *   Interfacing with auto-dialers.

7. Interface with an Official Check Printer system to prepare Cashiers Checks on loan proceeds, closed accounts, or CD redemption's. Describe any experience you have with interfacing with Official Check Printing systems.

8. Creation of very complex forms (e.g. loan documents) which have the ability to include or exclude sections based upon customer data.

9. Fulfill sales by sending data to host systems for boarding of the new account(s).

10. Create 'What If' scenarios, including graphs, of:

    * FNAX vs. competitor products.
    * Results of alternative investment decisions.
    * Results of borrowing based upon different loans products or loan amounts.

11. Ability to print graphs (locally, remotely, FAX) which might be generated from the 'What If' scenarios.

Supplemental information

S1. Describe your ability to provide Auto, RV, or Boat loan blue book rates on-line. Include listing of any interfaces to third party providers of this data you support today.

2.1.15 Imaging support

Describe your products ability to handle document images including what graphical and imaging /compression standards are currently supported by your software. Specifically, can your software:

1. Interface with an external DBMS which contains images of documents (such as checks)

2. Receive one or more images as part of the data returned in the response to a query or transaction sent to that DBMS.

3. Display the image(s) received from a DBMS or image system.

4. Does your product interface with any Check Imaging systems? Which ones? Is this capability in production at any site?

5.   Provide any future plans that you have for interfacing with imaging or
        Check Imaging systems in your product line and when that support is
        estimated to occur.

2.1.16   Miscellaneous

1.   A basic business on-line calculator should be available on a pop-up
        screen via quick keystroke or an on-screen icon.

2.   Reference numbers uniquely identifying an event or customer call for
        audit and recall purposes must be created. These reference numbers
        are provided to customers at the end of each call.

3.   Develop an interface to the FNAX Microfilm systems to support the
        ordering of check copies. This would include forwarding a file of
        check copy requests to the MSA system and the ability to look up the
        status of check orders in the Procar microfilm system.

Supplemental Information

S1.   Does your software provide the ability to perform screen prints to a
        printer connected to the local network?

S2   Can you support flexible keyboard arrangements and varying use of
        keys?

2.1.17   Reporting and data availability

1.   The software environment must capture information which will allow
        the following reports and on-line queries to be supported. Note: the
        data for calls received in both the Xzzum and Axxum locations must
        be consolidated.

2.   All terminals, based upon user class, must have the ability to display
        in real time the following:

        *   System status
        *   Agent Status
        *   Queue status
        *   Trunk status

3.   When customer calls are received by a representative, the ability to
        display the following information must be supported:

        *   Transfer path (e.g. VRU to CSR to second CSR).

* Total call time
* Wait time

4. Reporting and tracking by event such as:

* Type of event
* Length of calls for an event such as fee reversals or refunds by operator, group, time frame, department, etc. If multiple events occur during a call then the tracking may be requested for the length of time spent during that event within the overall call time. If multiple transactions occur within an event (e.g. a letter is generated, a fee is charged, etc.) then data about the individual transaction must be tracked.
* Tracking of the path an operator took to complete an event. Describe alternatives for this tracking ability and how you would recommend displaying this type of information.
* Statistical correlation of events to determine what types of events tend to occur in the same phone calls and in what order.

5. Productivity reporting by operator, group, location, or department including:

* Average length of call broken out by VRU, CSR, and individual queue time
* Average length of call wrap-up
* Idle times
* # of events/call
* Pathing of event navigation
* Specific actions taken by operators during phone calls such as fee waivers, reversals of fees, referrals, etc.
* # of calls/hour (day, week, month, etc.)
* # of calls/hour vs. number of calls in queue
* # of transfers
* Outbound call statistics
* All time spent by CSRs including lunch, breaks, training, etc.

6. Reporting and queries of customer contact history including:

* date of contact
* events during contact
* staff contacted
* status: (closed/pending) for each event, tickler items, etc.
* notes regarding customer contact such as whether they tried to obtain a fee reversal

7.   Tracking of customers who hang up while in queue. Tracking of customers who hang up while using the VRU in the middle of a transaction (e.g. they do not complete the activity). Keep track of ANI data for analysis of these types of calls.

8.   Lists of customers who have multiple or repeat problems to aid in retention.

9.   Describe how your report writing tool supports each of the following features:

* Selection of data across multiple tables. Hides database structure from user area.
* Building of multiple table reports.
* Filtering of data.
* Ability to build standard filters for dynamic application to query results.
* Sorting of data.
* Ability to build standard sorts for dynamic application to query results.
* Automatic totals on breaks.
* Labeling of data.
* Ability to easily set performance goals for unit (group, department, division) and build exception reports of events, service levels, productivity statistics which do not meet those goals.

10.   Describe reports that are delivered with your solution on a turnkey basis.

11.   Must support the ability to upload all data from the Contact History Database to external databases.

2.2   Sample event flow development

Appendix E contains a detailed description of potential requirements for an event. Provide a detailed description of the development steps which would be taken, tools which would be utilized, the amount of effort it would take, etc. to develop the event per the requirements.

Also describe any suggested design criteria for screen flow, screen design, etc. based upon the detailed event description.

2.3   Overall requirements

2.3.1   System and application security

2.3.1.1 Security overview

1.   Describe how you would support single sign-on by user which enables access to multiple host applications or sessions and the ACD.

2.   Security architecture should be compliant with standard Distributed Computing Environment (DCE) security services, as defined by the Kerberos standard. If your security architecture is not in compliance, list your plans for becoming compliant. If you do not have plans to become compliant, describe your reasons for not doing so.

3.   Describe your software's abilities to support the following and how you would implement these features:

*   Limiting physical access to your environment including workstations, servers, etc.
*   Limiting direct logons to the server (e.g. support use of a NTAS security server or equivalent to perform logons). List options currently supported.
*   Security software provided by the server application or database software and not the operating system.
*   Access RACF to authenticate users. Keep passwords in synch with RACF.

Note: existing mainframe systems such as IBM and Tandem will retain their internal security controls. Native security services will continue to control access to mainframe resources, i.e. RACF and Tandem.

2.3.1.2 Client Workstation Security

Indicate your ability to meet each of the following workstation security standards. If you would address these requirements through the use of third party software, indicate your recommendations for such software.

1.   Logon should require authentication with a password of at least 7 alpha numeric characters.
2.   There should be a logon failure process that prevents logon after a predetermined number of attempts (maximum of 5 to 10 logon attempts).
3.   Initial passwords set by administrators should be pre-expired, requiring the owner to change default passwords at first logon.

4.   Passwords expiration should be definable by the security administrators (30 to 90 days).
5.   Passwords should be encrypted for storage.
6.   Passwords should be masked at entry.
7.   There should be the ability to authorize more than one employee to the work station without sharing an individual userid.
8.   There should be a way for a guest to use a workstation for network access without accessing the owner's data files and proprietary programs.
9.   Access control should provide for the protection of data files and programs by individuals and groups.
10.   Security software should be enabled at start-up and should be protected from alteration without prior security administrator authorization and prevent boot from removable media.
11.   There should be the ability to perform password resets from a remote location.
12.   The software must support pre-configuration.
13.   Software should provide a quick lock feature that allows for temporary absence from the workstation.
14.   The software should provide for locking of an unattended/inactive workstation.
15.   The software should support single sign-on across the network.
16.   Product should allow for multiple administrator ID's.
17.   Password history should be maintained at least for 20 generations to prevent password reuse.
18.   Password changes can be performed by the ID owner for routine password changes.
19.   Product keeps an audit trail that can be accessed remotely for reporting and investigation.
20.   Encryption support for both fixed drives and removable media (floppies and tape).
21.   Controls for deciphering data.
22.   Supports centralized distribution and minimizes user interaction.

2.3.1.3 Virus Protection Standards

Indicate your ability to meet each of the following virus detection standards. If you would address these requirements through the use of third party software, indicate your recommendations for such software.

1.   Software must run in an active mode that provides constant screening.
2.   Software must detect known viruses and support cleanup of identified viruses.
3.   Software should have a feature that will allow it to identify suspicious activity.
4.   The software should be tamper resistant.
5.   Supports centralized distribution and minimizes user interaction.

2.3.1.4 File Server Security

The server operating system is viewed as the primary means to implement data security objectives over and above complementary functionality found in network, application and database products.
Indicate your ability to meet each of the following file server security standards. If you would address these requirements through the use of third party software, indicate your recommendations for such software.

1.   Logon to any department server from the server keyboard should require authentication with a password of at least 7 alpha/numeric characters.
2.   There should be a logon failure process that prevents logon after a predetermined number of attempts (maximum of 5 to 10 logon attempts).
3.   Initial passwords set by administrators should be pre-expired, requiring the owner to change default password a first logon.
4.   Passwords expiration should be definable by the security administrators (30 to 90 days).
5.   Passwords should be encrypted for storage.
6.   Passwords should be masked at entry.
7.   Access control should provide for the protection of data files and programs by individuals and groups.
8.   Security software should be enabled at start-up and should be protected from alteration without prior security administrator authorization and prevent boot from removable media.
9.   There should be the ability to perform password resets for administrators and users from a remote location.
10. The software must support pre-configuration.
11. The software should provide for locking of the server keyboard if left unattended/inactive.
12. The software should support single sign-on by accepting pre-authenticated users from an external source.

2.3.1.5 Network Security

Network Security will be provided by software that will support network encryption and user authentication. Components of the software will be housed on each workstation and server in the environment. Indicate your ability to meet each of the following network security standards. If you would address these requirements through the use of third party software, indicate your recommendations for such software.

1.   The software should provide for integrity and/or the privacy of a message (message authentication/encryption).

2. The software should provide for transport of a users credentials (single sign on support).
3. Software should support extended authentication.

2.3.1.6 Application security

1. Discuss application level security that your system provides. Include, at minimum, the following abilities:

    *   Controlling access to transactions or procedures by individual or group.
    *   Controlling the ability to complete transactions based upon criteria such as dollar amount or customer value by individual or group. Customer value may be determined from a mainframe based indicator.
    *   A history of access levels for each individual or group and audit trails as to who affected changes to access levels.

Supplemental information

S1. What physical workstation security products is your software currently running in production?

S2. Do you have the ability support single sign-on by allowing the use of an external security software product for user authentication? Which software packages does your software currently interface with?

S3. How do you prevent CSRs or other end users from using the workstation for any applications other than the system you provide? How do you prevent CSRs from by-passing this and possibly harming the system during system failures, e.g. during restarts?

2.3.2 System reliability

2.3.2.1 System Uptime

[CSD is open for customer calls 24 hours a day/7 days a week. Any downtime has a significant impact on our customers.]

1. Describe your ability to support the following requirements.

    *   System administrative and maintenance activities must not take the system down.

> * Ability to make changes to software and system without taking down whole system. Specifically, list which features and maintenance activities can be performed while the system is live. Include listing of what user parameters can be changed such as scripts, help screens, pick list tables, etc.

2. For software updates which are not user controlled (e.g. involve code changes), changes must minimize impact on production. Describe how you would implement changes without impacting the rest of the system.

3. Can the system support two different Client systems running simultaneously while downloads of new client software are being made (assume that the interface between the client and server may change as part of the new software)?

4. Describe any tools which support notice of possible impending failures (e.g. monitoring of network or disk access failures which exceed certain parameters).

2.3.2.2 Restart/recovery

Provide complete descriptions of how your system would support the following requirements:

1. The ability to recover from various component crashes including server, workstation, power failures, disk crashes, host, ACD. Include ability to switch to alternate devices. Describe the events that take place upon a failure of each component.

2. System crash recovery processes must allow for reconstruction of all files to the last checkpoint.

3. Should a server fail, automatic switching to a backup server must occur. How long does it take for the backup system to become operational? Does this take manual intervention?

4. The system must have the capability of handling damaged files gracefully. Can it continue to function while providing notice to a system administrator that a problem exist? For which files? Which files would cause a system failure if broken?

5. The phones and VRU must continue to function even though the network or server is down. Describe how you would accomplish this and any ACD or VRU functionality lost as a result of such a failure.

What incoming phone data (e.g. source of call) is available when the server/CSD automation system is down?

6.	Support for remote recovery must be provided, if appropriate. Support for all Xzzum systems occurs from Axxum.

Supplemental Information

S1.	Explain operational and system recovery procedures for when the power or equipment fails during operation.

S2.	Explain redundant hardware capabilities and how these capabilities are utilized.

## 2.3.2.3	Store and Forward and off-line Capabilities

1.	What are the off-line capabilities of each component of your architecture? Separately describe the ability of the server(s), workstation, or other architectural components to function when:

*	The Host is unavailable.
*	The host is only partially available (e.g. specific applications are down but the host is generally functioning).
*	The Server is unavailable.

2.	Describe your software capability to (and the development required to support):

3.	Recognize that the host has not responded on a particular transaction and based upon the event being processed, backout other related transactions which may have been completed with the host and provide unique error messages back to the agent for the particular failure which has occurred. Describe the development tools used to customize this capability.

4.	Describe store and forward capabilities including:

*	Practical limits to the length of time the system can store and forward.
*	Retry controls and capabilities upon multiple transaction (full or partial) failures.
*	The ability to manage system workload upon store and forward. For example, pacing transactions a few at a time to the host or at controllable intervals in order to prevent

degradation in system performance upon re-instatement of mainframe availability.

* The ability to run without manual intervention except in exception conditions.
* The ability to inform designated areas or personnel of an off-line condition.
* Workstations must run independently of server including the ability to perform store and forward. What capabilities would they have?
* The ability to inform a designated area of off-line transaction exceptions (e.g. store and forward transactions which are rejected by the mainframe) so that they can research and process accordingly.

Supplemental information

S1.   If a workstation crashes while it has store forward transactions queued up, how are these transactions accounted for?

S2.   Provide alternatives and recommendations which you can support for insuring that the host has received all activity which is performed by CSRs.

S3.   Provide alternatives and recommendations which you can support for insuring that the host does not process duplicate activity (consider issues with store and forward transactions or retries upon no response from host).

S4.   Do you support the ability to access data (e.g. a daily download of customer identification data such as personal security codes which has been loaded onto the server) when the host is down in order to complete a transaction?

2.3.3   Disaster recovery requirements

1.   What are your backup and disaster recovery recommendations?

2.3.4   Volume requirements

The following projected transaction daily volumes must be supported by the CSD automation system:

Activity	1995	1996	1997	1998
Total Call Volume	100,000	120,000	145,000	175,000
Calls handled by VRU	70,000	88,000	110,000	137,000
Calls handled by CSR	30,000	32,000	34,000	38,000
Host transactions generated by Calls	415,000	500,000	600,000	720,000
Host transactions generated by VRU	120,000	150,000	190,000	240,000
Transferred calls (within CSD)	8,000	9,000	10,000	11,000
Transferred calls (total)	47,000	51,000	55,000	60,000

Notes:

* 60% of the volume is at the Axxum Site vs. 40% at the Xzzum site.
* The system will need to handle no less than 300 simultaneous operators in production.
* The above represents nearly 14 host transactions for each customer call handled by a representative today. VRU usage results in approximately 2 host transactions being generated per call.

Based upon these numbers, a peak 1/2 hour call volume is projected to be:

	1995	1996	1997	1998
Peak Volume	6,200	7,500	9,000	11,000
Peak Mainframe transaction volume	30,000	35,000	42,000	50,000

1. Describe your system's ability to process the above volumes.

2. The most difficult system load may be after a system recovery when as many as 300 CSRs may attempt a logon at in an extremely short period of time. Describe how your system would handle an extremely high peak transaction load and what the client would experience should the system capacity be exceeded for a short period of time.

See Appendix A for detailed volume statistics.

2.3.5   Response time requirements

1. Current response time for host access by CSD representative is .8 seconds including host and network time. No degradation in this response time is acceptable. Describe the expected response time overhead added to host access by a properly configured system using your architecture. Include screen refresh time.

2. For a transaction which requires no host update (but will require accessing the Contact History Database, identify the amount of time utilized between the time a request is generated by a client workstation (e.g. a CSR presses 'enter') and the CSR receives a fully refreshed response screen back from the server. Assume a Contact History database storing 6,000,000 calls for 1,000,000 customers.

3. Describe how you would configure the Computer Based Training environment to avoid conflict with the production environment.

4. Describe how you would configure the report writing and query access on the CSD automation system database to avoid conflict with the production environment.

5. Describe how you would configure the CSD automation database (e.g. for customer contact history) to provide adequate response time to CSR staff.

2.3.6   System management, monitoring, and support

Describe the tools that you provide and their functionality for the following:

1. Network management
2. Configuration management
3. Performance monitoring and system tuning tools including identification of software, network, or hardware bottlenecks.
4. Full system backup while on-line.
5. Hardware monitoring

If you don't provide system management tools, which tools do you recommend?

2.3.7   Multiple site support

FNAX has Customer Service sites in Axxum and in the Xzzum area. Information about customers calls and contacts, is required in an integrated fashion for both sites. This means that even if a prior call originated in Xzzum, a Axxum CSR must have transparent and complete visibility to that call data in real time. Customer and call statistics need to be integrated across both sites, as well. Note: a call may arrive in the Xzzum location, be answered in Axxum, and transferred back to the Xzzum.

1. Provide explicit detail on how your system will manage call and customer data in such a way that both sites will have access to all

Contact History data including that from the current call (e.g. in a transfer situation across sites).

2.   Describe how your system will handle call transfers and call Conferences (with associated data) which are cross-site in nature.

3.   Describe any distance specific issues such as server location in relation to client workstations, e.g. is their a maximum distance that your recommended configuration will support (keep in mind our dual site situation).

2.3.8   Other functionality supported

1.   The vendor should describe other significant application functionality not covered above which may help differentiate their product.

2.4   Implementation

2.4.1   Implementation strategy

1.   The vendor's implementation proposal is to begin with a brief
      narrative on the strategy recommended for installing a CSD
      automation solution. Alternatives can be recommended on all items.
      It is important that the following information be part of the vendor's
      response:

   *   Methodology to be used for all aspects of the project from
        requirements through implementation and a description of
        each phase.
   *   Migration procedures the vendor would use for converting the
        current CSD environment to the new one.
   *   What portions of the implementation can be or should be
        phased

Note: FNAX will expect to pilot functionality for 4-8 weeks.

2.4.2   Project methodology

1.   Describe each phase and the deliverables to be included. Include a
      sample project plan and a typical list of deliverables. Include an
      example of well written requirements documentation.

2.4.3   Quality assurance strategies

Describe what strategies you use for insuring that your delivered product will be
error free. High quality includes issues of meeting our objectives. Include a
discussion on:

1)   Approach to testing (during each phase).
2)   Error log/tracking methodology.
3)   Change control methodology.
4)   Performance and volume testing.
5)   Quality assurance strategies before you deliver code or product.
6)   Automated testing tools.

2.4.4   Expected FNBA system changes

1.   Describe the possible changes that we might have to make to our
      systems to support this project. Although our intent is to minimize

changes to our ACD, VRU, and mainframe environments, what types of changes do you recommend?

Include changes to the ACD, VRU, network, mainframe, etc. Describe the possible extent of those changes. In the case of issues such as 3270 emulation vs. LU 6.2, describe what conditions would cause us to want to convert to LU 6.2.

2.4.5   Recommended training for FNAX staff

1.   Please describe the training program, and what classes would be required to allow FNAX to be fully independent from a customization and development standpoint. Include recommended classes, whether or not your company performs the course in-house. Include video training or equivalent to reduce training cost. Include specific identification of the pre-requisites for staff attending the courses (technical or business backgrounds).

2.   Clearly identify training which can be provided to client areas (the system owners) which would allow them to make changes independent of FNAX technical staff. Insure that this information cross references clearly to Section 4.2, General Package Information.

3.   Include a full course listing.

4.   Describe the extent and type of training that you will recommend for our Customer Service Representatives to adapt to use of the new system. Describe the training required to 'train the trainer' should we decide to perform the training in-house.

3.0   Contractual issues and expectations

The contract governing this project will be developed specifically to encompass this RFI and your Response. Standard contracts may be used as reference, but will **not** be the basis for negotiations. The General Terms and Conditions included in Appendix D forms the basis upon which the Special Terms and Conditions (project-specific) will be attached.   Please review and note any changes you would propose or exceptions you have to those General Terms and Conditions.

Your Response you present will be made a basis for an exhibit to the contract in the event FNAX elects to proceed and you are the vendor of choice. As contracts typically state, the final contract encompasses the complete and exclusive agreement as to the products and services being acquired and the contract will supersede all communications, oral or written, between the parties. In support of this clause, FNAX Bank may require your Response or sections thereof and any additional documentation which describes the project framework, products, services, guarantees, warranties, response times, support, etc., to be made a part of the contract.

The following sections are key components of a contract that would be addressed in any subsequent agreements that we would make with your firm. Please indicate your firm's position on each of these issues and respond directly to any questions.

1.   **Pricing and Payments:** Prices are subject to discounting. Wherever possible, to affect more attractive pricing, you are encouraged to be creative, including price bundling. Payments shall be tied to project milestones, with final payment of not less than 40% of the contract due after final acceptance.

2.   **Development, Installation, Testing, and Training:** These tasks may be scheduled for off-hours. No incremental charges will be assessed.

3.   **Scope Changes:** There will be a formal section dealing with scope changes covering the opportunity to re-price in the event the scope is reduced or expanded. Scope changes must address not only price but also project impact and deliverable dates. How does your firm formally incorporate changes into a project?

4.   **Warranty:** 3 year on-site warranty is required at no additional charge.

5.   **Maintenance:** You must be willing and capable to contract for maintenance and support for both hardware (if you provide) and software. (If approved in advance by FNAX Bank, a qualified subcontractor may be used.) Due to the critical nature of this installation, response time from the time the problem call is received to the time a service technician arrives on FNAX's site must be not

more than **2** hours. Additionally, escalation procedures for unresolved critical problems will be addressed.

6. **Escalation:** There will be a formal escalation procedure to be followed during the project and subsequent to acceptance. Problem logs, status meetings, and open communication will be a part of this section.

7. **Acceptance Testing:** This will be developed prior to the installation of the products. You will be required to comply with the acceptance testing. In the event you will not contract for acceptance testing, an indication on your Proposal must clearly state why and what you propose as an alternative to acceptance testing. No acceptance test may disqualify you as a supplier under this project.

8. **Documentation:** Manufacturer standard manuals will be required. In addition, you may be required to develop a "project specific" user manual. The contract will not be considered complete without proper documentation.

9. **Trade-in policy:** You may propose a framework for trade-ins for any hardware included as part of your proposal, particularly if a manufacturer discontinues a product line.

10. **Liquidated damages:** Once the project milestones have been established, you must agree to liquidated damages if you're solely responsible for missing or delaying a milestone.

11. **Performance Bond:** Indicate your willingness to post an adequate performance bond to ensure that the project will be completed in the event you withdraw or are unable to complete the installation.

12. **Performance Warranty:** Indicate what performance warranty would remain in place after your proposed system had been installed and accepted by FNAX (i.e. uptime, response time for inquiries, reliability etc.)

13. **Third Party Agreements:** Provide samples of any third party agreements that FNAX would need to execute, as part of your response, such as third party software or hardware maintenance agreements.

14. **Bank of America Agreements:** Are any or all of the components contained in your proposed system currently being utilized by Bank of America? Please provide copies of any Bank of America contracts related to your proposed system. In addition, it is expected that any terms and conditions reached with FNAX as a part of an agreement will also apply to Bank of America should they decide to utilize your product at a future time.

15. **Configuration Errors and Omissions:** Are your prepared to offer a warranty that all the necessary components (hardware, software, network cards, interfaces, etc.) that will be required for FNAX to test and implement your proposed solution will be included in the contracted price [or if not included in the contracted price, identified as required elements in your formal response?].

16. **Software** Please describe whether each software component that you are proposing would be delivered to FNAX in Object and/or Source Code.

17. **Escrow Agreement:** Describe any existing Escrow agreement for your proposed software that would be incorporated into overall agreement with FNAX.

18. **Ownership of Custom Developed Applications:** If your proposal involves the development of a custom application by your organization then described who would retain the rights to re-license this application and how do you envision supporting it.

4.0   Vendor information & questions

Provide detailed responses to each of the following subject areas.

4.1   Corporate information

1.   Provide a brief narrative about your company. This narrative should contain information about the company's background, its current size and the products and services it offers.

2.   Provide information that demonstrates the expertise of the company and its personnel, including a discussion of the size and expertise of those technical staff whom would be candidates to support an implementation of your product at FNAX.

3.   Provide information that demonstrates the company's financial stability. As part of this information, we request a copy of the company's most recent audited financial statement.

4.2   General package information

In addition to responding to the following questions, specifically identify whether any feature, development capability, or characteristic of your environment would need development in order to be supported. Identify whether or not that development is part of the quoted price estimates to follow in Section 5. If in any case, support for a function is provided by third party products, identify which products you recommend.

4.2.1   System architecture

The vendor is to provide an introduction to their system including descriptions of all significant system components.

1.   Include pictures which describe all hardware and software aspects of the proposed system including those functions for which FNAX is responsible (mainframe, VRU, etc.)

2.   Describe the role of each component and the specific functionality implemented as a part of that component. Components should include any significant hardware, software packages or subsystems; especially any component requiring independent development to customize or integrate. Describe the standards and manner in which each component communicates and interacts. Note any limits to expansion or issues associated with scale.

3.   Describe the development tools used to customize each aspect of the system. What does the development package provide without having to incorporate the use of user exits or 3GL's? What types of functionality typically require the use of a 3GL or user exit? Do you have a visual development tool and/or 4GL and what are their capabilities?

4.   Explain the mechanics of how your system manages the Computer Telephony Integration (CTI) including Screen Pop, Conferences of calls and data, etc. Describe the different components that help manage screen pop, their role, how these components would interact with our ACD, etc. If your CTI capability can function as a separate module, i.e. interfacing with other third party software, describe the functionality which would be provided by the CTI module alone.

5.   Identify any third party tool sets which are included in your tool set.

6.   Describe what you consider to be strengths and weaknesses of your current offering.

7.   Explain exactly why use of your product set would make us more productive than developing the CSD automation system in house using tools such as:

    *   Standard visual development tools, i.e. Visual Basic.
    *   A standard middleware package such as MDI.
    *   Sybase as a local database engine.

The ideal solution must integrate with FNAX's standard distributed computing environment (see Section 4.2.5) and internally developed client/server applications. These applications are currently targeted for development using Visual Basic and Sybase System 10.

8. Can your system use Visual Basic for the presentation tool and Sybase System 10 as the server database? If not, why not? What is the impact of using either of these tools? If you would recommend against use of either of these tools, please explain?

9. Describe how your system will integrate within our client/server application environment with the following capabilities:

 * Share data
 * Share objects and modules
 * Call or launch one application from another
 * Implement Computer Telephony Integration across applications (e.g. transfer the voice and data to a telemarketing representative who is using a FNAX developed application from a CSR using the CSD automation system.)
 * Implement a common look and feel
 * Run under common platform

4.2.2 Documentation

What kinds of software documentation standards are used in the following areas:

1. User manuals.

2. Module or subroutine headers.

3. Comments in the source code.

4. Program design languages.

5. Audit trails of modifications to code.

6. Include a section of a sample user manual in your response for our review. Include any other samples which would provide us with a feel for the quality of your documentation.

4.2.3 Software standards

1. Describe how your application design supports portability across platforms. For example, does the application make direct calls to the Operating System (O/S)? Are calls to the O/S isolated in separate modules?

2. What compiler is used by your development tools to generate executable code? What platforms does this compiler run on?

3. What functions must run on client, server, host, other? How much flexibility is there in where application modules operate?

4. Are your applications developed in a modular basis? Which of them function independently and can interact with other vendor applications? What are the interfaces and are they documented for third parties?

5. What operating systems does the product work with today?

6. Does the product conform to the OSF standard? What other open software standards does the product conform to? Assuming that your products are only partially compatible with these standards, how do they vary?

7. Which network drivers does your product work with (e.g. Named Pipes, TCP/IP)?

4.2.4   Hardware standards

1. What type of hardware does your software currently run on? What hardware, in your experience, provides the best price/performance?

2. Describe in detail benchmarking results (and source) which support identification of appropriate processing power required to run your software based upon varied volumes. Identify the highest volume production shop using your software in a fashion similar to FNAX's direction, the volume of transactions currently being supported, the platform being used, and response time to the client for representative transactions.

4.2.5   Compliance with FNAX distributed computing standards

For consistency in our computing environment and to leverage our existing support resources, we prefer that the vendor solution conforms as much as possible to existing Bank computing standards. If the solution recommended by the vendor departs from the standards listed below, the vendor should describe plans for bringing the system into conformance. If the vendor has no plans for bringing their product into performance, describe the reasons for not doing so.

Existing distributed standards or preferred solutions:

1. Server Operating System: MS Windows NT Server

    (The Bank also has an installed base of NetWare 3.12 systems; if a UNIX solution is required by vendor, HP-UX is preferred solution)

2. Server Hardware: Compaq Proliant

    (Proliant 2000 is typical; 4000 is acceptable; should be rack mount)

3. Network Protocols: TCP/IP on Token Ring (16Mb/s)

    (IPX is alternative; NetBEUI is not permitted; DLC for direct FEP access is available)

4. Workstation Operating System: MS Windows 3.11

    (Win NT Workstation, Windows 95, or OS/2 3.0 will be considered)

5. Workstation Hardware: Minimum 486/50 with planned migration to 586/60.

    (Compaq XLs are preferred. IBM PS/2s are alternative; amount of RAM or video subsystems are optional; TR NIC is the Madge card)

6. Server Database: Sybase System 10 or most recent version

    (Microsoft SQL version 4.9 or most recent version will be considered)

4.2.6   Database specifics

4.2.6.1 Data Architecture

The new teleservicing environment will require the development of a number of new data repositories. For example, new data repositories will be required for contact history, pending activity, future activity and payroll information. There is the possibility that data can be stored in the mainframe environment, at the server, at multiple servers and at multiple servers in multiple physical locations.

1.   Does your existing architecture specify the location of new data repositories?

2.   What strategy do you use and what factors do you consider when you determine where databases should be located?

3.   How would you fulfill the requirement to have all data available to all CSRs in both locations.?

4.2.6.2 Database management system

1.   Does your product include or require a proprietary database management system (DBMS)?

2.   What third party DBMS products do you support? Given our requirements, what DBMS would you recommend? What experience do you have with the recommended product? Specifically, how many production implementations have you completed?

3.   Can you support Sybase System 10 if that were to be a project requirement? What impact would that requirement have on your architecture, application functionality, application development time and cost?

Respond directly to the following questions if your product includes a database engine. If your product utilizes third party database engines, then identify whether any of the following capabilities are precluded from use by your system.

4.   Does the database support DBMS conversion, including automated assimilation of data structures and data? For which DBMS'?

5.   Are there any restrictions to the size and/or number of records that can effectively be used in your database engine without affecting performance?

6.   Does the Database support (yes or no answers are permissible unless otherwise indicated):

Synonyms or aliases
Headings, titles, or labels
Comments or remarks
Date formats
Time formats

Money formats
Variable-length fields
Keyed or indexed files
Data structure management
Ability to read, query, or report from ASCII files
Ability to import ASCII files
Ability to export ASCII files
Ability to translate EBCDIC files to ASCII and vice versa
Ability to preserve versions of data model and applications
Cross reference for dictionary objects
Ability to read, query, or report from formatted files
Ability to import formatted files (what types?)
Ability to export formatted files (what types?)
Ability to modify files while loading
File check when loading
File modification
BLOBS
Parallel query
Provides Parallel Data Loader or a high performance loader
Parallel index builder
Non-Blocking Sequence Generator.
Adheres to ANSI SQL, which version (extensions are to be described)
Control access by user ID and password and user groups.
Data dictionary based triggers.
"Like" SQL statements.
Non-Blocking queries.
Unique key generator.
Parallel sort
Cascading updates and deletes.
Referential integrity
ODBC
DRDA

7. Describe your backup and recovery capability including:

Roll back capability.
On line (during regular processing) backup and recovery.
Unattended backups.
Automatic database recovery (automatic, manual, semi-automatic)
Mirroring regardless of hardware and UNIX operating system variations.
On-line recovery
Database re-organization
Archiving capabilities
Compression

Remote recovery, such as recovering a database in the Xzzum
remotely from Axxum.
Archive medium.

8.   Describe the support of performance management including:

Ability to support a 24 hours a day 7 days a week availability.
Resource limiter
Performance monitoring tools
Describe alternatives for minimizing network utilization which your
DBMS supports.
Path analysis

9.   Describe facilities and strategies for aging information off the database
and the decision criteria that can be used.

4.2.6.3   Database development

1.   Do you provide or recommend a data modeling tool? Does your
modeling tool interface with your preferred DBMS?

2.   Do you provide or recommend a Data Dictionary? Is there
connectivity between your recommended modeling tool, Data
Dictionary and DBMS?

3.   What features does the Data Dictionary include? Include its
capabilities at defining or capturing:

logical and physical characteristic of the data
relationships amongst data
business rules
blobs
error handling and messaging

4.   Is the Data Dictionary centrally stored and accessible by more than one
developer? Can it control access to all data?

5.   Can the Data Dictionary activate changes to data definitions during
run time?

6.   Describe your database application development tools, including
support for the following:

Thorough 4GL that conforms to modular programming techniques.
Quick prototyping capability

Graphical user interface which insulates developers and end users from native SQL.
Utility to display relationships, dependencies, triggers, procedures, and views.

7.   What other tools do you provide or recommend that facilitate database development?

4.2.6.4   Database performance

Detail performance characteristics of your database environment. Include responses to the following questions:

1.   Assume that you must deal with a database that must store 100,000 new 2K transactions per day. How many days worth of data can your system maintain in the database without affecting performance given your recommended hardware configuration (see Section 5)? What factors would affect this?

Respond to questions 2-6 for the following scenario:

*   100,000 new 2K transactions each day.
*   Storage of those transactions for 60 days.
*   Data stored on multiple tables (assume four tables updated for each transaction).
*   20,000 - 30,000 inquiries against a combination of the four tables each day.
*   The inquiries are on the call critical path, for example, part of the screen pop and intelligent routing process.
*   Data must be accessible by at least three criteria groups such as: CSR identifier, client account number and activity or event type.

2.   What effect would this have on your recommended architecture?
3.   What would be your concerns?
4.   What restrictions would you want to apply in order to provide acceptable performance?
5.   Using your recommended backup facility, how long would it take to create a backup of the database previously described?
6.   How long would it take to recover?
7.   What strategies do you recommend for insuring that simultaneous logging, queries and reporting do not affect OLTP performance?
8.   Describe the largest database environment you currently have in production? How many rows of data does that database contain?

What is the transaction volume, in terms of logging and inquiring, for that database environment?

4.2.4.5 Database Access

If your software can access multiple database backends, what access standards does it support such as ODBC and DRDA?

4.2.7   Development tools and integration

4.2.7.1 Development tools description

1.   Describe tools used for customizing the system to FNAX' needs. For each tool, clearly identify the pre-requisite technical expertise, training, and time required for FNAX staff to become fully productive in its use. Specifically identify development tools and capabilities which are expected to be usable by the user area. Specifically describe tools required for the following (in sequence, if applicable):

Forms development and management
General development tool support
Computer based training
Reporting:
Work flow
Presentation tools (graphical user interface)Database access
Development of scripts and user help screens

2.   Which of your tools are proprietary? How long have they been in production?

3.   Describe what functionality specific to a bank call center has been pre-built. What objects are currently supported and in production that would be applicable to our use?

4.2.7.2 Graphical user interface

1.   What options to you support for adding color to the user interface? How many colors do you support and what color parameters (e.g. text vs. background) can be controlled? What are the limiting factors and are there any performance considerations?

2.   Are colors customizable by the user area and if so, for any screens and windows features? How does the user area maintain screen colors? Can colors be reset to default schemes?

3.   List all controls supported as objects by your development environment.

4.   Does the product support the following User Interface features (yes or no answers are permissible unless otherwise noted):

      Graphical Debugger
      Moveable forms
      Control Panel (Separate windows of buttons for common commands)
      Definable Control Panels
      Push buttons
      Check buttons
      Large graphic images
      Icons
      User defined data types:
      Standard data types (list):
      Boiler Plate definitions
      Active field indicator
      Intuitive date/time constructs
      Keystroke macros

5.   How does your forms development tools support multiple table forms including multiple rows within an embedded form? Does this include the following:

      Automatic table:table coordination
      Automatic referential integrity enforcement
            Automatic cascade processing
            Automatic restrict processing
            Automatic nullify processing

4.2.7.3 Development language support:

1.   Does the product support the following language features:

      SQL Implementation
      Simple queries on one file
      AND/OR logic - one file
      Relational join
      AND/OR logic - two files
      Complex Boolean logic
      Traps command or statement errors
      Compiles code
      Interprets code
      Condition logic

While constructs
Repeat Until constructs
Labels
Field Layout definitions
Relational and arithmetic operators
Intrinsic date/time functions
Intrinsic numeric functions
Statistical functions
Ability to process missing data
Procedural capabilities/constructs
3GL interaction allowing write to application fields from 3GL

4.2.7.4 General development environment support

1.   Does your development environment support "Self documenting" or "automated documentation"
2.   How do your tools support multi-threading?
3.   Is there a central repository accessible by all developers?
4.   Describe the ability to develop on one platform/operating system and deploy on another and how it would be accomplished.
5.   Describe the ability to develop using one DBMS and deploy on another and how it would be accomplished.
6.   Can we utilize our own text editor for development? Are there any restrictions?
7.   How do your tools support tracking and documenting of objects?

4.2.7.5 Integration with external software packages/tools

1.   Describe your support of OLE 2.0 and DDE.
2.   Describe other API's that your product provides or supports.
3.   Does your product provide a VBX(s) to allow features to be used within Visual Basic?
4.   Describe any features that your system has for integrating foreign packages into your system such as word processor, spreadsheets, or custom applications to include menuing, launching, and sharing of data.

4.2.7.6 Application development features

1.   Does your system support the following application development environment features? (yes or no answers are permissible unless otherwise noted)

Interface to other languages
Interface to operating system

POSIX Compatibility
On-line HELP
Clear and concise documentation
Error messages and warnings
Product standard
User defined error messages and warnings
Ability to call a 3GL including C and COBOL
Ability to be called from a 3GL including C and COBOL
Ability to pass parameters to a 3GL
Ability to receive parameters from a 3GL
National Language Support (list):
Branching logic
Looping logic
Language integration
Ability to call subroutines
Ability to imbed queries in procedures
Ability to share temporary data
Ability to assign global variables
Ability to create local variables
Ability to define calculations using field values
Module re-usability via sharable libraries
Cross reference of common modules used in different applications
Ability to simply define keyboards by capturing key escape sequences
and prompting for key function
Ability to switch keyboard definitions on demand
Ability to restrict field entry or modification based upon data values
Query by Example
Query by Form
Data location transparency
Pre-defined event triggers
> Field level event triggers
> Form level event triggers
> Entity level event triggers

Ability to redefine event triggers to place objects in libraries and reuse
as a library
Ability to automatically generate stored procedures

4.2.7.7 Debugging Tools

1.   Describe tools for helping debug problems after the system has been
       installed
2.   Describe the product's debugging tools including:

       step capability
       step forward

step backward
step in steps
set a break point at <u>module</u> on <u>line</u>
cancel a break point
set break points on call instruction
cancel break points on call instruction
allow messages to accumulate in a known area
return from a 4GL procedure without executing any further
instructions
dump statements of a current procedure module
dump the procedure statements of a named central procedure library
display contents of the next register/variable
display ;contents of a named register/variable
display contents of a field
set contents of a register/variable
display break point settings
send performance benchmarks to the message area
examination of functions
extend trace capability, showing:
    trigger procedure is in
    module
    any arguments given to procedure statement
Dial-in capability for deployed applications

4.2.7.8 Computer Telephone Integration scripting tools

1.   Provide a detailed description of how CTI related scripts are developed which control the disposition of phone calls. It is expected that control over call routing, alternative routing for problem resolution, which queue receive incoming calls (e g based upon source of call), etc. are all user area controllable dynamically. Include a sample of a script and explain what it controls. Explain how control over phone calls in your system interacts with control over calls inherent in the scripting capabilities of our current ACD. Include consideration for our VRU environment.

4.2.8   Computer based training

(See functionality described in Section 2.1.11.)

1.   Describe the technology (hardware and software) used for your Computer Based Training product.

4.2.9   Report and query writing tool

1. Describe the tools which support end-user creation of queries and reports.

4.2.10   User flexibility and control

1. Clearly identify those functional changes which can be made without programming, specific tools utilized for those changes, and the method for putting such changes into production. This category will exclude any changes requiring use of a procedural language (e.g. 3GL) or changes that if implemented incorrectly could significantly affect the stability of the production environment. Differentiate between changes that the end-user (e.g. CSR) can make versus those changes that are global in nature and would be changed by a central staff person in the user area.

4.2.11   Communications

1. What remote communication line speeds are accommodated by the system?

2. What communication protocols are supported by your product and which ones are in production today?

3. Which ACD interfaces are supported (e.g. TSAPI, TAPI)? If you support a proprietary interface then describe the reason and the incremental functionality that it allows.

4. Describe alternatives for communicating with the Intervoice VRU. List other supported VRU platforms.

4.3   List of current package users

1. Provide a list of all current institutions using the proposed system. Provide name, address, telephone number, and contact name for at least three financial institutions who are using your product in a call center of at least 200 workstations. Please select institutions who have deployed the product in a similar fashion as FNAX is considering.

4.4   Maintenance support description

1. Describe your release methodology for updated or new products. Include:

* How long you will commit to supporting old releases past the introduction of a new release. What is the impact to us of not upgrading?
* Whether you anticipate separate releases of individual components (such as visual front end tools, CTI tools, etc.) of your software or whether we will be required to update all software simultaneously.
* What is your typical release frequency? List dates of your previous three releases.

2. Do you provide a single point of contact for failure? Does this include hardware and software should you provide the hardware? If you do not provide the hardware, what expectations do you have regarding our role in determining whether the problem is a hardware or software problem, e.g. for performance problems?

3. Will you provide a dedicated account representative assigned to FNAX? Does the customer have input as to whom that representative will be?

4. Describe the trouble-recording, personnel-dispatching procedures which will be used in servicing your proposed products(s) at our facility.

5. Describe the following company procedures and services:

* Telephone support
* Installation/upgrade support
* Escalation procedures for problem resolution

6. Describe how workstation software is updated when changes are made, e.g. is it automated? Is downloading supported from a central server?

7. Do you support a CompuServe or Internet link for fixes?

8. If a problem involves a third party provider (such as language compilers or NTAS solutions), can we obtain the fix directly from the third party or from your firm? For which tools?

4.5   Architecture and/or vendor future direction

1. Describe the technology direction in which your company is headed. Include portability to different platforms, database technologies, open standards, connectivity, development tools, etc. in your response. Be as specific as possible.

2. What are the major elements of planned product release(s)? When are they due?

4.6   Other

1.   Describe any additional features or information about your company or
      products which would make your proposal more advantageous than others.

5.0   Proposal

Descriptions for varying scenarios and vendor options follow. The vendor should
provide estimates for each of the following combinations of these variations. Sections
5.1 - 5.9 should be responded to for each Option.

Option 1:   Scenario 1 with Vendor Option 1
Option 2:   Scenario 1 with Vendor Option 2
Option 3:   Scenario 2 with Vendor Option 1
Option 4:   Scenario 2 with Vendor Option 2
Option 5:   Vendor Option 3

In all estimates, include recommended development environment and testing laboratory
hardware and software in your responses. Appendix E, the sample detailed transaction,
is intended to provide the vendor with a sense of the level of complexity and
functionality which will be expected in each transaction.

Scenario 1

Scenario 1 includes all functionality included in the following sections only:

Section 2.1.1	Event and activity tracking
Section 2.1.4	Letter Generation
Section 2.1.5	Screen navigation and Context Sensitive events
Section 2.1.6	On-line User Help or reference information
Section 2.1.7	Scripting (Dialogue)
Section 2.1.8	Screen design capabilities
Section 2.1.10	ATM and branch location capabilities (does not include on-line graphical map capability)
Section 2.1.16	Miscellaneous
Section 2.1.17	Reporting

All Overall Requirements described in section 2.3 except Store and Forward

In addition, the estimate should include the above functionality only for the following
'Top Events' as described in Appendix C:

*	Verify account activity
*	Overdraft research
*	Changes to service charges/ product type
*	Copies of checks/statements
*	Stop payments
*	Balances
*	Error resolution
*	Provide Branch/ATM information

For further clarification, see pages 1-6 of Appendix B, Key Concepts.

Scenario 2

Scenario 2 includes all functionality in Scenario 1 **plus:**

Section 2.1.2	Computer Telephony Integration capabilities
Section 2.1.3	Check vendor interfaces
Section 2.1.9	Department message broadcasting
Section 2.1.10	FNAX ATM and branch location capabilities (with on-line graphical map capability)
Section 2.1.11	Computer Based Training
Section 2.1.12	Personnel scheduling adherence
Section 2.1.13	Time card system
Section 2.1.14	Telemarketing and sales specific requirements
Section 2.1.15	Imaging
Section 2.3.2.3	Store and forward

This functionality should be estimated for a project which would include all 'Top Events' in scenario 1 plus:

*	Support calls (SBS, RLSC, branches)
*	Check/Deposit slip orders
*	Address changes (personal)

Remaining Top Events do not need to be estimated.

For further clarification of the remaining functionality in this section, see pages 7-10 of Appendix B, Key Concepts.

Vendor Option 1

1)   The vendor performs all customization, development, and testing for software they provide. FNAX would:

   *   Manage the project

* Define requirements (the vendor would be expected to provide detailed product and teleservicing expertise during this phase).
* Develop any required changes in our own environment such as VRU or host.
* Manage and staff acceptance testing.

Describe how your bid would be affected if we required development using Visual Basic and Sybase.

Vendor Option 2

2) FNAX performs all customization, development, testing, and implementation of the product in addition to the functions assumed in Option 1. The vendor would only provide necessary training of the technology being licensed and respond to all technical questions throughout the life cycle of the initial implementation. For this scenario, provide a high level estimate as to the development time, in hours, FNAX technical development staff could be expected to spend in learning and customizing your software.

Describe how your bid would be affected if we required development using Visual Basic and Sybase.

Vendor Option 3

FNAX will consider alternatives which involve combining tools from multiple vendors with the idea of:

* selecting 'best of class' tools
* leveraging off of current FNAX initiatives, technical standards, and expertise.

Please describe alternatives which you would support which involve participating with other vendors as part of an overall CSD automation solution. Include options providing individual components such as a Front End - GUI, Local Database, CTI, Middleware, Computer Based Training, etc.

Include the following in your response:

* What role will you consider playing in these scenarios? Prime contractor? Sub-contractor?
* What experiences do you have with alliances with other vendors (list vendors)
* Which aspects of your software and services were used?
* Estimates ($'s, time) for each of the alternatives that you would support.

> * Describe where your strengths and weaknesses would be for this type of partnership.

In particular, can you provide CTI functionality only? Would you be willing to participate as the provider of that portion of the project? What would be the estimated cost of this alternative?

5.1 Equipment (hardware)

Describe recommended hardware specifications.

- Include separate specifications for client workstations and servers. Include memory, processor speed, video configuration, size of monitor, bus requirements, etc.

- Include recommended configuration for all hardware including backup server processors and network components.

- Include recommendations for all peripheral devices (printers, CRT's, tape drives, disk units, etc.) which can be attached to the proposed system.

- Describe any limitations or special restrictions in connecting multiple peripherals.

- Insure that you account for ability to use the PC (workstation) as a phone device.

- Identify recommended level of hardware redundancy and identify where that has an impact on our costs.

Provide pricing for any hardware components listed above for which you are a supplier or estimates for the above if you are not a supplier. Include maintenance expenses for years 1-5 for each of these components.

5.2 Vendor software

1. Describe expenses associated with the licensing and support of all software included in your response which is proprietary to your firm.

2. Should any specific functional requirements listed in Section 2 require substantial development, list the development cost for that portion as a separate line item. The intent is for us to understand if any specific requirements which we are requesting significantly affect the price of a delivered product.

Include maintenance and support expenses for years 1-5.

5.3   Non-vendor software

Identify operating systems, network software, or development environment components that are not proprietary to your firm which you <u>support or are embedded in your product.</u> Identify those software components you <u>recommend or are required</u>. Indicate whether or not you are a supplier of that software and provide an estimated cost for each component. Provide the number of installations you currently support for each configuration.

5.4   Other vendor expenses and services

Identify vendor expenses and services other than hardware or software which may be included in a proposal. Include in this section:

* Development services
* Integration services
* Installation services
* Training

    - Technical Staff
    - User Area Staff
    - Training for FNAX staff responsible for CSD training programs
    - Full initial training for all CSRs and end users (by your firm)

* Other services or expenses

Under each category, describe your services in detail and the cost of your different support options. Include expertise of staff and estimate headcount of staff you would provide for each of these services, should FNAX contract for them.   Differentiate between staff that are full time employees of your company and those with whom you would contract to service FNAX. If you include any of these services as part of overall product pricing, describe what is included. The limits to your commitment (number of hours, months, etc.) should be identified along with the costs to FNAX of exceeding those parameters. Include hourly rates for any category, as appropriate.

5.5   Other non-vendor expenses

1.   Identify any expenses that we might incur that are not included in your service or identified above. Include an estimate of the percentage increase in ACD utilization we might experience as a result of this project and the factors which will affect that percentage.

5.6 Upgrade and expansion expenses

Address costs relating to expansion or upgrades after the initial implementation (additional or upgraded equipment, software, documentation, etc.) At minimum, describe and list estimates for expenses which we are likely to incur related to your proposal if:

1. The number of data centers increases from two to four.
2. The volume of transactions triples
3. The number of workstations doubles

5.7 Leasing

1. FNAX would be interested in exploring the idea of leasing the system from you, including customization expenses. Provide us with information regarding your willingness to explore this option and what types of terms and conditions you would consider.

5.8 Expected implementation schedule

1. Provide an estimated implementation schedule to final product including time frames for each phase and milestone for each Scenario listed in Section 5.0.

2. Identify at what point in the project you would be willing to commit to a specific schedule and budget for completion. Describe what information and level of detail you will require before such a commitment. **Provide an estimate of the cost to perform the work necessary to develop a firm budget for completion.**

3. If you believe that there will be differences in project time frames depending on which portions of the project are contracted to you, describe those differences and why they exist.

4. State any restrictions on when we would be able to start this project with your firm, or limits to your ability to fully staff the project.

5.9 FNAX resource requirements

1. Describe the level of involvement which you will expect from the business client at FNAX especially focusing on up front requirements and the testing phases. Provide an estimate of the time that will be expected from FNAX staff to support requirements and acceptance testing.

2.   Include estimates for the time required from FNAX technical staff to support this project. Assume minimal system changes on our part (we will estimate the time for any such changes). Rather, focus on the needed expertise to describe technical interfaces and to participate in the testing phases of the project.

5.10   Laboratory evaluation

Upon selection of finalist vendors, FNAX would like to perform laboratory work with each of the vendors remaining under consideration. The purpose of this effort would be to obtain a hands on feel for the tools and software of each vendor and to understand how difficult it will be to customize that package to our environment. The effort will likely be based upon the 'Account Activity' transaction detailed in the Appendix E.

1.   Please indicate your willingness to support such a laboratory effort at your cost and your conditions for support (e.g. where, how long you would recommend, etc.).

2.   FNAX would prefer this laboratory work be performed on our premises. Describe the needed hardware configuration at our location required to support such an effort.